Regulating Health Foods

This book is dedicated to

William A. Kerr

Eleni and Ioanna Malla-Tran and Kien Tran

Sarah Asumadu, Eric Sogah Jnr and Clarence Rockson Sogah

Man Sing Yeung and Wendy Fung

Regulating Health Foods

Policy Challenges and Consumer Conundrums

Jill E. Hobbs

Professor, University of Saskatchewan, Canada

Stavroula Malla

Associate Professor, University of Lethbridge, Canada

Eric K. Sogah

Research Associate, University of Lethbridge, Canada

May T. Yeung

Research Associate, Estey Centre for Law and Economics in International Trade, Canada

Edward Elgar

Cheltenham, UK • Northampton, MA, USA

Published by
Edward Elgar Publishing Limited
The Lypiatts
15 Lansdown Road
Cheltenham
Glos GL50 2JA
UK

Edward Elgar Publishing, Inc.
William Pratt House
9 Dewey Court
Northampton
Massachusetts 01060
USA

A catalogue record for this book
is available from the British Library

Library of Congress Control Number: 2014941547

This book is available electronically in the ElgarOnline.com Economics Subject Collection, E-ISBN 978 1 78347 472 1

ISBN 978 1 78347 471 4

Typeset by Columns Design XML Ltd, Reading
Printed and bound in Great Britain by T.J. International Ltd, Padstow

Contents

Preface

With ageing populations, rising incomes and a growing recognition of the link between diet and health, consumers are increasingly interested in new food products, supplements and ingredients with health-enhancing properties. The food industry has responded with an ever-increasing array of new food innovations, formulations and enhancements that comprise the growing health food market: omega-3-enhanced juices and dairy products with heart health benefits; dairy products containing probiotics for enhanced digestive health; breakfast cereals containing soluble fibre and oat bran for lower cholesterol and heart health; delicious spreads fortified with B vitamins for energy or high in folic acid for foetal development; foods high in calcium for healthy bones and teeth; vitamin C supplements offering antioxidant benefits. The list goes on.

Innovation in food markets brings both opportunities and challenges, particularly from a regulatory and policy perspective. The purpose of this book is to bring a social science lens to those opportunities and challenges. The opportunities lie in increased choice and product availability for consumers, in the potential to address the growing health care cost burden through foods that assist with the management or prevention of disease or improve general health and wellbeing and growth opportunities for the food industry through innovation and product differentiation.

Challenges lie in establishing a regulatory framework that creates the appropriate incentives for research and development leading to successful innovation and commercialization strategies in the sector, while balancing the need to protect and inform consumers. It is critical that health claims are genuine and not misleading, are supported by science and are understood and considered credible by consumers. As countries have each navigated this regulatory path, different regulatory frameworks have emerged, albeit often based on the same underlying science but resulting in different processes for the approval of new products and technologies and differences in allowable health claims and food labelling requirements. The words functional food, nutraceutical, dietary or food supplement, natural health product and bioactive substance have variously been used to describe the category of 'health food products' considered in this book. What is considered a functional food in one market may be treated as a supplement in another market and a natural health product elsewhere, with a different set of regulatory requirements depending on the categorization. For firms interested in tapping into export markets, this means unpacking a complex array of allowable health claims, product approval processes and product positioning strategies that differ across international markets.

Our purpose in writing this book is to provide an overview and assessment of the policy and regulatory environment governing the health foods sector in various countries. We examine the different definitions and categorization of 'health food', product approval processes and health claims regulations in a number of developed and emerging markets. Against this backdrop, the book also offers insights into the nature of the health foods sector in selected countries and examines the drivers of consumer demand for foods offering health benefits. The analysis draws on insights from the discipline of economics in understanding motivations for policy intervention, as well as understanding incentives for decisions at the individual consumer and firm levels. Of course, this can never be a comprehensive assessment, and regulatory and commercial environments will continue to evolve over time. By design, our analysis has needed to be selective, with a focus on the current state of policy and industry development in major developed markets, as well as a number of interesting emerging markets. Taken together, our book offers a big picture overview of the key policy issues surrounding innovation in this segment of the food industry, alongside a more detailed and nuanced analysis of the regulatory approach in key markets.

Jill E. Hobbs, Saskatoon, Canada

Stavroula Malla and Eric K. Sogah
Lethbridge, Canada

May T. Yeung, Calgary, Canada
April 2014

Acknowledgements

The background research for this book was made possible by a research grant from the Canadian Agricultural Innovation and Regulation Network (CAIRN), an Enabling Research for Competitive Agriculture (ERCA) network funded by Agriculture and Agri-Food Canada (AAFC). The authors wish to thank Richard Gray for his vision and leadership in the establishment of CAIRN, which ran for eight years until 2013. Thanks also go to numerous staff within AAFC for their enthusiastic support of the ERCA networks and the research made possible through the networks, including in particular Tulay Yildirim and Margaret Zafiriou. We would also like to thank Cecil Nagy and Robbie Rolfe for their research assistance. Finally, thanks go to Matthew Pitman and all of the people at Edward Elgar for their support and hard work during the preparation of this book.

Abbreviations

AAFC	Agriculture and Agri-Food Canada
ADA	American Dietetic Association
ANOVA	analysis of variance method
ANZTPA	Australia New Zealand Therapeutic Products Authority
BAFS	biologically active food supplements (Russia)
BNSFD	Bureau of Nutritional Sciences Food Directorate (Canada)
BRIC	Brazil, Russia, India and China
CFDA	China Food and Drug Administration
CFIA	Canadian Food Inspection Agency (CFIA)
CHD	coronary heart disease
CIN	claim identification number
CIPO	Canadian Intellectual Property Office
CLA	conjugated linoleic acid
CRAFT	Co-operative Research Action for Technology (EU)
CV	Contingent Valuation
CVD	cardiovascular diseases
DCE	Discrete Choice Experiment
DIN	drug identification number
DSHEA	Dietary Supplement Health and Education Act (USA)
EC	European Commission
EFSA	European Food Safety Authority
EHCR	European Health Claims Regulation
EU	European Union
FAO	Food and Agriculture Organization (United Nations)
FDA	Food and Drug Administration (USA)
FDAMA	Food and Drug Administration Modernization Act
FDR	Food and Drug Regulations (Canada)
FF	functional food
FFNet	Functional Food Net (EU)
FFNHP	functional food and natural health product(s) (Canada)
FNFC	food with nutrient function claims (Japan)
FOSHU	food for specified health uses (Japan)
FSANZ	Food Standards Australia New Zealand (Agency)
FSDU	food for special dietary use (USA)

FSSA	Food Safety and Standards Act (India)
FSSAI	Food Safety and Standards Authority of India
FUFOSE	European Commission Concerted Action on Functional Food Science in Europe
GM	genetically modified
GMP	good manufacturing practices
HFCA	Health Food Control Act (Taiwan)
HFF	health functional food (South Korea)
HFFA	Health Functional Food Act (South Korea)
IFIC	International Food Information Council
IFT	Institute of Food Technologists
IP	intellectual property
IPR	intellectual property rights
JAFRA	Japan Functional Food Research Association
JHCI	Joint Health Claims Initiative (UK)
KFDA	Korean Food and Drug Administration
MAFF	Ministry of Agriculture, Forestry and Fisheries (Japan)
MFDS	Ministry of Food and Drug Safety (South Korea)
MHLW	Ministry of Health, Labour and Welfare (Japan)
NHP	natural health product (Canada)
NHPD	Natural Health Products Directorate (Canada)
NHPR	Natural Health Products Regulations (Canada)
NLEA	Nutrition Labeling and Education Act (USA)
NPN	natural product number (Canada)
OECD	Organisation for Economic Co-operation and Development
R&D	research and development
RBA	risk-based approach
RDA	recommended dietary allowance (Canada)
RDI	recommended daily intake
SFDA	State Food and Drug Administration (China)
SSA	Significant Scientific Agreement standard (USA)
STREPS	Specific Targeted Research Projects (EU)
UK	United Kingdom
USA	United States of America
USPTO	United States Patent and Trademark Office
WHO	World Health Organization
WTO	World Trade Organization
WTP	willingness to pay

1. Introduction

1.1 MOTIVATION

With ageing and increasingly affluent populations, there is a growing awareness and recognition of the link between diet and health. For consumers, this means seeking out food products with new or enhanced health attributes and navigating through the sometimes confusing maze of food health claims. For the food industry, this creates opportunities for product differentiation and drives incentives to invest in the research, development and commercialization of healthier foods. For regulators, this creates challenges in designing appropriate regulatory frameworks to encourage investment and facilitate innovation, while protecting consumers from fraudulent or misleading health claims. These issues form the backdrop to this book. The primary objective of the book is to examine the policy and regulatory environment governing the health foods sector internationally and examine key trends and industry developments in leading markets.

In researching the book, it became evident that the 'health foods sector' is a diverse concept: it is defined differently, is regulated differently and encompasses different types of products, in various countries. As will become clearer in the material that follows, the terms 'functional foods', 'nutraceuticals', 'supplements', 'natural health products', 'medical foods' are used variously and interchangeably across different countries to refer to products with health-enhancing attributes. The inconsistencies in definitions across countries is more than merely pedantic: it affects how these products are regulated and positioned in the market, determines what health claims are permissible and creates complexities for firms seeking to navigate export markets. For the purposes of this book, therefore, we have taken the deliberate decision to refer to these products under the catch-all term of 'health foods'.

In this chapter we lay out the primary issues that are dealt with in more detail in subsequent chapters. Before doing so, it is useful to consider the factors that have driven interest in the health foods sector.

1.2 DIET AND HEALTH: DRIVERS OF INTEREST IN HEALTH FOODS

Science has shown fairly clearly that diet affects human health and, therefore, healthy diets help promote good health. Conventionally, the primary role of the human diet has been the biological provision of nutrients to maintain metabolic function and wellbeing. Scientific evidence increasingly suggests, however, that some foods and food ingredients provide physiological benefits over and above that of conventional foods (ADA, 2004; Health Canada, 2009b; IFIC, 2009). Examples include food products with enhanced levels of omega-3 fatty acids for heart health or foods enhanced with probiotics for digestive health, or calcium for bone health. Previous studies[1] have pinpointed several drivers of the interest in health foods, which can be loosely grouped into four categories: (1) health drivers, including increased incidence of chronic diseases such as diabetes, cancer, cardiovascular diseases (CVD) and respiratory diseases; (2) lifestyle drivers, including sedentary lifestyles, which lead to an increase in lifestyle-related diseases, ageing populations and rising consumer incomes; (3) scientific advances, including new research and development (R&D) applications that create opportunities for product differentiation in the food industry; and (4) economic factors, including rising public health care costs and awareness of the link between diet and health.

A number of indicators related to disease, obesity rates, life expectancy and health expenditures set the scene for increased global interest in the health foods sector. According to the World Health Organization (WHO, 2013), CVD are the leading cause of death worldwide, with an estimated 17.3 million deaths caused by CVD in 2008, predicted to rise to 23.3 million by 2030. The majority of these deaths occur in low- and middle-income countries. Lifestyle factors, including tobacco and alcohol use, but also unhealthy diets, obesity and physical inactivity are leading contributory factors of CVD (WHO, 2013). Indeed, rising levels of obesity continue to present health challenges, with the WHO estimating that the worldwide prevalence of obesity doubled between 1980 and 2008. High levels of obesity are concentrated in the Americas, with around 30 per cent of the United States of America (USA) population over the age of 20 now considered obese.[2] Globally, the WHO estimates that 2.8 million people a year die as a result of being overweight or obese, with many more developing diet-related diseases and long-term health problems (WHO, 2012a).

With improvements in life expectancy, nutrition and disease reduction, the world population continues to age; the number of people aged 60 and over has doubled since 1980 and is forecast to reach 2 billion people by 2050 (WHO, 2012b). This places an ever-increasing burden on health care systems, particularly in high-income countries. Global expenditures for health are estimated to top US$6.5 trillion, with the highest total spending per person per year on health occurring in the USA at US$8362 in 2012. These expenditure levels are in sharp contrast with the lowest spending per person per year of only US$12 in Eritrea. The disparity in global health spending worldwide is reflected in the fact that Organisation for Economic Co-operation and Development (OECD) countries, representing just 18 per cent of the world's population, account for 84 per cent of the world's total financial resources devoted to health (WHO, 2012c).

The significant increase in lifestyle and diet-related diseases poses a challenge to governments around the world seeking effective ways to reduce health care costs and improve citizens' health. At the same time, opportunities are burgeoning in the health foods sector as the relationship between diet and health is becoming increasingly important in the context of ageing populations, particularly in the developed world. As healthier diets today may lead to fewer diseases tomorrow, the consumption of health-enhancing foods provides an avenue for improving the welfare of citizens.

The importance of the health foods sector is evident in the growth of the industry worldwide. Available food technologies, scientific discoveries and increased consumer desires/interest for healthier food products provide opportunities for the development of healthier food products, while industry foresighting analysis suggests a continued upward trajectory for the industry (Arias-Aranda and Romerosa-Martinez, 2010; Hobbs, 2002; IFT, 2005). With the caveat that robust estimates are notoriously difficult to come by in part due to differences in the definition of the health food category, the global market size for the health foods sector is estimated to have ranged from US$30 to US$60 billion in 2004, representing 1–3 per cent of the total food market (Kotilainen et al., 2006). The sector has continued to grow. More recent estimates put the global health food market at around US$151 billion in 2011, with the sector forecast to grow to US$207 billion by 2016 (BCC Research, 2011). Currently, the leading markets are the USA, the European Union (EU) and Japan.

A burgeoning literature on health-enhancing food products indicates strong prospects for the health foods sector. There is growing evidence of consumer acceptance of these products and willingness to pay a premium for their benefits. Consumer acceptance is critical and should in turn lead to additional R&D and product development. Increased consumption of nutrient-enhanced products (for example, trans fat-free designer eggs, high conjugated linoleic acid (CLA) dairy products, golden rice, probiotics, functional cereals, phytoalexin-enriched foods and high oleic oil peanuts) offer potential health benefits and improvements in areas where considerable public and private sector health spending occurs (including CVD and cancer).

The health foods sector is not without its challenges, which include resources for product development, transparent and enforceable property rights systems to protect patents, regulations that differ across jurisdictions with respect to the number of permissible health claims, slow and cumbersome approval processes and maintaining consumer confidence in the face of a proliferation of products and health claims. These issues are examined in later chapters.

1.3 ISSUES EXPLORED IN THE BOOK

The book covers three main themes: the different approaches to defining the health foods sector; policy challenges and the regulation of health claims and new product approvals; and drivers of industry growth and consumer acceptance.

1.3.1 Defining 'Health Foods'

A central objective of this book is to provide an overview of the policy and regulatory environment governing the health foods sector internationally. This regulatory environment, particularly with respect to health claims and new product approvals, is evolving at different rates internationally. Various countries permit health claims declaring an association between a food or food ingredient and a health benefit; however, different definitions, terminologies and regulations are in use. Chapter 2 provides a comprehensive discussion of the terminology used to define health foods in various countries. Below we provide a broad overview.

Generally speaking, the health foods sector is characterized by two broad categories of products: so-called 'functional foods' and 'supplements' or 'nutraceuticals'. The term functional food has become a fairly widely accepted term to describe enhanced foods. Functional food usually refers to food that is intended to be consumed as part of a normal diet and contains ingredients that have the potential to enhance human health or reduce the risk of disease beyond basic nutritional functions (ADA, 2004; Health Canada, 2009b; IFIC, 2009; Stein and Rodríguez-Cerezo, 2008).

Nutraceuticals, also known as food supplements, or natural health products (NHPs), are products that have been isolated or purified from food and may include ingredients such as amino acids or vitamins; they are often marketed in the form of pills, powders, capsules or tablets. Nutraceuticals/supplements are intended to have a physiological benefit or to provide protection against chronic disease (EFSA, 2010; Health Canada, 1998).

Consumption of products from either category provides additional health benefits beyond the supply of basic nutrients. We devote an entire chapter to explaining how these products are defined in various countries because this is an important context for the remaining chapters of the book. In particular, it underpins the discussion of the regulatory environments in developed and emerging markets in later chapters. As such, Chapter 2 presents the varying definitions used for these health food products in the USA, Canada, EU, Japan, Australia and New Zealand, Brazil, Russia, India, China, South Korea and Taiwan.

1.3.2 Policy Challenges: Health Claims and New Product Approvals

The health foods sector embodies the outcome of scientific discoveries and new technologies leading to the creation of new products. While this creates obvious opportunities for market growth, it also brings with it a set of policy issues including the process for new product approvals, the establishment of regulatory frameworks to govern allowable health claims for these products and determining whether the rules around the protection of intellectual property rights (IPR) provide appropriate incentives for innovation. Labelling and novel food registration procedures have a direct bearing on the incentives for firms to innovate. Different regulatory treatment of these products in different countries creates the potential for trade barriers; for example, if a product, an ingredient or a process is approved for use in one jurisdiction but not in another, or if a health claim is permitted on a product label in one jurisdiction but not in another.

Consumers seeking improved health will likely see food with health benefits as superior to food without health benefits, thereby providing opportunities for food innovations that meet consumer demands. In order for consumers to choose foods with health benefits over conventional foods, they must be provided with credible, useful information about a product's health and nutrient benefits upon which to make informed decisions. The role of credible information is therefore critical but susceptible to manipulation, hence many countries have moved to regulate health and nutrient content claims on food products. Such claims are usually permitted on labelling and in advertisements to inform consumers about the health benefits of the consumption of the food or the food constituent.

Recent policy responses include measures to better inform consumers about the nutrient content of foods to facilitate healthier eating choices – for example, the introduction of mandatory nutrition labelling on prepackaged foods and the requirement to label the presence of trans fat in these foods. Enhancing the information provided to consumers is an important policy response to improving health by changing what consumers eat. Policies to encourage R&D into healthier foods also have a role to play. This may include changing the nutritional composition of diets by lowering the cost of producing food that is more nutritious and by improving the nutrient composition of existing foods. Policy issues are explored in Chapter 3, which also charts the evolution of regulatory frameworks in a number of countries through a review of the literature examining regulatory developments.

How do regulatory frameworks in key markets differ? This is the subject of Chapters 4 and 5, which describe the regulatory environments in key developed country markets and emerging markets, respectively. Specifically, Chapter 4 focuses on the USA, Canada, EU, Japan, Australia and New Zealand, with a particular focus on allowable health claims and the processes for new product approval. Chapter 5 presents a comparable analysis of the regulatory frameworks in Brazil, Russia, India, China, South Korea and Taiwan.

While Chapters 4 and 5 provide a detailed treatment of these topics, it is useful to provide a broad overview of the different types of health claims in use. Health claims can be either generic or product-specific. Generic claims usually specify relationships between a food constituent and a health effect and can be claimed by a food product so long as it meets the conditions for using the claims. Product-specific claims, on the other hand, can only be used by products that have undergone a registration process for use of the claim, which usually specifies a relationship between the food or food constituent and a health benefit (Subirade, 2007).

Beyond generic or product-specific distinctions, health claims are usually further divided into two different categories: disease risk reduction claims and structure/function claims (Subirade, 2007). A disease risk reduction claim usually specifies the relationship between the consumption of a nutrient and its effects on mitigating disease risk. For example, several countries (USA, Japan, Canada, Australia and New Zealand) permit claims linking the presence of calcium and/or vitamin D and the reduced risk of osteoporosis. Structure/function claims, on the other hand, link the presence of a nutrient to normal growth, development or functioning of the human body. For example, several countries (Japan, Canada, Australia and New Zealand) permit claims linking the presence of calcium and/or vitamin D and proper bone structure.

Nutrition content claims or nutrition claims can also often be made on food and sometimes on supplements/nutraceuticals. Nutrition claims simply describe the presence or absence of a nutrient. Permitted nutrition claims tend to indicate positive implications for health. In a way, nutrient content claims are implied health claims. For example, in some countries (for example, USA, EU, Japan, Canada), firms can claim a food to be 'high in potassium and low in sodium', both of which contribute to reduced risk of high blood pressure and CVD.

Nutrition labelling regulations vary from country to country. Of specific focus are nutrition facts tables, which display information about levels of nutrients per serving. A number of countries (for example, USA, Canada, EU, Brazil, Russia, India) have implemented mandatory nutrition labelling. Labelling is deemed an essential means of imparting information to consumers about the foods they eat and also confirms that the claims that firms make on their health food products are not misleading.

Labelling requirements for the products categorized as nutraceuticals/supplements (see Chapter 2) often differ from that of food and vary from country to country. Some countries have implemented labelling that treats these products more like drugs than food (for example, Canada, Australia), while others have implemented the reverse. There are also broad regulatory differences across countries when it comes to functional food regulations. Some countries have a body that regulates the use of health claims (for example, the Food and Drug Administration (FDA) in the USA, the Ministry of Health, Labour and Welfare (MHLW) in Japan, Health Canada in Canada, the Ministry of Food and Drug Safety (MFDS) in South Korea, the State Food and Drug Administration (SFDA) in China). Historically, some governments permitted health claims but allowed private interests to regulate their use (United Kingdom). Other countries have developed regulations cooperatively on health and nutrition claims (EU, Australia and New Zealand). All countries examined in this book no longer permit self-regulation. Future regulatory trends appear to be leaning towards regulatory cooperation between countries, which will be particularly important in countries with close trade relationships.

A final regulatory hurdle to new health food products may be novel food approval. If a food meets certain conditions (for example, it lacks a history of safe use as a food), then it may be subject to novel food registration before entering the market, which generally requires a safety assessment. Details of the novel food registration procedures in several countries are also provided in Chapters 4 and 5.

1.3.3 Drivers of Industry Growth and Consumer Acceptance

The health foods sector has experienced rapid growth, with an increasing array of products available in the marketplace. Chapter 6 charts the growth of this sector in four markets – the USA, EU, Japan and Canada – in terms of size, market trends and research directions. Ultimately, it is consumers that determine the long-run market success of these products, therefore understanding the factors that influence consumer acceptance of products with new health attributes is critical. These issues are explored in Chapter 7, which draws upon a growing body of literature examining the receptivity of consumers to new health attributes in food products, their willingness to pay (WTP) for these attributes and the drivers of trust in health claims. The chapter reveals growing evidence that consumers are willing to pay a premium for health benefits provided by foods and by supplements. An understanding of consumer attitudes towards health foods, including the extent to which traditional influences on consumer acceptance – such as convenience and taste – remain relevant, is important to the long-run growth of the sector.

1.4 ROADMAP

As outlined in more detail above, this book is organized into eight chapters. Chapter 2 explains the terminology used within the 'health foods sector' internationally and forms the backdrop for the subsequent discussion of policy and regulatory issues. Chapter 3 outlines key policy issues surrounding the health foods sector and charts the evolution of regulatory frameworks through a review of relevant literature. Chapters 4 and 5 discuss health claims regulations in selected developed and emerging markets, respectively. Chapter 6 examines industry trends in selected developed markets. Chapter 7 explores consumer responses to the health foods category and is informed by a comprehensive review of consumer literature in this area. Chapter 8, 'Through the looking glass', offers a synthesis and concluding thoughts with respect to common themes and differences in regulatory environments for the health foods sector globally and future issues that are likely to arise as new food innovations emerge. We invite the reader to grab a (healthy) bran muffin, pour a glass of omega-3-enhanced orange juice and read on.

NOTES

1. See, for example, AAFC (2009), ADA (2004), Cinnamon (2009), Evani (2009), Hobbs (2002), NBJ (2007a), West and Larue (2004) and WHO (2002).
2. Obesity is defined as a body mass index $\geq 30\text{kg/m}^2$ (WHO, 2012a).

2. What are 'health foods'?

The health food products sector is plagued by a lack of consensus or harmonization across countries with respect to the terminology used to describe and define these foods. Terms such as functional food, dietary supplements, nutraceuticals, natural health products (NHPs), food for special dietary use and novel food are used; each term often has slightly different meanings or synonyms with subtle differences. What may be considered an NHP in one country may be known as a functional food in another and a nutraceutical but not a dietary supplement elsewhere. That same NHP may be considered an over-the-counter product in one country, a prescription drug in another and banned in a third. As such, a prevailing state of confusion exists in the industry internationally, making informed choices difficult for consumers and complicating the efforts of both regulators and researchers alike. Firms wishing to diversify beyond their home markets must navigate a different regime of definitions, terminology and regulations in each potential new market. In order to reduce potential reader confusion for the remainder of this book and to inform the subsequent discussion of health claims regulations, this chapter explains terminology used to define the 'health food category' across a number of countries, including the USA, Canada, EU, Japan, Australia and New Zealand, Brazil, Russia, India, China, South Korea and Taiwan.

2.1 UNITED STATES OF AMERICA

The US FDA does not provide a legal definition for functional food. Depending on the health claims that are made and the basis thereof, a functional food could be considered a food, a dietary supplement or a drug and regulated accordingly by the FDA. However, a number of working definitions for functional foods have been developed by different organizations including the American Dietetic Association (ADA), the International Food Information Council (IFIC) and the Institute of Food Technologies (IFT). According to these organizations, a functional food is any food that moves beyond necessity (basic nutrition) to provide additional health benefits that may reduce disease risk and/or promote optimal health (ADA, 2004; IFIC, 2009). The IFT defines functional food as 'foods and food components that provide a health benefit beyond basic nutrition (for the intended population). These substances provide essential nutrients often beyond quantities necessary for normal maintenance, growth and development and/or other biologically active components that impart health benefits or desirable physiological effects' (IFT, 2005, p. 6).

In the USA, there are also dietary supplements that would be classified as nutraceuticals or NHPs in other countries. According to the US Dietary Supplement Health and Education Act (DSHEA), dietary supplements are vitamins, minerals, herbs or other botanicals, amino acids and other dietary substances intended to supplement the diet by increasing the total dietary intake or as any concentrate, metabolite, constituent, extract or combination of these. They are products that are 'intended for ingestion in pill, capsule, tablet, powder or liquid form' and should not be represented for use as a conventional food or as the sole item of a meal or diet (DSHEA, 1994; Ross, 2000).

The USA has other categories of food products with health benefits beyond basic nutrition, including medical foods and food for special dietary use (FSDU). According to the Orphan Drug Act 1988, medical foods are defined as 'a food which is manufactured to be consumed or administered entirely under the supervision of a physician and which is intended for the specific dietary management of a disease or condition for which distinctive nutritional requirements, based on recognized scientific principles, are established by "medical evaluation"'. In this context, an example of a medical food is Lofenalac, a product that was designed for use in the dietary management of a rare genetic condition known as phenylketonuria. To be considered a medical food, a product must, at a minimum, meet very specific criteria: the product must be a food for oral or tube feeding; the product must be labelled for the dietary management of a specific medical disorder, disease or condition for which there are distinctive nutritional requirements; and the product must be intended to be used under medical supervision (FDA, 2010).

Foods for special dietary use are defined as 'a particular use for which a food purports or is represented to be used, including but not limited to: supplying a special dietary need that exists by reason of a physical, physiological, pathological or other condition; supplying a vitamin, mineral or other ingredient for use by humans to supplement the diet by increasing the total dietary intake; supplying a special dietary need by reason of being a food for use as the sole item of the diet' (FDA, 2009a). Examples include infant foods, hypoallergenic foods such as gluten-free foods and lactose-free foods and foods offered for weight reduction.

The FDA does not have a formal definition for novel food. These foods are often referred to as new and emerging food/biotechnology products and a pre-market notification with the FDA is usually recommended (FDA, 2005a).

Types of permitted health claims in the USA include disease risk reduction claims, structure/function claims and nutrient content claims, all of which can be used for either food products or dietary supplements but regulations and requirements change depending on whether the claim is used on food or a dietary supplement and the basis upon which the claim is being made. A more detailed discussion of health claims regulations in the US is provided in Chapter 4.

Key terminology in the USA: dietary supplement, food for special dietary use (FSDU), novel food, functional food, medical food, disease risk reduction claims, structure/function claims, nutrient content claims.

2.2 CANADA

In Canada, categories of healthier foods and food derivatives have been evolving over time, with references commonly made to functional food, nutraceuticals, natural health products and novel food. Health Canada (1998) defines a functional food 'as similar in appearance to, or may be, a conventional food, is consumed as part of a usual diet and is demonstrated to have physiological benefits and/or reduce the risk of chronic disease beyond basic nutritional functions' (p. 3).

Prior to 2003, NHPs were commonly categorized as 'nutraceuticals' in Canada, which are 'product(s) isolated or purified from foods, that is generally sold in medicinal forms [pills, capsules or tablets], not usually associated with food. A nutraceutical is demonstrated to have a physio-logical benefit or provide protection against chronic disease' (Health Canada, 1998, p. 3). The introduction of the Natural Health Products Directorate (NHPD) of Health Canada in 2000 signalled a change in focus away from the use of the term nutraceuticals, officially replacing it with 'natural health products' in 2003. An NHP is defined by the 2003 Natural Health Products Regulations (NHPR) as being 'a substance or a combination of substances in which all the medicinal ingredients are made up of natural substances. This includes homeopathic medicine or a traditional medicine that is manufactured, sold and represented for use in:

- The diagnosis, treatment, mitigation or prevention of a disease, disorder or abnormal physical state or its symptoms in humans.
- Restoring or correcting organic functions in humans.

- Modifying organic functions in humans such as modifying those functions in a manner that maintains or promotes health' (Canada Gazette, 2003).

NHPs include over-the-counter products used to diagnose/treat and mitigate or prevent diseases such as vitamins and minerals, herbal remedies, traditional medicines and essential fatty acids (Health Canada, 2004; Laeeque et al., 2006).

In Canada, a novel food was originally defined by Health Canada in 1999 (Canada Gazette, 1998) and refers to foods resulting from a process not previously used for food. This includes products that do not have a history of safe use as a food. In addition, foods that have been modified by genetic manipulation, also known as genetically modified (GM) foods, genetically engineered foods or biotechnology-derived foods, fall under the novel food category (Health Canada, 2010).

A health claim is any claim that correlates the consumption of a food or ingredient and health. Permitted health claims in Canada include disease risk reduction claims, structure/function claims and therapeutic claims, all of which are governed by specific standards and regulations. Disease risk reduction claims relate the consumption of food (or a food component) and the risk of developing a diet-related disease (CFIA and Health Canada, 2009). Function claims describe the nutrient's importance in promoting normal, healthy growth and functioning. Therapeutic claims suggest that the consumption of a certain nutrient will treat or mitigate a disease or condition or restore or otherwise modify an existing function.

Key terminology in Canada: functional food, natural health product (NHP), novel food, disease risk reduction claim, therapeutic claim, function claim.

2.3 THE EUROPEAN UNION

In the EU, the European Commission Concerted Action on Functional Food Science in Europe (FUFOSE) defines a food as functional if 'it is satisfactorily demonstrated to affect beneficially one or more target functions in the body, beyond adequate nutritional effects, in a way that is relevant to either an improved state of health and well-being and/or reduction of risk of disease. Functional foods must be in the form of conventional foods and they must demonstrate their effects in amounts that can normally be expected to be consumed in the diet: they are not pills or capsules, but part of a normal food pattern' (Stein and Rodríguez-Cerezo, 2008, p. 1).

The European Food Safety Authority (EFSA) defines nutraceuticals as food supplements that are concentrated sources of nutrients or other substances with a nutritional or physiological effect. The purpose of use should be to supplement the normal diet. They are marketed in dose form, that is, as pills, tablets, capsules or liquids in measured doses and so on (EFSA, 2010). In 2007, the EU formally defined novel food as 'a food that has not been used for human consumption to a significant degree before May 15, 1997' (EC, 1997). Novel food in the EU includes genetically modified products.

Permitted health claims in the EU are generic structure/function (Article 13.1) claims, product-specific/new/proprietary (Article 13.5) claims, disease risk reducing (Article 14.1.a) claims, children's health (Article 14.1.b) claims and nutrient content claims. Each has accompanying approval processes and requirements of use. The EU regulatory environment is discussed in more detail in Chapter 4.

Key terminology in the EU: food supplements, novel food, functional food, generic structure/function (Article 13.1) claims, product-specific/new/proprietary (Article 13.5) claims, disease risk reducing (Article 14.1.a) claims, children's health (Article 14.1.b) claims.

2.4 JAPAN

Japan was one of the first countries to recognize a different category of healthier food products. In the 1980s, the Japanese government formally accepted that food products could positively affect the physiological system of the human body and accepted approved health claims for food (MHLW, 2010). These foods are classified as 'food for specified health uses' (FOSHU). The Japanese government defines FOSHU as food that 'is intended to be consumed for the maintenance/promotion of health or for special health uses by people who wish to control health conditions, including blood pressure or blood cholesterol' (MHLW, 2010). This definition includes both functional foods and supplements and is referred to as 'Regular' FOSHU.

In order for a food to be approved as FOSHU, a safety assessment is required and the efficacy of functional attributes must be established. Furthermore, FOSHU can be categorized beyond Regular FOSHU to 'Qualified FOSHU', 'Standardized FOSHU' and 'Reduction of disease risk FOSHU' (sometimes called Specific FOSHU) reflecting different strengths of assurance regarding the link with health benefits. Qualified FOSHU is 'food with health function which is not substantiated on scientific evidence that meets the level of Regular FOSHU, or the food with certain effectiveness but without established mechanism of the effective element for the function' (MHLW, 2010). Standardized FOSHU is food where 'standards and specifications are established for foods with sufficient FOSHU approvals and accumulation of scientific evidence' (MHLW, 2010). Products are approved as Standardized FOSHU when they meet the requisite standards and specifications. Reduction of disease risk FOSHU are products permitted to carry a disease risk reduction claim 'when reduction of disease risk is clinically and nutritionally established in an ingredient' (MHLW, 2010).

The FOSHU claim must be approved by the Ministry of Health, Labour and Welfare (MHLW). Specifically, to qualify as FOSHU, a food must fulfil the following requirements:

- Effectiveness on the human body is clearly proven.
- Absence of any safety issues (animal toxicity tests, confirmation of effects in the cases of excess intake and so on).
- Use of nutritionally appropriate ingredients (for example, no excessive use of salt and so on).
- Guarantee of compatibility with product specifications by the time of consumption.
- Established quality control methods, such as specifications of products and ingredients, processes and methods of analysis (MHLW, 2010).

Food with nutrient function claims (FNFC) has also been introduced in Japan. An FNFC refers to all food that is labelled with the nutrient function claims stipulated by the MHLW, of which there are currently 17, consisting of 12 vitamins and five minerals. As long as the product meets the requisite standards and specifications, no further notification to or permission from the MHLW is necessary (MHLW, n.d.b). An FNFC is comparable to a product with a generic structure/function claim in the USA, EU or Canada.

Both FOSHU and FNFC are, by definition, not only categories of products but also types of health claims allowed in Japan. FOSHU claims are product-specific health claims that require approval prior to use. A Regular FOSHU claim is neither qualified nor standardized but may include disease risk reduction claims (sometimes called Specific FOSHU). A Qualified FOSHU claim is one for which there exists supporting but inconclusive evidence and a Standardized FOSHU claim is one that is proven and well established. FNFC claims are comparable to generic structure/function claims that do not require approval prior to being used on a product. Nutrient content claims are statements applying to nutrients that are useful for healthy living. Nutrition labelling was initially optional unless a health claim was made but became mandatory in 2013. Additionally, Japan defines novel foods as 'foods and food additives that have been produced through the use of recombinant DNA techniques' (MHLW, 2010).

Key terminology in Japan: (Regular) FOSHU, Qualified FOSHU, Standardized FOSHU, Reduction of disease risk FOSHU (or Specific FOSHU), novel foods, food with nutrient function claims (FNFC), nutrient content claims.

2.5 OTHER NATIONS

Terminology used for the health foods category in Australia and New Zealand, Brazil, Russia, China, India, South Korea and Taiwan is explained below.

2.5.1 Australia and New Zealand

Australia and New Zealand have established a joint food regulation agency, Food Standards Australia and New Zealand (FSANZ), which has jurisdiction over the health foods sector. Although there is no universally accepted definition for functional food in Australia and New Zealand, FSANZ uses a working definition for functional food as being 'similar in appearance to conventional food and intended to be consumed as part of a normal diet, but modified to serve physiological roles beyond the provision of simple nutrient requirements' (FSANZ, 2006). A nutra-ceutical is defined as a food designed to provide health benefits that may contain ingredients such as specific amino acids or vitamins. Nutra-ceuticals can be marketed in the form of pills, capsules or tablets (FSANZ, 2001).

FSANZ refers to novel food as '*a non-traditional food* for which there is insufficient knowledge in the broad community to enable safe use in the form or context in which it is presented, taking into account:

- The composition or structure of the product;
- Levels of undesirable substances in the product;
- Known potential for adverse effects in humans;
- Traditional preparation and cooking methods; or
- Patterns and levels of consumption of the product' (FSANZ, 2010c).

In general, a non-traditional food is defined as 'A food which does not have a history of significant human consumption by the broad community in Australia or New Zealand' (FSANZ, 2010c). Australia uses the term therapeutic goods or complementary medicines to describe complementary (in other words, vitamins, minerals, amino acids, homeopathic medicines) and alternative medicines, including dietary supplements (nutraceuticals). New Zealand defines dietary supplements as any amino acid, edible substance, herb, mineral, nutrient or vitamin normally available in food that is put into a controlled dosage form and is intended to be taken orally.

Australia and New Zealand allow 'general-level' health claims and 'high-level' health claims. General-level claims are comparable to structure/function claims as they describe the relationship between a nutrient and a health function. High-level health claims are disease risk reduction claims. They elucidate a relationship between the consumption of a nutrient and the risk of a disease. Nutrition content claims are also allowed.

Key terminology in Australia and New Zealand: functional food, nutraceutical, non-traditional food, therapeutic goods, complementary medicines, dietary supplement, general-level claims, high-level claims, nutrient content claims.

2.5.2 Brazil

Brazil has no legal definition for functional foods, supplements/ nutraceuticals or novel foods. Functional foods and supplements are generally referred to as any healthful product that is not a drug but part of a normal diet and provides a health benefit beyond basic nutrition. Novel foods often refer to food with no history of use in Brazil (Lajolo, 2002). Supplements are called bioactive substances in Brazil and are substances that have a particular physiological or metabolic function and must be extracted and isolated from their original source. Brazil allows nutrient content, generic disease risk reduction and structure/function claims but prohibits therapeutic claims. Nutrition labelling is mandatory.

Key terminology in Brazil: healthful product, novel foods, bioactive substances.

2.5.3 Russia

In Russia (The Russian Federation), food products with health benefits (functional food and supplements) are known as 'biologically active food supplements' (BAFS). Russia defines BAFS as nutritive substances and minor food components used to ameliorate deficiencies, decrease risk of debilitating diseases and improve the quality of life (Zawistowski, 2008). The food product and its components should be natural or identical to natural. They should be consumed along with food and incorporated into food. BAFS are not regarded as medicines and are not meant to treat or diagnose diseases. BAFS are equivalent to supplements in many other countries; however, in Russia the definition used for supplements also applies to functional foods and novel foods. BAFS are further categorized as nutraceuticals or parapharmaceuticals. Nutrition labelling is mandatory for BAFS, nutrient content claims and structure/function claims are allowed but disease risk reduction claims are prohibited.

Key terminology in Russia: biologically active food supplements (BAFS), nutraceuticals, parapharmaceuticals, nutrient content claims, structure/function claims.

2.5.4 India

In India, functional food is defined as food that encompasses potentially healthful products, including any modified food or food ingredient that may provide a health benefit beyond that of the traditional nutrients it contains (MWCD, 2010). Functional food, health supplements, nutraceuticals and food for special dietary use are used interchangeably in India to define foods that are specially processed or formulated to satisfy particular dietary requirements that exist because of a particular physical or physiological condition. The Food Safety and Standards Act (FSSA) defines functional foods (including foods for special dietary uses/ nutraceuticals/health supplements) as:

> foods which are specially processed or formulated to satisfy particular dietary requirements which exist because of a particular physical or physiological condition or specific diseases and disorders ... wherein the composition must differ significantly from the composition of ordinary foods of comparable nature ... does not claim to cure or mitigate any specific disease, disorder or condition (except for certain health benefit or such promotion claims) as may be permitted by the regulations made under FSSA. (Palthur et al., 2009, p. 4)

Novel food, on the other hand, refers to an article of food for which safety standards have not been specified but are not unsafe. These products should not contain any food or ingredient that is prohibited under the Food Safety Standards Act 2006 (FSSA, 2006). Nutrient structure/function claims are permitted but disease risk reduction claims are prohibited.

Key terminology in India: functional foods, novel foods, health supplements, nutraceuticals, food for special dietary use, nutrient structure/function claims.

2.5.5 China (The People's Republic of China)

The China Food and Drug Administration (CFDA) refers to functional food as health food, defining it as 'food with specific health functions that are suitable for consumption by specific groups of people and that has the effect of regulating human body functions without treating diseases' (Patel et al., 2008, p. 4). Novel foods in China are defined as ingredients that have not traditionally been part of the Chinese diet. There are four different categories of novel foods, which usually refer to ingredients used in ready-to-consume products. The first category is animals and microorganisms. The second is for rarely used ingredients. The third entails newly discovered microorganisms applied to food processing. The fourth category covers food ingredients whose structure has been modified by new technology (AP, 2007). The CFDA has no specific definition for nutraceuticals/supplements. China permits the use of disease risk reduction claims, structure/function claims and recently, nutrient content claims. Nutrition labelling is required when claims are made.

Key terminology in China: health food, novel food, structure/function claims, disease risk reduction claims, nutrient content claims.

2.5.6 South Korea (The Republic of Korea)

In South Korea, the Health Functional Food Act (HFFA) 2004 defines food products and supplements with health benefits as health/functional food products. They are food supplements containing nutrients or other substances (in a concentrated form) that have a nutritional or physiological effect whose purpose is to supplement the normal diet. A healthier food product in South Korea is similar to a (dietary/food) supplement in the USA or EU or an NHP in Canada. The HFFA requires these products to be marketed in measured doses, such as in pills, tablets, capsules and liquids (MHW, 2004). The definition used for supplements and functional foods also applies to novel foods. Disease risk reduction, structure/function and 'other function' claims are permitted. Other function claims have three different levels of scientific evidence. Nutrient function claims are also permitted.

Key terminology in South Korea: health/functional food (HFF) products.

2.5.7 Taiwan

The Taiwan Health Food Control Act (HFCA) 2006 refers to both functional food and supplements as health foods. In Taiwan, health food should be in the form of a food product or consumed along with food. Health food in Taiwan is defined as food that possesses special nutritious elements (bioactive components) or specific health care abilities to improve and/or reduce the risk of disease. To be considered a health food and granted a permit, these products must satisfy the following conditions:

● Bioactive components that provide the health benefit should be clearly identified. If the specific ingredients cannot be identified, then the health benefits should be listed and research supporting them provided to the health authorities for verification.
● The health benefit should be scientifically proven.
● The product must be safe and harmless to humans when consumed. All manufacturing, effectiveness and safety methods should be approved by health authorities (HFCA, 2006).

Health foods should not be used for mitigation, curing and/or treating human disease. In Taiwan, the definition used for supplements/nutraceuticals and functional foods also applies to novel foods. Taiwan permits health maintenance claims, which are claims that the product promotes health by reducing the risk of serious illness (structure/function claims) as well as nutrient content claims. Therapeutic claims are not permitted. Nutrition labelling is regulated.

Key terminology in Taiwan: health foods, health maintenance claims.

2.5.8 FAO

In 2007, the Food and Agriculture Organization (FAO) of the United Nations provided a working definition for functional food as 'foods which are intended to be consumed as part of the normal diet and that, contain biologically active components which offer the potential of enhanced health or reduced risk of disease' (Subirade, 2007, p. 4). The FAO does not have formal definitions for supplements/nutraceuticals or novel foods.

2.6 NAVIGATING THE CONFUSION

Since the introduction of healthier food products, a myriad of different terminologies and definitions to describe such products have emerged across various countries. Although broadly referencing foods with health benefits or new attributes, no consensus exists regarding the definitions of functional foods, nutraceuticals, supplements or NHPs. Neither is there consensus as to what constitutes a 'novel' food. Table 2.1 presents a summary of the terminology used across the 11 jurisdictions discussed in this chapter.

While there is no universally accepted definition for functional food, some similarities in the terminology used across countries do exist. The differences in the definitions are often cultural and regulatory in nature. All definitions require that the food product provide benefits beyond that of conventional food; while it should not be perceived as a drug, it should have some physiological functions. In the USA, Canada, EU, Australia and New Zealand, Brazil, India and China, functional foods are expected to be similar in appearance to conventional food and must provide benefits beyond basic nutrition. Many countries have an official defin-ition for functional foods (EU, Japan, Canada, India, China), while others have a set of specifications that a food should possess to qualify as a functional food – in other words, a working definition only (the USA, Australia and New Zealand, Brazil). Lastly, in other countries, there is no distinction made between a functional food and a supplement (Russia, South Korea, Taiwan).

Therefore, in the USA, foods and dietary components that have health benefits beyond basic nutrition – that is, they furnish energy, sustain growth or maintain vital processes – are classified as functional food. In Canada, functional food should be part of a usual diet and have physiological benefits and/or reduce the risk of diseases beyond basic nutrition. In Japan, they are foods containing ingredients claimed to have physiological effects on humans. In the EU, functional foods are regarded as food with beneficial effects on the human body beyond basic nutrition. In Australia and New Zealand, functional foods should be similar in appearance to conventional foods but modified to provide particular benefits. China refers to functional food as food with special health functions. Brazil and India refer to functional food as foods that can provide benefits beyond basic nutrition.

Some consensus exists regarding the definitions of supplements/ nutraceuticals. Though the terminology may be different, the underlying intent appears similar among countries. The most common characteristics of nutraceuticals or supplements are that they should be sold in measured

Table 2.1   Definitions of functional foods, supplements/nutraceuticals and novel foods, various countries

Location	Functional food	Nutraceutical/dietary supplement/ NHP/medical foods/ FSDU	Novel food
UNITED STATES OF AMERICA Key terms: dietary supplement, food for special dietary use, novel food, functional food, medical food	The US FDA does not provide a legal definition for the term functional foods, which is currently more of a marketing idiom for the category. Working definitions have been developed by different organizations. ADA classifies all foods as functional at some physiological level because they provide nutrients or other substances that furnish energy, sustain growth or maintain/repair vital processes. However, functional foods move beyond necessity to provide additional health benefits that may reduce disease risk and/or promote optimal health. IFIC considers functional foods to include any food or dietary components that may have health benefits beyond basic nutrition. IFT defines functional foods as foods and food components that provide a health benefit beyond basic nutrition (for the intended population). These substances provide essential nutrients often beyond quantities necessary for normal maintenance, growth and development and/or other biologically active components that impart health benefits or desirable physiological effects.	A dietary supplement is defined by the DSHEA as a product that is intended to supplement the diet and contains any of the following dietary ingredients: a vitamin, a mineral, a herb or other botanical (excluding tobacco), an amino acid, a concentrate, metabolite, constituent, extract or combination of any of the above. Furthermore, it must also conform to the following criteria: be intended for ingestion in pill, capsule, tablet, powder or liquid form and not be represented for use as a conventional food or as the sole item of a meal or diet labelled as a dietary supplement. Foods for special dietary use are defined as a particular use for which a food purports or is represented to be used, including but not limited to supplying a special dietary need that exists by reason of a physical, physiological, pathological or other condition; supplying a vitamin, mineral or other ingredient for use by humans to supplement the diet by increasing the total dietary intake; supplying a special dietary need by reason of being a food for use as the sole item of the diet. Examples include infant foods, hypoallergenic foods such as gluten-free foods and lactose-free foods and foods offered for reducing weight.	No official definition for novel food but often referred to as new and emerging food products derived from biotechnology.

	Medical foods are defined by the Orphan Drug Act as a food that is formulated to be consumed or administered entirely under the supervision of a physician and that is intended for the specific dietary management of a disease or condition for which distinctive nutritional requirements, based on recognized scientific principles, are established by medical evaluation.		
CANADA Key terms: functional food, natural health product (NHP), nutraceutical, novel food	A functional food is similar in appearance to, or may be, a conventional food, is consumed as part of a usual diet and is demonstrated to have physiological benefits and/or reduce the risk of chronic disease beyond basic nutritional functions.	Natural health product (NHP) means a substance or a combination of substances in which all the medicinal ingredients are natural products, a homeopathic medicine or a traditional medicine, that is manufactured, sold or represented for use in (a) the diagnosis, treatment, mitigation or prevention of a disease, disorder or abnormal physical state or its symptoms in humans; (b) restoring or correcting organic functions in humans; or (c) modifying organic functions in humans, such as modifying those functions in a manner that maintains or promotes health. A nutraceutical was previously defined as a product isolated or purified from foods that is generally sold in medicinal forms not usually associated with food. A nutraceutical is demonstrated to have a physiological benefit or provide protection against chronic disease. (Note: The term NHP replaced nutraceutical in the 2003 NHP Regulations.)	Foods resulting from a process not previously used for food OR products that do not have a history of safe use as a food OR foods that have been modified by genetic manipulation, also known as genetically modified foods, GM foods, genetically engineered foods or biotechnology-derived foods.

Location	Functional food	Nutraceutical/dietary supplement/ NHP/medical foods/ FSDU	Novel food
EU Key terms: functional food, food supplements, novel food	A food can be regarded as functional if it is satisfactorily demonstrated to affect beneficially one or more target functions in the body, beyond adequate nutritional effects, in a way that is relevant to either an improved state of health and wellbeing and/or reduction of risk of disease. Functional foods must be in the form of conventional foods and they must demonstrate their effects in amounts that can normally be expected to be consumed in the diet: they are not pills or capsules, but part of a normal food pattern.	Food supplements are concentrated sources of nutrients or other substances with a nutritional or physiological effect whose purpose is to supplement the normal diet. They are marketed 'in dose' form, that is, as pills, tablets, capsules, liquids in measured doses and so on.	Defined as a food that has not been used for human consumption to a significant degree before.
JAPAN Key terms: (Regular) FOSHU, Qualified FOSHU, Standardized FOSHU, Reduction of disease risk FOSHU, novel foods	Foods containing ingredients with functions for health and officially approved to claim physiological effects on the human body. FOSHU is intended to be consumed for the maintenance/promotion of health or special health uses by people who wish to control health conditions, including blood pressure or blood cholesterol. In order to sell a food as FOSHU, a safety assessment is required, along with an assessment of the effectiveness of the functions for health and the claim must be approved by the MHLW. FOSHU can be classified as Regular, Qualified, Standardized or Reduction of disease risk.	The terminology for functional food/FOSHU also applies to supplements. In addition to FOSHU, supplements may also be categorized as follows. • Food with nutrient function claims refers to food products that require no pre-market approval but is restricted to approved vitamins and minerals. • Medical drugs that require prior approval. • All other foods or general food category includes nutritional supplements and all other food products not in the other categories.	In Japan, there is no official definition for novel food but it is often referred to as foods and food additives that have been produced through the use of recombinant DNA techniques (GM).

Country / Key terms	Functional foods	Nutraceutical / supplement	Novel food
AUSTRALIA and NEW ZEALAND Key terms: functional food, nutraceutical, dietary supplement, non-traditional food (novel food)	FSANZ defines functional foods as being similar in appearance to conventional foods and intended to be consumed as part of a normal diet, but modified to serve physiological roles beyond the provision of simple nutrient requirements. In other words, functional foods look like their conventional counterparts but have a nutrient or other health-promoting substance (or substances) added, or have undergone some other significant modification to provide a particular health benefit.	A nutraceutical is a food that has been designed to provide health benefits. It may contain beneficial ingredients such as specific amino acids or vitamins and so on. Nutraceuticals can be marketed in the form of pills, capsules or tablets. In New Zealand, a dietary supplement is any amino acid, edible substance, herb, mineral, nutrient or vitamin normally available in food that is put into a controlled dosage form and is intended to be taken orally.	Novel food is defined as a non-traditional food for which there is insufficient knowledge in the broad community to enable safe use in the form or context in which it is presented, taking into account: (a) the composition or structure of the product; (b) levels of undesirable substances in the product; (c) known potential for adverse effects in humans; (d) traditional preparation and cooking methods; or (e) patterns and levels of consumption of the product, where a non-traditional food is defined as a food that does not have a history of significant human consumption by the broad community in Australia or New Zealand.
BRAZIL Key terms: healthful products, novel foods	Functional foods have not been defined, but the norms were based on the idea of a product that is a food and not a drug, that is part of a normal diet and that can produce benefits beyond basic nutrition. They are generally referred to as healthful products.	Included as healthful products.	Food with no history of use in Brazil.
RUSSIA Key terms: BAFS	Included as BAFS.	Biologically active food supplements (BAFS) is defined as nutritive substances and minor food components used to ameliorate deficiencies, decrease risk of debilitating diseases and improve life quality. They are meant to be consumed along with food or be incorporated into foodstuffs.	Included as BAFS.

Location	Functional food	Nutraceutical/dietary supplement/ NHP/medical foods/ FSDU	Novel food
INDIA Key terms: functional foods, novel foods, health supplements	Food that encompasses potentially healthful products, including any modified food or food ingredient that may provide a health benefit beyond that of the traditional nutrients it contains.	N/A	An article of food for which standards have not been specified but are not unsafe. These products should not contain any food or ingredient that is prohibited under the Food Safety and Standards Act 2006.
CHINA Key terms: health food, novel food	Referred to as health food and is defined as foods with specific health functions that are suitable for consumption by specific groups of people and that have the effect of regulating human body functions without treating diseases.	N/A	Novel foods in China are defined as ingredients that have not traditionally formed part of the Chinese diet. Four categories exist: for plants, animals and microorganisms; for rarely used ingredients; newly discovered microorganisms applied to food processing; food ingredients whose structure has been modified by new technology.
SOUTH KOREA Key terms: health/ functional food (HFF)	Included as HFF.	The term health/functional food (HFF) refers to food supplements containing nutrients or other substances (in a concentrated form) that have a nutritional or physiological effect whose purpose is to supplement the normal diet. These are products to be marketed in measured doses, such as in pills, tablets, capsules and liquids.	Included as HFF.

TAIWAN Key terms: health food(s)	Included as health food.	Health food is defined as food products that possess 'special nutritious elements' (bioactive components) or 'specific health care abilities' to improve health and/or reduce the risk of disease. Health food should be in the form of food products or consumed along with food. These products should not be used for mitigation, curing and/or treating human diseases.	Included as health food.
FAO	Functional foods are generally considered as foods that are intended to be consumed as part of the normal diet and that contain biologically active components that offer the potential of enhanced health or reduced risk of disease.	N/A	N/A

Source: Adapted from the following. USA: ADA (2004), FDA (2005a, 2010), IFIC (2009), IFT (2005); Canada: Canada Gazette (2003), Health Canada (1998, 2009a); EU: EC (1998), EFSA (2010), FUFOSE (1999); Japan: MHLW (2010); Australia and New Zealand: FSANZ (2001, 2006, 2010c); Brazil: Lajolo (2002); Russia: Zawistowski (2008); India: MWCD (2010), The Gazette of India (2006); China: AP (2007), Patel et al. (2008); South Korea: MHW (2004); Taiwan: HFCA (2006); FAO: Subirade (2007).

doses and in the form of pills, tablets, capsules or liquids, as well as have some physiological benefits or provide certain health benefits. In the USA, dietary supplements are also marketed in the form of pills, tablets or capsules and are intended to supplement the diet. In Canada, NHPs should be in a medicinal form (pills, tablets or capsules) and used for the prevention or treatment of diseases. In the EU, similar to Canada, the USA and South Korea, food supplements should be marketed in a dose form as pills, capsules or tablets. However, in contrast, Russia (BAFS) supplements should be in the form of food products or consumed along with food.

The terminology governing these products is evolving and remains contradictory in places. Canada now classifies a nutraceutical as a natural health product, which is equivalent to a food supplement in the EU; is still often called a nutraceutical in Australia and New Zealand; and is equivalent to a dietary supplement in the USA. Confusingly, in Japan, Russia, South Korea and Taiwan, the terminology used for health-enhancing food products applies to both functional food and nutraceuticals/supplements.

Novel foods are most commonly categorized as foods not previously used by humans or lack a history of use as food in the country in question. Something akin to this definition is used in the USA, Canada, EU, Australia, New Zealand, Brazil, India and China. However, in some countries, notably the USA, Canada, EU, Japan and China, novel foods also include food products that are genetically engineered or derived through biotechnology. In Japan and the USA, there is a working definition only for novel foods. In countries like Russia, South Korea and Taiwan (without a distinct definition for novel food), the definition used for supplements/nutraceuticals and functional foods also applies to novel foods.

The absence of uniform terminology for these food products or ingredients reflects differences in the underlying approaches to food regulation across countries, as well as perhaps a lack of scientific consensus on the presence, efficacy and measurement of the health benefits derived from these products. Differences in terminology raise costs and create uncertainty for firms marketing across international borders and, as such, can hinder the expansion of international trade in these products. Certainly, a firm contemplating developing export markets for a functional food or supplement/nutraceutical needs to be fully cognizant of the food category in which its product will be defined and the specific regulatory approvals required for marketing the product with a health claim. More in-depth discussion of differences in regulatory environments internationally is provided in Chapters 4 and 5.

3. Evolving policy issues and regulatory frameworks

This chapter outlines the key economic and governance issues surrounding regulatory approvals for new health food products, the regulation of health claims and the protection of intellectual property rights (IPR). It begins by outlining how these issues arise and why they are important, drawing upon the economic concepts of market and non-market failure. A major theme of the chapter is the challenges facing regulators in developing new policy frameworks and insights from the literature are used to examine the state of flux within policy environments. Three case studies are then used to illustrate different aspects of regulatory development. Canada is used as one of the case studies to examine the gradual process of regulatory adaptation in response to the relatively new category of health food products. An example of regulatory harmonization is provided within the context of the development of EU regulations that supersede previously disparate individual country regulatory approaches. The issues explored in this chapter serve as a backdrop for Chapters 4 and 5, which provide a detailed examination of the regulations pertaining to health claims and new product approvals in selected developed and emerging markets, respectively.

3.1 WHY DO GOVERNMENTS INTERVENE?

The emergence of the health foods sector has raised a number of policy issues for governments. Beyond simply providing a regulatory definition for categories of health foods, as discussed in Chapter 2, governments intervene in the regulation of allowable health claims, in new product approval processes and in establishing rules for the protection of IPRs that influence incentives for R&D in the sector. Why do governments intervene and how much intervention is optimal?

The notion of a market failure is a fairly standard concept in economics whereby markets sometimes fail to produce a socially optimal allocation of resources. In this situation, it is argued, government intervention is justified to correct the market failure provided that the benefits of that intervention outweigh the costs. The concept of market failure, and the consequences of government intervention to address market failures, is well established in the economics literature. Coase (1964) observed, however, that whereas the category of market failure was prevalent in the economics literature, no category of 'government failure' existed. He went on to document the ineffectiveness and poor performance of a number of US regulatory commissions in this regard.

Economists have subsequently paid more attention to the notion of government or regulatory failures, with the theory of 'non-market' failures gaining prominence (for example, Wolf, 1979, 1987). Wolf's theory of non-market failure shows how collective choice can lead to socially inefficient outcomes; it redresses the apparent asymmetry in the standard treatment of market failures by showing that government (regulatory) failure can also occur.

The traditional notion of market failure recognizes that self-interested individual behaviour may lead to an economically inefficient allocation of resources generating a need for government (or collective) intervention to correct the market failure, with the objective of achieving a Pareto improvement.[1] Four sources of market failures provide the standard rationale for government (non-market) intervention in remedying the failure of the market to allocate resources efficiently: externalities and public goods; monopoly rents; market imperfections (including imperfect information); and distributional equity (Wolf, 1987).

In parallel, Wolf posits that there are four sources of non-market (government or regulatory) failures: the disjunction between costs and revenues (such as government tax revenues); the existence of 'internalities' and private or organizational goals (in other words, self-interested behaviour within organizations); derived externalities; and distributional inequities (Wolf, 1987).[2] Consequently, in determining the extent to which policy interventions will yield a Pareto improvement in the face of market failures, it is also necessary to consider the non-market failures, or inefficiencies, created by the policy intervention.

Applying this framework to the health foods product sector, a number of potential sources of market failure exist and form the rationale for policy interventions. Layered on top of this discussion is the recognition that policy interventions may also be the source of non-market failure, particularly if over-regulation stifles investments in new food innovations. Market failures are conceptualized as consequences (either positive or negative) of the actions of individual producers (or consumers) that affect other producers (or consumers), while non-market failures arise as a result of the actions of the regulator and may affect all producers (or consumers).

The market failures related to the consumption and production of health foods include negative externalities and information asymmetry in consumption, as well as positive externalities (spillovers) in production. A consumption-related market failure is the information asymmetry that arises due to the credence attribute[3] nature of health foods. In the absence of labelling, consumers are unaware of the potential health benefits associated with the consumption of a specific product, resulting in under-consumption from a societal perspective. Labelling and credible health claims enable consumers to identify food with health benefits and are a solution to this type of market failure. Countries have moved to establish regulatory frameworks around the approval of specific health claims and the type of information that can be provided on food labels to better inform consumers about the nutrient content of foods and to facilitate healthier eating choices. At the same time, however, an overly complex or onerous regulatory process for the approval of new products and new health claims introduces elements of non-market (regulatory) failure by increasing costs for firms or by adding complexity to the consumer's decision-making process. If consumers do not trust the regulatory system for health claims, question the truthfulness of health claims or are confused by contradictory or obtuse language in health claims, demand for these products will be below the socially optimal level.

The second form of consumption-related market failure is the negative externality due to under-consumption of health foods if the costs of poor health are not borne entirely by the individual. This would be the case for countries with publicly funded health care systems such as the UK and Canada but also with private health care insurance markets where an insured individual does not bear the full costs of poor health. In both cases, consumption of foods with health benefits will be less than the social optimum. Simply labelling a food as healthier may do little to alleviate this market failure.

The technological spillovers in the development of new functional food and natural health products are a potential source of positive production externalities and therefore of market failure. A technology spillover is a positive externality that exists when a firm's innovation or research into a new technology contributes to reduced research costs for other firms who can free-ride on the efforts of the innovating firm, thus leading to suboptimal private investments in new food innovations. This will be the case where it is difficult to establish or protect IPRs to innovations. In the case of functional foods in Canada, for example, it has been noted that firms have tended to use trade secrets rather than formal patent protection as a means to protect their research investments, in part due to weaker

IPR protection (Cinnamon, 2009; Malla et al., 2013a). A lack of effective patent protection or well-established property rights protection markedly affects decisions to undertake R&D as firms cannot capture all the rents from their R&D investments.

The registration process for novel foods and the approval process for new health claims can introduce an element of both market and non-market (regulatory) failure. For example, there may be positive spillover effects from the approval process for new health claims; these are sunk costs to the individual innovating firm that reduce entry costs for subsequent firms entering or innovating in this market. Since the benefits of pursuing a novel food or a health claim through the approval process accrue to others in addition to the innovating firm, there will be suboptimal levels of resources allocated to new product and new health claim approvals. This is a form of market failure.

On the other hand, if the regulatory processes for approval of a new health claim or to register a new product are slow, demanding and expensive, this raises costs for all firms. The inefficiencies introduced by the regulatory process result in a lower output of health foods than is socially optimal. This is a source of non-market (regulatory) failure. The bureaucracy surrounding the approval process for new health claims, the stringent requirements and a relative lengthy approval process often mean that it is very difficult to get approval for a new health claim or that firms face significant costs in navigating the regulatory process. If this is the case, the bureaucracy becomes a form of non-market failure due to internalities and/or derived externalities.

Health claims can be classified as generic or product-specific (see Chapter 1). Product-specific claims specify a relationship between a specific food or food constituent and a health benefit, whereas generic claims apply to more than one product. Generic health claims create a free-rider problem because many firms can benefit but, depending on the regulatory requirements, if the claim must be submitted to and approved by a regulatory agency, then only one firm must initiate and undergo the application process to obtain approval for a new claim. Post approval, other firms may then use the claim.

The market and non-market failures associated with consumption and production in the health foods sector are presented in Figure 3.1. Considering first the demand for health foods, the private marginal benefit (demand) curve without labelling/health claims is MB_P^1; while the social marginal benefit curve with credible labelling/health claims is denoted by MB_S^1. Addressing information asymmetry through policies that facilitate credible health claims shifts the marginal benefit curve to the right. Even in the presence of credible labelling, however, marginal

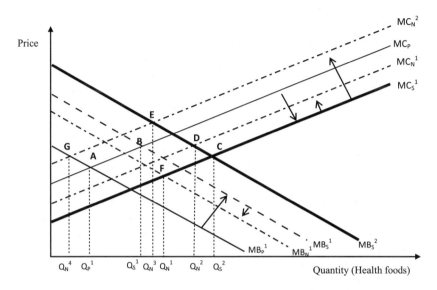

Figure 3.1 Market and non-market failures in the health foods sector

benefit may still lie below the optimal social marginal benefit if there remains a market failure due to consumption externalities; for example, when the social benefits of healthier food consumption decisions are larger than the private benefits, thus MB_S^1 still lies below the optimal social marginal benefit curve MB_S^2. The optimal social marginal benefit is greater than the private marginal benefit due to both asymmetric information and health care consumption externalities, as described above. The marginal benefit curve in the presence of regulatory failure (in other words, incorporating non-market failures) is labelled MB_N^1 and reflects a situation where regulatory complexity muddies the consumer quality signal or reduces consumer confidence in the truthfulness of health claims, thereby introducing an inefficiency that shifts marginal benefit below the credible labelling scenario, MB_S^1.

Turning to the supply side of the market, MC_P is the private marginal cost curve for health foods, MC_S^1 is the (optimal) social marginal cost curve in the absence of non-market failures and MC_N^1 and MC_N^2 are social marginal cost curves in the presence of non-market (government) failures of different magnitudes. The private marginal cost (MC_P) lies above the social marginal cost MC_S^1 due to the presence of market failure (production externalities) pertaining to technological spillovers and spillovers from the registration process for new health claims. These spillovers lower costs for subsequent firms but are not captured in the cost curves of the original innovator.

The regulatory system for approval of new functional foods or new health claims, however, may be a source of non-market failures, increasing costs for firms and shifting the (social) marginal cost curve away from its optimum, for example, from $MC_S{}^1$ to $MC_N{}^1$. In the case of extreme non-market failure, the (social) marginal cost curve may even lie above the original private marginal cost curve, for example, at $MC_N{}^2$. In this case, the non-market-derived externalities and internalities, or regulatory burdens, not only negate any positive spillover effects but significantly add to firms' costs, resulting in a large leftward shift in the social marginal cost curve and a general rise in industry costs.

The intersection of the private marginal benefit curve and the private marginal cost curve yields a market outcome at point A (corresponding to output level $Q_P{}^1$). In the presence of information asymmetry and positive consumption externalities, however, this outcome is suboptimal due to market failures. If consumers are informed about health benefits through labelling, but do not bear the full costs of poor health outcomes, then the private equilibrium is determined at point B on $MB_S{}^1$ (corresponding to output level $Q_S{}^1$).

The socially optimal equilibrium (in the absence of market and non-market failures) is determined at point C, where the marginal social cost ($MC_S{}^1$) is equal to the optimal marginal social benefit ($MB_S{}^2$). The socially optimal equilibrium quantity ($Q_S{}^2$) is higher than the market equilibrium quantity ($Q_P{}^1$). Labelling is expected to address one aspect of the consumption-related market failure (information asymmetry) but it would not lead to the socially optimal consumption level if other market failures (positive externalities from healthier food consumption choices) are present. On the other hand, if poorly defined or ineffective health claims regulations introduce consumer confusion, marginal benefit shifts back to $MB_N{}^1$ and equilibrium occurs at point F, corresponding to output level $Q_N{}^1$.

When unintended non-market failures associated with government intervention increase firms' costs, then the equilibrium may be at point D. Regulatory-induced inefficiencies shift the marginal (social) cost curve back to $MC_N{}^1$, resulting in inefficient outcome $Q_N{}^2$ rather than the socially optimal outcome $Q_S{}^2$. If regulatory interventions create significant non-market failures, the marginal social cost curve shifts to $MC_N{}^2$ at point E, with output falling to $Q_N{}^3$. In this case, although the interventions successfully addressed information asymmetry and consumption externalities, the interventions themselves were costly, reducing the consumption of functional foods below its socially optimal level.

The 'worst case' scenario is represented by point G at output level $Q_N{}^4$. In this case, policy interventions failed to address either the information asymmetry or the consumption externality market failures (labelling was ineffective and behaviour did not change), thereby leaving marginal benefit at $MB_P{}^1$, yet the interventions imposed costs on the industry, increasing marginal social costs to $MC_N{}^2$. Points G and C represent two extremes: policy that completely fails to address market failures while introducing significant non-market (regulatory) failures (G) and policy that perfectly addresses market failures and avoids the introduction of non-market failures (C). The reality is likely to lie somewhere in between these two extremes as policy interventions balance the benefits of improving market signals and incentives to innovate, with the pitfalls of introducing bureaucratic inefficiencies and institutional rigidities. With this context in mind, the next section provides insights from the literature examining the disparity in regulatory approaches to the health foods sector across different countries. Section 3.3 then illustrates the complexity of developing regulations for the health foods sector through a case study of the evolution of the Canadian regulatory environment.

3.2 POLICIES IN FLUX: INSIGHTS FROM THE LITERATURE

The widespread inconsistencies in terminology and definitions characterizing the health foods industry globally is reflected in significant differences in regulatory and policy environments. Individual countries have developed their own regulatory frameworks and policy agendas concerning labelling and approval of health foods, novel food application procedures, nutritional contents, health claims and the enforcement of these regulations. Efforts to harmonize regulations across borders have been hampered by a vast array of differences in approach and systems. This section reviews literature dealing with regulatory policies affecting the health foods sector.

In a report prepared for the World Health Organization (WHO), Hawkes (2004) reviews global regulations on nutrition labelling and health claims and provides an overview of approaches to developing and implementing these regulations. The analysis reveals regulations in over 70 countries with some degree of harmony but also significant variations. There appears to be a consensus among countries on the need to declare nutrition information on labels, based on the belief that nutritional labelling will help consumers make informed choices. Health claims, however, are more internationally controversial; nutrient function claims are more accepted than structure/function and disease risk reduction claims, based upon the premise that referencing diseases will imply the ability of food to treat or prevent diseases. There are constant changes in health claims (due to ongoing developments in national, regional and international regulations, as well as the possibility of misleading and confusing claims) making attempts by regulatory authorities to harmonize health claims regulations internationally extremely challenging.

In an assessment of the challenges of policy development for the health foods sector, Veeman (2002) recognizes that the industry suffers from market failures due to uncertainty and information asymmetry associated with health claims. The author notes that while the USA, Japan and other nations implemented policies that enabled manufacturers to make health claims on functional foods, nutraceuticals and supplements, often there are significant variations in approaches. For example, prior to the development of EU-wide regulations, Germany[4] treated supplements as drugs that were sold through pharmacies as prescription medications but in contrast, in the USA, the same products (referred to as dietary supplements) are sold without pre-clearance and health claims are permitted. In another example, S-adenosylmethionene (SAMe) is regarded as a dietary supplement in the USA but classified as a drug in Canada, requiring a drug identification number (DIN) and licence from Health Canada, while in Europe it is available as a prescription medication. That policy harmonization is possible, however, is illustrated by the example of the coordination of food standards between Australia and New Zealand, discussed in the next chapter.

Farrell et al. (2009) illustrate the confusion and ambiguities surrounding the regulatory framework governing foods and NHPs in Canada, using probiotic yoghurt and green tea as examples. The authors argue that the regulatory distinctions between conventional foods, NHPs, functional foods and nutraceuticals are unclear. For example, the definition of an NHP in Canada does not include conventional foods, yet NHPs are commonly marketed in a conventional food format (for example, probiotic yoghurt), becoming a source of confusion. NHPs are considered a subcategory of drugs in Canada and the National Health Product Regulations (NHPR) indicate that any product whose effect on humans has not been investigated may have to undergo clinical trials in order to obtain approval from Health Canada. In contrast, clinical trials are not required on food products (including functional foods). Firms conducting clinical trials on food products face uncertainty due to the conflict between NHPR and the Canadian Food and Drugs Act regulations. Should the trial results be negative, then the product remains a conventional food item; should the results be positive or indicate that the product contains an ingredient with medicinal/health properties (or health-enhanced ingredients), then the ingredient could become an NHP, potentially requiring further trial and approval. The product could also potentially require pre-market approval if it is classified as an NHP, but generally not as a conventional food, unless the product is a novel food (foods with no history of use), food additive or infant formula.

The case of probiotic yoghurt is used to illustrate the confusion surrounding regulations. Probiotic yoghurt is sold in the Canadian market without a health claim, yet the term 'probiotic' is included in the definition of an NHP. Should a researcher decide to conduct a clinical trial to ascertain whether probiotic yoghurt can relieve certain gastrointestinal problems, confusion exists regarding whether NHP approval is needed as it will not be clear whether the product is considered a probiotic and therefore an NHP requiring approval, or yoghurt, in which case an approval is not necessary as yoghurt is a conventional food.

The same conflict exists for green tea. As tea is a plant extract, it is considered an NHP, but since tea is also a beverage, it can be considered as food. This situation is likely to create confusion for consumers and manufacturers as there could be some green teas marketed as NHPs while other green teas are marketed as food. Farrell et al. (2009) conclude that existing regulations in Canada do not provide adequate distinctions between food and NHPs and recommend closer collaboration between the Food Directorate and the Natural Health Products Directorate (NHPD) to resolve these issues.

The risk of consumer confusion from health claims is discussed by Mariotti et al. (2010), who identify several sources of potential confusion based upon discrepancies between how consumers interpret a health claim and what the health claim is actually trying to communicate. These include the use of scientific jargon that is difficult for consumers to understand, a misperception that 'more is better' in terms of a nutrient, the assumption that a nutrient guarantees a health effect without considering other factors that may influence the health outcome and an assumption that a health claim refers to the general population rather than a target population. Consumer responses to health claims are discussed in more detail in Chapter 7.

In a report to the FAO, Subirade (2007) examines the regulatory developments for health, nutrients or functional claims relating to foods on both a global and regional basis. The analysis is based on information provided by regulatory authorities in Europe, the USA, Canada, Japan and other Asian countries and finds a general consensus that regulatory frameworks should focus on the protection of consumers, promotion of fair trade and innovation. There is also a general recognition among countries that health claims should be scientifically validated. Nevertheless, the report points to rampant confusion and distrust among health professionals and consumers that has been generated by the proliferation of health claims and identifies a need for greater international harmonization and uniformity in nutrient descriptions, disease risk reduction health claims and structure/function claims.

In a relatively early assessment as the health foods sector was emerging, Smith et al. (1996) analyse the regulatory frameworks for functional foods in the USA, Canada, EU and Japan. During this 1996 period, the regulatory regime governing the manufacture, packaging, labelling and advertising of functional foods in Canada was found to be relatively restrictive, thereby limiting product development and marketing. Few disease risk reduction health claims had been approved for use and novel food application requirements were strenuous. The study argued that consumer access to functional foods had been limited while investment and competition in the industry was restricted under the Food and Drugs Act, which offered the option of licensing and selling functional foods as 'drugs', thereby necessitating that a product undergo an extremely strenuous approval and registration process.

The regulatory framework in the USA, though restrictive in comparison to Japan's, was considered by Smith et al. (1996) to be more supportive of the development and marketing of functional foods compared to that of Canada. Legislation pertaining to the approval, labelling and advertising of dietary supplements, which may be applicable to certain functional foods, was relatively well defined. The divergence in regulatory approaches between Canada and the USA and the relatively limited opportunities for firms in Canada to utilize health claims on food products resulted in increasing pressure for reform of the Canadian regulatory framework governing the health foods sector. The development of a new regulatory landscape in Canada provides an interesting case study and is discussed in the next section.

3.3 EVOLVING POLICY FRAMEWORKS: A CASE STUDY OF THE CANADIAN REGULATORY ENVIRONMENT

In Canada, Health Canada (a federal government department) is responsible for establishing policies, regulations and standards pertaining to the health, safety and nutritional quality of food in Canada, while the Canadian Food Inspection Agency (CFIA) is responsible for enforcing the policies and regulations developed by Health Canada, including enforcement of food labelling regulations. Recognizing the need to reform regulation of the health foods sector in Canada, a long process of review and consultation began with the publication of a 1998 Health Canada policy paper (Health Canada, 1998). As a joint project involving government, industry, consumer groups, academia and health professionals, the development of a policy framework to address the lack of specific regulations for health claims on functional foods and nutraceuticals (as they were then known) was the goal.

Definitions were proposed for both nutraceuticals and functional foods as well as what constitutes a health claim. The absence of a definition for 'health claim' in Canada at that time led the group to use the term in a broader sense similar to its use in the USA: 'A health claim specifically characterizes the relationship between the nutrient and a disease or medical condition that is related to the diet' (Health Canada, 1998, p. 7). Health claims were further categorized into therapeutic, risk reduction and structure/function claims. A therapeutic claim could apply to either functional food or NHPs/nutraceuticals and suggested that a product can cure/treat/mitigate/prevent a disease. A risk reduction health claim was defined as the ability to significantly change recognized risk factors involved in the development of a chronic disease. A structure/function claim was defined as the ability of the product to affect the structure or any function of the human or animal body. Any of these claims could be generic or product-specific, where product-specific claims are made for a single commercial product and cannot be generalized to other similar products unless acceptable supporting evidence was provided. It was recommended that generic claims could be applied to any food, provided that it met the criteria for the claim (Health Canada, 1998, pp. 17–18).

Prior to this 1998 policy paper, the status quo practice in Canada was to regulate any products making health claims (including food) as drugs. A final policy proposal at that time was to permit both disease risk reduction and structure/function claims for food and food components while all other products with therapeutic health claims (in other words, said to cure, treat, mitigate or prevent illness) should continue to be regulated as drugs, regardless of their form. Appropriate standards for evidence and the development of a regulatory framework to measure and ensure compliance with the proposed policy for risk reduction and structure/function claims, the development of an implementation strategy, standards of evidence and composition for claims on food in consultation with industry stakeholders were also suggested.

In 1999, Health Canada began an evaluation process for ten generic health claims that were permitted in the USA, based upon consultation workshops, industry input and the recommendations of the 1998 Health Canada policy paper to permit risk reduction claims and structure/ function claims on foods. Health Canada (2000) proposed conditions for the use of five generic health claims, all of which were supported by scientific agreement. Opinions on claim credibility, consumer education and a review of scientific evidence were also presented.

With the successful identification of specific health claims, the Bureau of Nutritional Sciences Food Directorate (BNSFD) proposed a framework for the evaluation of foods with health claims with the purpose of ensuring product safety, the validity of claims, quality assurance in production methods and product testing (BNSFD, 2000). It was decided that all food products should undergo at least a basic evaluation to determine the safety of the product with respect to nutritional and toxicology effects; novel foods or those with greater uncertainty with respect to safety would be subject to further testing. Processes to demonstrate the efficacy and effectiveness of the product, as well as to ensure the validity of the claim were proposed. These included evidence-based evaluations to support the causal relationship between the food and the claimed benefit as well as the determination of whether the strength and quality of the evidence is sufficient to support the claim. Quality assurance programmes to ensure product safety and efficacy, as well as the consistent presence of the bioactive constituent were also proposed and could be achieved via testing, meeting of standards, utilizing good manufacturing practices (GMP) and documentation.

A framework to evaluate foods with health claims was also created by Health Canada to ensure product safety and claim validity, as well as establish procedures for product testing to support health claims. The framework is based on the product-specific 'authorization' approach, where the product with the intended health claim is assessed on its own merit, instead of an entire food group being the subject of a claim. All products with health claims, once approved, are required to carry a claim identification number (CIN).

Based upon these prior studies and proposals, the NHPD was created within Health Canada in 2001 with the responsibility of regulating NHPs.[5] In 2004, the NHPR came into force and is based on five basic elements (Health Canada, 2004). A product licensing system requires all NHPs to display a product identification number on the label, identified by the prefix NPN[6] (or DIN-HM, for homeopathic preparations) after it is approved for sale in Canada, with the premise that identification numbers will assist in ensuring that quality products are sold to consumers, as well as facilitate quick and effective product recalls if necessary. A site licensing system requires all manufacturers, packagers, labellers and importers to be licensed to ensure that producers and distributors have the appropriate procedures and facilities in place. GMPs are to be employed to ensure product safety and quality. Standardized labelling requirements are stipulated, ensuring consumers can make informed choices. Finally, an adverse reaction system requires product licence holders to monitor all adverse reactions associated with their products and report the serious reactions to Health Canada. Labelling requirements under the NHPR include product name, quantity, ingredient listing and recommended conditions of use, which include purpose, dosage, route of administration and any cautionary statements, all of which are to assist consumers in making informed choices.

Mine and Young (2009) examine Health Canada's 2009 risk-based approach (RBA) of assessing NHPs; products are classified according to either of two risk levels and issued an appropriate product licence. Class I refers to products that have available and authoritative evidence concerning safety and quality that require minimal assessment, while Class II products are considered high risk due to lack of evidence and require thorough safety, efficacy and quality assessments. Certain NHPs, whose effects on humans have not been investigated, may be required to undergo a clinical trial to ascertain the safety and efficacy of the product; clinical trials are not the norm as the NHPR allow for other 'range of evidence' to support an NHP license application.

The prior regulatory system had restricted the health claims that could be made on vitamins and minerals; the new NHPR repealed this by including vitamins and minerals in the definition of NHPs, thereby allowing health claims. The new regulatory framework included transition periods for the implementation of GMPs, obtaining site licences for industry members and for the implementation of the new product licensing system. NHPs that had a product licence as a DIN were expected to have transitioned to an NPN or a DIN-HM (homeopathic medicine) (Health Canada, 2004).

In summary, the regulatory landscape in Canada has evolved steadily. Prior to 1998, neither official definitions of functional foods nor nutraceuticals nor specific regulations pertaining to these products existed in Canada. Any product that made a health claim was considered a drug, with the exception of nutrient function claims. Health Canada now allows function, risk reduction and therapeutic health claims.

After establishing the ability for the Canadian health foods sector to make health claims, Health Canada initially evaluated ten, and following consultations adopted five disease risk reduction health claims that were already permitted in the USA. Additional health claims have been added and currently, 11 disease risk reduction or therapeutic claims are permitted in Canada (Health Canada, 2014). Further discussion of these health claims is provided in Chapter 4.

Prior to the enactment of the NHPR in Canada in 2004, NHPs were not officially defined (only nutraceuticals were defined), such that by default, all NHPs that carried health claims were regulated as drugs. With the NHPR in place, there is greater clarification regarding the categorization and regulation of NHPs.

Currently, a major challenge facing Health Canada concerns the development of new products that have both food and NHP characteristics and the conflicts that arise due to the inability to properly categorize or define them as they can be subject to both the NHPR and the Food and Drugs Act for the purposes of health claims (Farrell et al., 2009; Mine and Young, 2009). Health Canada classifies these controversial products based on their composition, representations, format, public perception and history of use to determine which regulations apply. This incongruity exists in other areas, causing further conflicts. For example, some NHPs must undergo clinical trials[7] in order to obtain approval from Health Canada but food products do not; NHPs require pre-market approval whereas, in general, food does not, with the exception of novel foods (foods with no history of use), food additives and infant formulas. A potential incongruity also exists in the treatment of health claims on food versus on NHPs. Health claims on functional foods are generic and do not require proof of ingredients or pre-market approval, but health claims on NHPs are product-specific, for which manufacturers must prove ingredient content in order to obtain mandatory pre-market approval.

Regulatory review and reform is an ongoing process in most countries, particularly as scientific advancements continue to open new possibilities and the ways in which consumers seek and process information about food changes. Canada is no exception in this regard. A review of food labelling regulations in Canada is underway through the Food Labelling Modernization Initiative, while Health Canada continues to review and update its food regulatory framework, including regulations affecting health and nutrition claims and labelling under the Regulatory Roadmap for Health Products and Food (CFIA, 2013; Health Canada, 2012).

The challenges encountered in establishing a regulatory framework for the health foods sector in Canada are not atypical. Many countries have gone through similar processes of regulatory development, usually initiated by a recognition that existing regulations have failed to keep pace with scientific advancements in the enhancement or purification of health food ingredients. The need for regulatory reform is also often intensified by a recognition that domestic regulations are falling behind or are inconsistent with those of other countries, hampering the ability of domestic firms to compete internationally and creating regulatory burdens that hinder cross-border movement of products. The need to balance consumer protection against fraudulent or misleading health claims, while facilitating the creation of innovative food products with health-enhancing attributes, has also motivated regulatory reforms internationally. Establishing a regulatory framework within a single country is challenging enough; the next section discusses the development of a harmonized regulatory system across multiple countries in a case study of regulatory harmonization across the EU.

3.4 POLICY HARMONIZATION: THE CASE OF THE EU

For a considerable period of time, regulations affecting the health claims presented on functional foods and supplements were not consistent between EU member states. The lack of a unified set of EU regulations pertaining to the health foods product sector meant that member states instead developed separate national regulatory frameworks for their domestic sectors. Even the means by which claims were regulated varied, for example, with Belgium regulating all foods through one national authority in contrast to Germany's individual federal lands having their own authorities. As a result, in 2000, the EU began a controversial and lengthy process to assess and harmonize the regulation of health claims, which resulted in a new regulation governing the assessment and approval of health claims, the European Health Claims Regulation (EHCR) that came into force in December 2012 (Gruenwald, 2013). The path towards regulatory harmonization was a gradual process, fraught with many challenges.

In 2006, the EU issued a regulation (EC1924/2006) on nutrition and health claims made on food and food supplements, with two objectives:

(1) to keep the regulation standard with that of the international community, whereby unsubstantiated health claims are prohibited, along with claims that are not approved by the European Commission (EC); and (2) to allow health claims on food products whose effects are strongly substantiated. Generic structure/function claims in use domestically were gathered by member states and provided to the European Food Safety Authority (EFSA) for evaluation. The EC initially was to compile a list of acceptable claims by the end of January 2010 in consultation with the EFSA, but the process was considerably delayed until the end of 2011. Mariotti et al. (2010, p. 627) note that: 'By early 2009, the European call for applications for inclusion on the claims register had resulted in approximately 10,000 health claims, based on 4,185 main relationships, all of which need to be reviewed'. Eventually the Commission received lists with more than 44 000 health claims from the member states.[8] This suggests there were many overlapping functional ingredient–health claim relationships within the 44 000 applications. Concerns raised by industry stakeholders regarding the rewording of the health claims submitted to the EFSA, the significant volume of submitted health claims and the necessary due diligence to be conducted on the scientific backing of the claims contributed to the delay (EurActiv, 2010).

The EHCR became effective in December 2012 and currently restricts the use of health claims to 222 approved generic health claims that can be applied to all foodstuffs on the market; all other claims are illegal, with some exceptions for botanical claims on products on the market prior to 2007. New products can only carry these generic health claims if they meet the conditions of use (EC, 2012; Gruenwald, 2013). Companies are still able to apply for individual health claims subject to individual scientific evaluation and pre-market approvals by the EFSA. Otherwise, all other claims are illegal. A more detailed discussion of EU health claims is provided in Chapter 4.

The EHCR was drafted to mitigate the lack of harmonization in regulation of supplements and functional foods between member states, yet its implementation is occurring at different rates across EU countries during the transition period as member states vary in the administration and timing of full implementation. Consequently, it is expected that intra-EU differences in the regulation of the industry will continue in the interim. These challenges notwithstanding, the EU provides a fairly unique example of the harmonization of health claims regulations across a large number of countries, made possible by the cooperative governance structure of the EU.

3.5 CONCLUSIONS

Increased consumer interest, scientific developments and market opportunities in the health foods sector have provided incentives for firms to develop a greater variety of products with enhanced health attributes, thereby necessitating an overhaul of policies regulating this sector. These policies are in large part motivated by the recognition that markets work imperfectly due to uncertainty and information asymmetry with respect to the health outcomes from consumption of these products, or from weak incentives to invest in R&D. A primary motivation of regulation is to inform consumers and to protect and ensure consumer safety, while providing incentives for continued innovation and industry growth. Reconciling these objectives, however, is not always straightforward: overly stringent regulations pertaining to allowable health claims or new product approvals, or regulations that diverge markedly across jurisdictions, raise costs for businesses, stifling innovation and resulting in non-market (regulatory) failure.

Regulatory frameworks for the health foods sector have been evolving globally, with considerable variance in approaches, implementation and enforcement. A summary of literature examining regulatory and policy environments can be found in Appendix 5 (Table A5.1). A number of studies assert that Japan and the USA have relatively well-advanced regulatory regimes.[9] Canada is viewed as having a relatively more restrictive regulatory environment for the development and marketing of functional food compared to the USA, EU and Japan, while Japan's regulatory system is considered by some commentators as the most supportive, with high levels of collaboration between government, industry, academia and research organizations. The development of new EU-wide regulations and enforcement mechanisms is expected to reduce confusion and remove inconsistencies across member states. A more detailed exposition of the current regulatory landscape in the USA, Canada, EU, Japan and Australia and New Zealand is provided in the next chapter.

NOTES

1. A Pareto improvement makes at least one individual better off without making another individual worse off.
2. The 'disjunction between costs and revenues' results in inefficient production, redundant and rising costs. The revenues that finance non-market activities are derived from government tax income and donations and since these are unrelated to the costs of the non-market activities there is a tendency to use more resources than is necessary to produce a given

output, or more of the non-market activity may be provided than is warranted. 'Internalities', or private or organizational goals, result from self-interested behaviour within organizations, where the goals that resonate often relate to the evaluation of agency performance and the performance of agency personnel, rather than the achievement of socially optimal market outcomes. 'Derived externalities' are unintended side-effects of public policy that are not taken into account by public agencies. Finally, 'distributional inequities' arise when power and privilege are key drivers of decisions rather than the income and wealth incentives that are typically generated by markets (Wolf, 1987).

3. A credence attribute is one whose quality is difficult or impossible for the consumer to evaluate without additional information (for example, such as labelling or third party verification).
4. Initially, individual member states of the EU had their own sets of regulation for the sector, although EU-wide regulations have since been put in place, as discussed in Section 3.4.
5. See Chapter 2 for an explanation of the definition of NHP in Canada.
6. Natural product number.
7. Not all products are required to undergo clinical trials because the NHPD does allow other evidence to support an application for a natural health product licence.
8. Commission Regulation (EU) No. 432/2012, http://eur-lex.europa.eu/LexUriServ/LexUriServ.do?uri=OJ:L:2012:136:0001:0040:en:PDF.
9. For example, Bech-Larsen and Scholderer (2007), Mariotti et al. (2010), Smith et al. (1996), Subirade (2007), Veeman (2002).

4. Health claim regulations in developed markets

This chapter reviews the regulatory environment for the health foods sector in major developed markets, including the USA, Canada, the UK (prior to regulatory harmonization within the EU), the EU, Japan, Australia and New Zealand. A primary focus of the discussion is the regulations surrounding allowable health claims and product approval processes. Nutrient content labelling regulations, nutritional labelling and novel foods regulations pertaining to novel functional foods are also discussed. Tables offering country-by-country comparisons of structure/function claims, disease risk reduction claims and nutrient content claims can be found in Appendix 1.

4.1 UNITED STATES OF AMERICA

The US FDA has regulatory authority over the food sector in the USA and has established three categories of permitted claims: (1) health claims (disease risk reduction) describe the relationship between a food and a disease or health-related conditions; (2) nutrient content claims indicate the level of a nutrient in a food; (3) structure/function claims describe how a nutrient or dietary supplement affects the normal growth, development or functioning of the human body (Subirade, 2007).

According to the FDA, the regulatory status of a food product is determined primarily by its intended use, its label and accompanying labelling information, which include nutrient information, nutrient content claims and health claims. Manufacturers must therefore make a definitive choice in marketing their product as either a food or a drug, thereby choosing their regulatory classification. The FDA does not provide a legal definition for functional food and no formal regulatory category exists for such foods. While the FDA does not officially define functional food, the term is used by the US industry. If marketed as a food, a functional food can be regulated as a conventional food product, as a dietary supplement, as a medical food[1] or as an infant formula (Ross, 2000). Foods have also been defined as substances that provide taste, aroma or nutritive value and may present structure/function claims if the claim is based upon their nutritive value. However, if the health claim describes a structure/function benefit not derived from the food's nutritive value, the claim can be used only if the product is marketed as either a dietary supplement or as a drug (Ross, 2000).

In general, the US regulatory environment is less restrictive towards the approval of new health claims and novel foods than is the case in other countries. Qualified claims that have lower standards of scientific evidence for approval are permitted as a result of legal action on First Amendment rights for both food and dietary supplements. Structure/ function claims on food and dietary supplements do not require pre-market approval by the FDA. Novel foods are essentially viewed as extensions of conventional foods; therefore, firms are only encouraged to consult informally with the FDA to ensure the safety of the food. Nutrient content claims are regulated to roughly the same extent as in some other countries. Nutrition labelling is mandatory and covers a similar number of nutrients (FDA, 2003). These issues are discussed in more detail below.

4.1.1 Health Claims

The 1990 Nutrition Labeling and Education Act (NLEA) amended the US Federal Food, Drug and Cosmetic Act and established the FDA's ability to regulate nutrient content claims and health claims on food; the NLEA provides guidelines for regulatory control over health claims and nutrient content claims. General requirements are that nutrition labelling must not be misleading and must meet the Significant Scientific Agreement (SSA) standard to qualify as an SSA health claim. The FDA uses an evidence-based system for evaluating the quality of scientific studies on the substance/disease relationship and whether studies show a causal substance/disease relationship. To achieve SSA, the FDA must judge that:

> Qualified experts would likely agree that the scientific evidence supports the substance/disease relationship that is the subject of a proposed health claim. The SSA standard is intended to be a strong standard that provides a high level of confidence in the validity of the substance/disease relationship ... SSA occurs well after the stage of emerging science, where data and information permit an inference, but before the point of unanimous agreement within the relevant scientific community that the inference is valid. (FDA, 2009b)

The 1997 FDA Modernization Act (FDAMA) provides an alternative process to obtain SSA health claim authorization. An FDA review of scientific evidence would not be necessary if any US federal scientific agency (with responsibility for public health) or the National Academy of Sciences could provide an authoritative statement about potential disease risk reduction claims (Hoadley and Rowlands, 2008). The FDA has approved a number of SSA claims including the following health claims approved under FDA scientific evidence review (FDA, 2009b):

- calcium, vitamin D and osteoporosis
- dietary lipids (fats) and cancer
- dietary saturated fat and cholesterol and risk of coronary heart disease (CHD)
- dietary non-cariogenic carbohydrate sweeteners and dental caries
- fibre-containing grain products, fruits and vegetables and cancer
- folate and neural tube defects (in infants)
- fruits and vegetables and cancer
- fruits, vegetables and grain products high in fibre, particularly soluble fibre and risk of CHD
- sodium and hypertension
- soluble fibre from certain foods and risk of CHD
- soy protein and risk of CHD
- plant sterol/stanol esters and risk of CHD.

In addition, a number of health claims are approved based on Authoritative Statements by Federal Scientific Bodies as per FDAMA, including, for example:

- potassium and risk of high blood pressure and strokes
- wholegrain foods and risk of heart disease and certain cancers
- fluoridated water and reduced risk of dental caries
- saturated fat, cholesterol and trans fat and reduced risk of heart disease
- substitution of saturated fat with unsaturated fatty acids and heart disease.

The FDA also allows qualified health claims that undergo the same evaluation procedure as SSA claims; these do not require the same level of qualified expert consensus as health claims, but must be supported by some credible but inconclusive evidence. The FDA has approved a series of qualified health claims (FDA, 2009d) including, for example:

- tomatoes and/or tomato sauce and prostate cancer
- tomato sauce and ovarian cancer

- tomatoes and gastric cancer
- tomatoes and pancreatic cancer
- calcium and colon/rectal cancer
- calcium and recurrent colon polyps
- green tea and cancer
- selenium and cancer
- antioxidant vitamins and cancer
- nuts and heart disease
- walnuts and heart disease
- omega-3 fatty acids and CHD
- B vitamins and vascular disease
- monounsaturated fatty acids from olive oil and heart disease
- unsaturated fats from canola oil and heart disease
- corn oil and heart disease
- phosphatidylserine and dementia
- phosphatidylserine and cognitive dysfunction
- chromium picolinate and diabetes
- folic acid and neural tube defects (claim recommends twice the intake of approved SSA claim)
- calcium and hypertension
- calcium and pregnancy-induced hypertension or pre-eclampsia.

A summary table of disease risk reduction claims by country can be found in Appendix 1 (Table A1.2).

The FDA allows structure/function claims on food but does not evaluate them and does not need to be advised of the claim's use; therefore, they are not usually considered to be 'health claims'. The structure/function claim must not be misleading or untrue and must be substantiated, but in the case of food that substantiation does not need to be provided to the FDA. As a result, the FDA does not approve or keep a list of structure/function claims in use on food products (FDA, 2009c). For example, the relationships between vitamin A and night vision, calcium and bone and teeth development and vitamin E as an antioxidant are sufficiently substantiated for use as structure/function claims. The firm must collect scientific literature that substantiates the claim before using it. The food must also contain sufficient quantities of the nutrient and enough of the nutrient can be consumed in a day to have the claimed effect for the structure/function claim to not be misleading. The firm does not need pre-market approval from the FDA to use the claim on a food product.

4.1.2 Nutrient Content Claims and Nutrition Labelling

Nutrient content claims are regulated under the Code of Federal Regulations (21 CFR 101.13) and any nutrient content claims other than those approved by the FDA are prohibited. Claims can only be made using the wording or synonyms provided and must be accompanied by additional information, which varies from claim to claim, usually requiring nutrition labelling. 'Free', 'low', 'reduced' and 'less' have all been defined for use with calories, fat, saturated fat and sodium (FDA, 2008). Vitamins and minerals can also have a variety of nutrient content claims if they have an established recommended daily intake (RDI). A summary table of nutrient content claims by country can be found in Appendix 1 (Table A1.3).

'Comparative claims' are also permitted but, unlike in other countries such as Canada, there is no difference between the use of 'reduced' and 'less'; in either case, the food has been modified to achieve the reduction in the level of a given nutrient to make it eligible for the claim. The claims need not be explicit and there is a list of implied claims provided in the Code of Federal Regulations, or firms can petition the FDA for the use of new implied claims. The claim 'healthy' is treated as an implied nutrient content claim; food labelled 'healthy' must meet requirements for levels of total fat, saturated fat, sodium, cholesterol and beneficial nutrients. Additionally, products that make nutrient content claims are forced to include a disclosure statement if the total fat, saturated fat, cholesterol and sodium levels exceed certain standards. For example, if the food exceeds 13 g total fat per reference amount customarily consumed, then the statement 'See nutrition information for total fat content' must also be provided and must be placed immediately adjacent to the claim (FDA, 2008). Of particular importance for functional foods are the definitions for 'high potency', which has a higher standard for the use of the claim on foods than on dietary supplements (Hoadley and Rowlands, 2008).

The FDA also regulates and monitors mandatory nutrition facts tables. Tables must at least include calories, calories from fat, total fat, saturated fat, trans fat, cholesterol, sodium, total carbohydrates, dietary fibre, sugar, protein, vitamins A and C, calcium and iron. If any of the following are added to the food, then they must also be declared in the facts table: vitamins D, E or K, thiamin, riboflavin, niacin, vitamin B_6, B_{12}, folate, biotin, pantothenic acid, phosphorus, iodine, magnesium, zinc, selenium, copper, manganese, chromium, molybdenum and chloride. Optional nutrients and minerals (for example, mono- and polyunsaturated fat, soluble fibre, potassium) must be declared in the table if they are featured in a nutrient content claim (FDA, 2008). The FDA exempts certain food from the nutrition facts table requirement.[2]

4.1.3 Novel Foods

Compared to other countries, the USA has relatively minimal regulations concerning 'novel foods'. The position of the FDA is essentially that novel foods (including GM food) are extensions of conventional foods (Blakeney, 2009). The FDA policy statement interpreting its role in regulating foods resulting from new processes notes that the FDA is responsible for ensuring that food is safe and in compliance with regulations. It is recommended that firms informally consult with the FDA 'to ensure that the safety and regulatory status of a new food is properly resolved' (FDA, 1992). The FDA issued a proposed rule requiring a 120-day pre-market notification rule for bioengineered food[3] that would require developers to submit a scientific and regulatory assessment of the food, allowing the FDA to ensure food safety and regulatory compliance (FDA, 2001). This remains a proposed rule. The FDA also issued draft guidance in 2001 for the industry regarding voluntary labelling of bioengineered foods. These recommendations constitute guidance only and there are currently no requirements to label these foods. The regulatory situation regarding novel foods in the USA is in stark contrast to the EU where firms must achieve pre-market registration before a novel food can enter the market and mandatory labelling rules apply to food containing GM ingredients approved for human consumption.

4.1.4 Dietary Supplements

The term 'nutraceutical' is not defined in the USA but most nutraceuticals fall into the 'dietary supplement' regulatory category (see Chapter 2 for a full discussion). Dietary supplements contain an amino acid, a vitamin, a mineral, a herb or any combination or extract of these nutrients. Dietary supplements come in a measured dose form (pill, capsule, tablet, powder and/or liquid) (DSHEA, 1994). The FDA's Center for Food Safety and Applied Nutrition has regulatory oversight over dietary supplements, which are regulated under the 1994 DSHEA.

Generic SSA and qualified health claims (disease risk reduction claims) can be made on dietary supplements, providing they meet the appropriate scientific standards; the approval process for new SSA and qualified health claims is the same for dietary supplements or functional food. Structure/function claims are also permitted on dietary supplements; the FDA requires pre-market notification of at least 30 days before the firm can use the claim on a product (DSHEA, 1994). The firm must have scientific substantiation for the claim should the FDA want to investigate and verify the truthfulness of the claim and prevent misleading labelling. Nutrient content claims are also permitted on dietary supplements.

Regulations on dietary supplement product approval are also relatively relaxed; no FDA approval or registration is necessary prior to marketing and sale. Even when the key ingredient is novel, or some scientific evidence suggests that the ingredient may be harmful, the burden of proof is on the FDA to demonstrate that the dietary supplement is unfit for sale (DSHEA, 1994; FDA, 2009e). This creates a very friendly innovation environment for US dietary supplements manufacturers, although arguably at the expense of greater consumer protection.

Like nutrition labelling on food, labelling on dietary supplements must be truthful and not misleading. In 'supplement facts' tables, firms must list (if they are present in measureable amounts) total calories, calories from fat, total fat, saturated fat, cholesterol, sodium, total carbohydrate, dietary fibre, sugars, protein, vitamin A, vitamin C, calcium and iron. Nutrients must be listed if they are added to the supplement for the purposes of supplementation or if a health or structure/function claim is made about the nutrient. 'Serving size' and 'servings per container' must also be provided (FDA, 2005b).

In summary, the large number of approved generic disease risk reduction claims in the USA creates incentives for firms to pursue R&D in the health foods products sector. The fact that firms do not need pre-market approval from the FDA to use structure/function claims also increases the appeal of health foods product R&D, as does the relatively large size of the US market compared to smaller countries such as Canada. The ease of novel food introduction into the market makes the undertaking of R&D in functional foods produced from novel plant varieties more attractive than in more stringent regulatory environments (for example, the EU). While there are distinctions between food and dietary supplements in the USA, regulations on supplements are not significantly more stringent than on food and remain generic.

4.2 CANADA

The historical development of the Canadian regulatory system for the health foods sector is charted in Chapter 3. Health Canada has regulatory responsibility for health and nutrient content claims under the Food and Drug Regulations (FDR).[4] The Canadian Food Inspection Agency (CFIA) is responsible for enforcing food labelling regulations. A health claim is any claim that correlates the consumption of a food or ingredient and health. Permitted health claims include structure/function claims, disease risk reduction claims and therapeutic claims.

4.2.1 Health Claims: Therapeutic and Disease Risk Reduction Claims

Therapeutic claims suggest that the consumption of a certain nutrient will treat or mitigate a disease or condition or restore or otherwise modify an existing function and must undergo the same evaluation procedure as disease risk reduction claims. The approval of a therapeutic claim would require an amendment to the FDR (CFIA and Health Canada, 2009). Canada is unique in allowing therapeutic claims on food. This is in stark contrast to many other countries that explicitly prohibit the use of therapeutic claims on food. While this provides an opportunity for firms to innovate, it can also be construed as elevating food to the status of a drug; the standards of evidence for proving the therapeutic effects of food may simply be too high for most food products.

Disease risk reduction claims relate the consumption of food (or a food component) and the risk of developing a diet-related disease (CFIA and Health Canada, 2009). There are 11 disease risk reduction or therapeutic claims currently permitted in Canada as listed below, along with the date of approval (Health Canada, 2014):

- low sodium intake and reduced risk of high blood pressure (2000)
- calcium and reduced risk of osteoporosis (2000)
- a diet low in saturated fat, cholesterol and trans fatty acids and reduced risk of CHD (2000)
- consumption of fruit and vegetables and reduced risk of some kinds of cancer (2000)
- psyllium products and blood cholesterol lowering (2011)
- plant sterols (phytosterols) and blood cholesterol lowering (2010)
- oat products and blood cholesterol lowering (2010)
- barley products and blood cholesterol lowering (2012)
- unsaturated fat and blood cholesterol lowering (2012)
- sugar-free chewing gum and dental caries risk reduction (2014)
- ground whole flaxseed and blood cholesterol lowering (2014).

Potential disease risk reduction claims that have been assessed but deemed as unacceptable by Health Canada include links between consumption of whole grains and CHD, dietary fat and cancer and dietary fibre, grain products and cancer (Health Canada, 2014). Although all three of these health claims are approved in the USA, Health Canada ruled that the balance of scientific evidence does not support the claim.

In Canada, the use of generic disease risk reduction claims[5] must not be misleading; they must be based on adequate scientific evidence and it should be reasonable and feasible for an individual to consume an effective amount of the food in the context of a healthy diet. Except for a few exempt foods ('local', 'test market' or 'specialty' foods), claims must appear in both of the official languages of Canada: English and French. Where a disease risk reduction claim is made, the food must also declare a nutrition facts table, including the amount of nutrient, mineral or vitamin that has the disease risk reducing effect. The claims themselves must be written as regulated and cannot be modified to contain intervening information. These claims are not allowed on food intended for children under two years of age or for food intended for very low energy diets (CFIA and Health Canada, 2009).

4.2.2 Function Claims

Function (structure/function) claims are also permitted in Canada. Unlike disease risk reduction claims, function claims must not refer to disease risk mitigation or prevention. Instead, they describe the beneficial effects that the consumption of the food or food constituent (for example, a nutrient) has on the normal functions of the body. Nutrient function claims are a subset of function claims and are claims about known nutrients that are essential for the maintenance of good health or normal growth and development (CFIA and Health Canada, 2009). The conditions for making nutrient function claims differ from general function claims and are discussed separately below. It is recommended (but not mandatory) that function claims be in both English and French. Function claims must be accompanied by a nutrition facts table and Health Canada recommends (but does not require) that when a function claim is made about a food constituent, a quantitative declaration of the amount of the food constituent (per serving of stated size) is also provided on the label. Three function claims based on food or food constituents are listed as approved: coarse wheat bran and regularity; green tea and antioxidant effect on blood; and psyllium and regularity (CFIA and Health Canada, 2009).

Nutrient function claims, formerly known as 'biological role claims', have been allowed in Canada for a number of years and describe the well-established role of known nutrients or energy that are essential for the maintenance of good health or for normal growth and development. For example, a general nutrient function claim is 'Energy (or nutrient) is a factor in the maintenance of good health'. Nutrient function claims are not made for a food but for the energy value or nutrients in a food. For example, rather than claim that milk is good for building strong bones and teeth, an acceptable claim would be 'Milk is an excellent source of calcium, which helps build strong bones and teeth' (CFIA and Health Canada, 2009).

Acceptable nutrient function claims include the following (CFIA and Health Canada, 2009):

- protein and body tissues or antibodies or strong muscles
- fat and energy or absorption of fat-soluble vitamins
- ARA[6] and development of brain, eyes and nerves in young children
- DHA[7] and development of brain, eyes and nerves in young children
- carbohydrates and energy or utilization of fat
- vitamin A and bones and teeth or night vision or healthy skin and membranes
- vitamin D and bones and teeth or calcium and phosphorus utilization
- vitamin E as antioxidant or oxidation of fatty tissues
- vitamin C as antioxidant or bones and cartilage or teeth and gums or protection against free radicals
- thiamine (vitamin B_1) and carbohydrates or normal growth
- riboflavin (vitamin B_2) and metabolism or tissue formation
- niacin and growth and development or metabolism or tissue formation
- vitamin B_6 and energy metabolism or tissue formation
- folate and red blood cell formation or foetal neural development
- vitamin B_{12} and red blood cell formation
- pantothenic acid and metabolism and tissue formation
- calcium and bones and teeth
- phosphorus and bones and teeth
- magnesium and metabolism and tissue formation and bone development
- iron and red blood cell formation
- zinc and metabolism and tissue formation
- iodine and thyroid gland function
- selenium as antioxidant or protection against oxidative stress.

New nutrient function claims must be approved and are granted based on the petitioner demonstrating that the Institute of Medicine of the US National Academies has established a recommended dietary allowance (RDA), adequate intake or acceptable macronutrient distribution ranges for the nutrient. There must also be broad consensus in the scientific community with respect to the nutrient's functions. Approval is also contingent upon a scientific authority – either the Institute of Medicine of the US National Academies or the EFSA – having evaluated the nutrient and its function within the last 15 years (CFIA and Health Canada, 2009).

The approval of new health claims are subject to an evaluation and approval process before being adopted by the government of Canada. Firms or individuals interested in receiving approval for a new health claim must apply to Health Canada. There are three main criteria involved in assessing a health claim: causality; generalization; and quality assurance. Applicants must clearly establish a causal link between a food and healthiness by providing a comprehensive list of studies that involve original research in humans on the effects of the food on the health effect. The claimed effect must be meaningfully generalizable to the wider population or a subgroup thereof. The food must conform to quality assurance standards (Health Canada, 2009b).

4.2.3 Nutrient Content Claims and Nutrition Labelling

Nutrient content claims describe the level of a nutrient or nutrients, vitamin or vitamins and mineral or minerals in food and are not considered health claims. In Canada, nutrient content claims are relatively tightly regulated compared to other countries. The nutrient must be present per stated serving size of the food and per reference amount of the food. Claims must be in both English and French, unless the food is a 'local food', a 'test market food' or a 'specialty food'. Claims must also be accompanied by a nutrition facts table unless the food is non-pre-packaged, the claim is advertised in a generic advertisement that names no brands, the food is a one-bite confection, the food consists of certain bottled dairy products or is one of certain individually portioned foods (DOJ, n.d.; CFIA and Health Canada, 2009). A wide variety of claims are permitted on numerous nutrients (see Table A1.3 in Appendix 1) corresponding to minimum or maximum levels of those nutrients in a food per stated serving size and reference amount. The stated serving size is declared on each food's nutrition labelling (in the nutrition facts table). The reference amount is a regulated and standardized (by Health Canada) serving of food a person consumes at a sitting (CFIA and Heath Canada,

2009). In addition to these generalized requirements, certain nutrient content claims must also meet individually specific requirements.

Some nutrient content claims are similar across nutrients. For example, many claims utilizing the term 'reduced' mean that the food has been modified or processed to contain at least 25 per cent less of the nutrient than a certain reference food used in comparison. Claims involving 'lower' are similar except that the food has not been modified or processed to achieve the 25 per cent reductions. Different kinds of foods can be used as reference foods in different claims. Some claims require that the reference food be of the same food group, while others require a 'similar reference food'; regardless, reference foods are only necessary for comparative claims (CFIA and Health Canada, 2009).

Other common claims include the terms 'low' and 'free'. These can be used to describe the nutrient content levels of energy, fat, protein, saturated fat and trans fat (among others) with the exception that 'free' cannot be used to describe protein. 'Light' can only be used in energy and fat nutrient content claims and can only be used to replace the term 'reduced'. Saturated and trans fat claims are highly interrelated (to be 'low in saturated fat' the food has to have less than 2 g combined saturated and trans fat per serving size and reference amount and have less than 15 per cent of total energy sourced from fat). Nutrient content claims can be used for vitamins and minerals as well, provided that there is a RDI for that vitamin or mineral; there are some claims that uniquely apply solely to vitamins and minerals (in other words, 'added' or 'fortified') (CFIA and Health Canada, 2009).

In Canada, food must be labelled with a nutrition facts table unless the food is exempt.[8] Some food never loses its exemption (in other words, one-bite confections). Otherwise, food automatically must be labelled with a nutrition facts table when:

- a vitamin, mineral or nutrient is added to the food
- aspartame or other artificial sweeteners are added
- the food is ground meat or when the label or advertisement contains a nutrient content claim, a health claim, health-related statement or the phrase 'nutrition facts'.

Nutrition facts tables must be in both English and French, either in the same table or in two separate tables. A number of nutrients, vitamins and minerals must be included in the table including calories, total fat, saturated fat, trans fat, cholesterol, sodium, carbohydrates, sugars, fibre, protein, vitamins A and C, calcium and iron. There is also a long list of optional nutrients, vitamins and minerals that can be declared in a nutrition facts table, including poly- and monounsaturated fat, soluble fibre, vitamin D, niacin or zinc. Optional information must be declared when any reference is made to the nutrient on the label or in advertisements (including nutrient content, function and disease risk reduction claims). Additionally, potassium content must be displayed when it has been added or if there are claims about salt content (CFIA and Health Canada, 2009).

4.2.4 Novel Food

Should the food product result from a process not traditionally used for food, does not have a history of safe consumption as a food or is GM and deemed novel, then the food must undergo novel food registration, either before or in conjunction with a health claim application (Health Canada, 2009a, 2009b). The novel food registration process is more stringent in Canada than in the USA, but is not as stringent as elsewhere (for example, the EU).

4.2.5 Natural Health Products

The regulatory system for NHPs in Canada is essentially product-specific.[9] The same types of health claims (therapeutic, disease risk reduction, function) are permitted on NHPs as on foods, but the NHPD of Health Canada evaluates each NHP and its associated health claim separately; all NHPs must have a health claim (Health Canada, 2006a, 2006b).

The NHPD evaluates product licence applications for manufacturing NHPs and their associated claims. The NHPD approves the NHP only if it can be proven as both effective and safe (Walji and Boon, 2008). The benefits of the NHP must outweigh the risks. The level of assessed risk is dependent on several factors, including the seriousness of the condition it is meant to address and whether it is meant for sole use or in conjunction with other factors. The level of evidence required is also dependent on the claim (therapeutic claims require stronger evidence, including clinical studies, than function claims) (Health Canada, 2006a).

Applicants can choose between two different kinds of health claims: traditional use or non-traditional use. Traditional use claims require the applicant prove that the product is made according to tradition and has been used for at least 50 consecutive years. These claims are worded as 'Traditionally used ...' (Health Canada, 2006a). Non-traditional use claims require scientific substantiation in order to be approved. This may include clinical trials, observational studies and expert opinions. The strength of evidence required to substantiate the claim is dependent on both the severity and symptoms of the condition and whether it is a therapeutic, disease risk reduction or function claim (Health Canada, 2006a).

Labelling requirements differ for NHPs compared to food. The dosage form (for example, tablets) must be stated. The brand name and NPN (assigned after product licence approval) must also appear on the label. Medicinal and non-medicinal ingredients must be listed separately. The quantity of medicinal ingredients per dose must also be stated. Unlike food, NHPs must present a health claim. Recommended dosing should also be provided. Risk information, if determined necessary by the NHPD, must be displayed. Nutritional labelling is strictly prohibited (so as not to confuse people by implying that NHPs are food) (Health Canada, 2006b).

In summary, Canada has a fairly stringent regulatory procedure compared to that of the USA, as evidenced by the smaller list of approved disease risk reduction claims (although their number has been increasing) and the stronger requirements for the use of structure/function claims. Strict nutrient content claims rules and nutrition labelling rules also indicate a relatively strongly regulated market. Natural health products are more tightly regulated than functional foods as they fall under NHP regulations. However, NHPs are also subject to product-specific regulation, which reduces spillover benefits and increases incentives for firms to apply to use claims. This is because, unlike general claims, only the firm that applies for the claim can use it on that particular product. With generic claims, anyone can use the claim after it is approved, which may create free-rider problems, as discussed in Chapter 3.

4.3 UNITED KINGDOM (PRIOR TO EUROPEAN UNION HARMONIZATION)

The new harmonization European Health Claims Regulation (EHCR), which came into force in 2013, supersedes the domestic regulations of member states of the EU, including the UK. Nevertheless, a review of the prior regulatory environment in the UK is instructive as an example of how a EU member state previously approached regulation of the health foods sector and gives a sense of the scope of change encompassed by the new EU regulatory framework discussed in the next section.

Initially, the UK government did not explicitly regulate health claims. The Food Labelling Regulations Act (1996) established some guidelines for claims in the UK, but left much room for interpretation and application. Only claims that promised a medicinal or therapeutic effect were deemed illegal (OPSI, 1996). The government left room for firms to self-regulate, providing an alternative to the approach to regulation in many other countries. Generic disease risk reduction claims, structure/function claims, nutrient claims and innovative claims (qualified claims) were all permitted. Novel food regulations and nutrition labelling regulations were already largely governed by EU regulations during the time that the UK governed health claims domestically.

4.3.1 Health Claims

The Joint Health Claims Initiative (JHCI) was formed in 2000 as a self-regulatory agency for trade associations along with consumer organizations and enforcement authorities to regulate the use of health claims in the UK. The JHCI defined a health claim as a claim (expressed or implied in labelling or in advertising) that a food has a specific health benefit or reduces the risk of a specific disease or illness or other negative health impact. The JHCI regulated two kinds of health claims: generic and innovative. Generic health claims were based on established and widely accepted scientific knowledge of a relationship between a food/nutrient and a health effect. Innovative health claims were to be applied to new foods or in cases where the science was still emerging and scientific agreement was not near consensus (JHCI, n.d.).

The JHCI approved five generic health claims for use in the UK, all of which were disease risk reduction claims: reduced saturated fat and cholesterol; wholegrain foods and heart health; soy protein and blood cholesterol; oats and blood cholesterol; omega-3 fatty acids and heart health (JHCI, 2007). Only disease risk reduction claims were approved; the JHCI was assessing a list of structure/function claims and a list of 'well-established' structure/function claims was provided to the UK Food Standards Agency, but none were approved for use before the EU began regulating health claims (JHCI, 2003).

Health claims were partially regulated by UK legislation and also by the JHCI Code of Practice. These documents ensured that health claims could not be misleading, which is considered a criminal offence (OPSI, 1996). Claims could not denigrate other foods or imply that a balanced diet did not have a positive health effect. Claims had to be contextualized as part of the overall diet. They had also to be on foods with serving sizes reasonable enough to be consumed in one day to achieve the health benefit. It was recommended that firms provide the following information, in addition to the statutory labelling requirements:

- full nutrition declaration
- quantified serving size
- target population and any sectors that should avoid consuming the food
- safe maximum intake if eating too much could prove harmful
- quantity of food and pattern of consumption required to achieve the desired effect
- declare how much of the nutrient is required for the health benefit per 100 g or serving size (JHCI, n.d.).

There were several key requirements for firms desiring health claim approval. Firms had to demonstrate that:

- food or its components contribute to a positive health effect in the target population (as part of normal consumption and diet)
- the effect is long term and not short term
- the effect can be obtained by eating a reasonable amount of the food
- the group that can benefit from this effect (whole population, subgroup or at-risk group of elderly or lactating or pregnant women)
- how the effect occurs (although the precise mechanism is not needed) (JHCI, n.d.).

Claims approval was granted by the JHCI on the basis of the totality of scientific evidence. Claims were evaluated based on human studies (which were necessary), but also animal studies or cellular studies (JHCI, n.d.).

4.3.2 Nutrient Content Claims and Nutrition Labelling

Nutrient content claims were also permissible under UK law (UK nutrient content claims are now also governed by EU-wide regulation). The UK regulation provided a list of nutrition content claims whose use was restricted (a negative list) but the legislation did not prohibit the use of claims on other nutrients as firms saw fit. The restricted claims were on energy, protein, vitamins, minerals and cholesterol. Otherwise, foods making nutrition claims based on other nutrients simply had to be capable of fulfilling the claim and have nutrition labelling (OPSI, 1996).

Nutrition labelling tables were voluntary, unless the firm made a nutrition claim (under the Code of Practice of the JHCI, nutrition labelling was only recommended when health claims were used). Nutrition claims did not trigger compulsory labelling as long as they were in generic advertisements (in other words, no particular brands mentioned). Energy, protein, carbohydrate, fat and the nutrient subject to the nutrition claim declarations were compulsory when a nutrition claim was made. The government also recommended the inclusion of sugars, saturated fat, fibre and sodium.[10] Other declarable nutrients included polyols, starch, monounsaturates, polyunsaturates, cholesterol, vitamins and minerals (FSA, 1999).

Compared to the other jurisdictions examined in this chapter, the UK provided considerable latitude to firms using health claims. The government relied heavily upon self-regulation by firms with only a few restrictions (for example, no therapeutic claims, restrictions on some nutrient claims). This relatively more relaxed regulatory environment notwithstanding, it appears that the JHCI did not authorize misleading or erroneous claims. The JHCI halted operations in 2007 after the EU adopted Regulation EC 1924/2006 on health claims.

4.4 THE EUROPEAN UNION

As discussed in Chapter 3, prior to 2006, the EU did not have a harmonized health claim system, leaving the governance of health claims under the jurisdiction of individual member states. With the establishment of an EU-wide regulatory approach, the EU has since been assessing generic health claims according to four separate categories, establishing one of the world's most specialized health claims systems. The regulatory stringency of the EU system appears to be high: many more claims have been rejected[11] than accepted. The EU's strict novel and GM food regulations impose significant additional risks and costs on firms pursuing research and innovation in food categories that would fall under the jurisdiction of these regulations. Nutrition labelling regulations are changing in the EU, from minimal information provision unless a health claim is made, to a new regulation that requires nutrition labelling on processed foods, effective December 2014 (EC, 2013b). Previously, labels only needed a very short list of nutrients compared to the USA and Canada.

Despite the complicated regulatory landscape, the EU remains an attractive market for firms seeking to sell functional food: it is large and lucrative, and its ageing population has the resources and interest in investing in healthy food options. Harmonizing legislation across member countries significantly reduces the transactions costs associated with marketing products in multiple member states.

4.4.1 Health Claims

The European Health Claims Regulation (EC 1924/2006) aims to prevent misleading or untrue claims, avoid the perception by consumers that the benefits from nutrients cannot be achieved through a balanced diet or that some food is unsafe or nutritionally inadequate, and avoid condoning excess consumption of food. There are several conditions for making nutrient content claims (nutrition claims in the regulation) and health claims: the claim must have some established positive nutritional or physiological effect; nutrients in the food must be either high or low enough to achieve the desired effect; and the consumer need only consume a reasonable amount of the product to achieve the desired nutritive or physiological effect. This is similar to the requirement in both the USA and Canada that it be feasible for the consumer to ingest the product as part of a regular diet to obtain the effect in the claim. For all health claims, a disclosure statement must be made if consuming too much of a product may be hazardous to one's health, despite some of the positive physiological benefits (EC, 2006).

There are four different kinds of health claims permitted by EC 1924/2006: Article 13(1) health claims (generic structure/function); Article 13(5) health claims (product-specific, new or proprietary); Article 14(1)(a) health claims (disease risk reducing claims); and Article 14(1)(b) health claims (children's health claims).

Article 13(1) health claims are primarily generic structure/function claims, but also include claims on psychological or behavioural functions and claims about weight control through reducing hunger or increasing satiety (health claims regarding weight slimming products are banned in general). The EHCR has allowed 222 approved generic health claims for use on food initially; all other claims are illegal, with some exceptions for botanical claims on products on the market prior to 2007.

Initially, EC 1924/2006 approved three Article 14(1)(a) (disease risk reduction) claims. New health claims are assessed by the EFSA on an ongoing basis, for example, six new general structure/function claims were approved in June 2013 (Mailly and Blaszkiewicz, 2013). Food can be labelled with disease risk reduction claims regarding a relationship between plant sterols and heart disease, plant stanols and heart disease, gum sweetened with 100 per cent xylitol and dental plaque (and dental caries or cavities), sugar-free chewing gum and reduced risk of dental caries and, barley and oat beta-glucans and reduced blood cholesterol, which contributes to lower risk of CHD (EC, 2013a). New products wishing to use approved generic health claims may do so if they meet the conditions of use. Although pre-market approval is not mandatory, seeking guidance to ensure regulatory compliance is highly recommended (DH, 2011).

In contrast to other countries such as Canada, which prohibits the use of claims on products intended for children under the age of two, the EU has initially approved six health claims pertaining to the normal health and development of children under Article 14(1)(b). These claims show a relationship between essential fatty acids and growth and development, calcium and vitamin D, individually and jointly, affecting bone growth and development, phosphorus and bone growth and development, and protein and normal growth and development (EC, 2013a).

To seek approval of any new health claims, whether a new generic structure/function claim (Article 13(1)), a new product-specific or proprietary claim (Article 13(5)), a disease risk reduction claim (Article 14(1)(a)) or a claim pertaining to child development (Article 14(1)(b)), applicants provide information to a national authority in a member state, which then forwards the application to the EFSA. An opinion is issued by the EFSA based on whether or not the health claim is substantiated by scientific evidence and whether or not the health claim is in compliance with EU 1924/2006. EFSA-approved health claims are then forwarded to the EC, which decides whether or not to permit the health claim, based on consideration of EFSA's opinion, other EU law and other relevant factors (EC, 2006). Under the new EHCR, firms may still apply for approval of new individual health claims under Articles 13(5) and 14(1) and 14(2); they must provide at least one EFSA-approved, product-specific study that substantiates the health claim (Gruenwald, 2013). Firms seeking approval of proprietary health claims must also provide reasons as to why the information is proprietary (EC, 2006).

Thus far, the EU's health claim approval/rejection process has been characterized as unpredictable and piecemeal, creating uncertainty for firms as their ability to market, label and communicate about their products is constrained during the transition to a harmonized regulatory system (Mailly and Blaszkiewicz, 2013). As the number of approved claims increases, however, firms should face greater regulatory stability, while the ability to use the same health claim across multiple member states further reduces barriers to market penetration.

4.4.2 Nutrient Content Claims and Nutrition Labelling

EC Regulation 1924/2006 provides for some explicitly listed nutrient content claims, including claims related to energy, fat, saturated fat, unsaturated fat, sugars, fibre, protein and sodium, as well as claims on vitamins and minerals (see Table A1.3 in Appendix 1). It also allows for comparative claims on nutrients (for example, fat, protein) but not on vitamins or minerals. The use of the term 'light/lite' means the same as 'reduced'. The use of 'reduced' is more stringent than in other countries such as the USA and Canada. Food must have at least 30 per cent less of a nutrient than a comparable food to qualify for the term (unless it is a micronutrient, in which case a 10 per cent reduction is all that is needed). The use of the term 'natural' is conditional upon the nutrients in the nutrient content claim being present without modification to the food (EC, 2006).

EU nutrition table regulations were originally given in the European Council Directive 90/496/EEC with subsequent amendments. Originally, nutrition labelling was optional, but became mandatory when either a nutrient content claim is made on the label or in advertisements or when health claims are made (EC, 1990). Regulation 1169/2011 repeals 90/496/EEC and amends 1924/2006 to include the addition of vitamins and minerals and certain other substances as referenced in 90/496/EEC. Nutrition labelling is now mandatory on pre-packaged foods and must provide information on energy value, fat, saturates, carbohydrates, sugars, protein and salt, in this order, expressed per 100 g or ml of product. Information on other nutrients may be provided voluntarily. The new regulation also includes requirements for location of information provision as well as font size, units of expression and allergen labelling. Pre-packed foods that previously provided nutrition information must comply with the new requirements as of December 2014, while those that did not previously provide information must do so by December 2016. Extremely small food packages, as well as unprocessed foods, are currently exempted from the new labelling regulations (EC, 2013b; EUFIC, 2012).

4.4.3 Novel Foods

Novel food regulation in the EU is governed by EC Regulation 258/97 and is highly restrictive, making the EU one of the most challenging markets worldwide for novel foods. A wide range of food is considered novel, including GM food, food produced from GM organisms, food produced by algae, fungi or microorganisms, food isolated from plants and animals without a history of safe use as food or food that has been processed and the process has dramatically changed the food (EC, 1997).

To obtain novel food registration, the food must achieve three criteria. The food must not pose a hazard to the consumer, mislead the consumer or differ significantly from other products on the market that it is intended to replace to the extent that it would have a nutritionally disadvantageous impact on the consumer. The applicant must apply to a member state for permission to sell the good in that market. The member state will then assess the food based on the three aforementioned criteria and if it passes the assessment, then permit the sale of the food in that particular member state's market. The report is then given to the EC and other member states where they have 60 days to file comments or objections. If there is an objection, or if it is determined that the food requires further assessment, an additional assessment will then be carried out (EC, 1997, 1998). Scientific requirements for the novel foods application are given in Commission Recommendation 97/618/EC.

Food that is GM, contains GM organisms or food that is produced from ingredients produced by GM organisms must also receive pre-market approval, which is obtained through a separate process. The EFSA issues an opinion on whether or not the GM food meets the same three criteria for novel food applications. After issuing the opinion, the Commission makes a draft decision based on EFSA's opinion. A final decision is later made to authorize or reject the food (EC, 2003). Foods that have come into incidental contact with GM foods are permitted in the EU, but the food must be 0.9 per cent or less GM (EC, n.d). The EU has stringent GM monitoring and testing protocols for all food and feed products (Viju et al., 2012).

4.4.4 Food Supplements

Four years before harmonizing food health claims regulations, the EU developed harmonized regulations for 'food supplements' (comparable to nutraceuticals, as discussed in Chapter 2). In Directive 2002/46/EC, the EU began establishing harmonized regulations for the labelling of food supplements and introduced specific rules on vitamins and minerals in food supplements (EC, 2002). Food supplements are concentrated doses (for example, tablets, pills, capsules, powders and so on) of vitamins and minerals with the intention of achieving nutritive or physiological effects. Food supplements are legally considered food (not drugs or an inter-mediate category) (EC, 2002), thus, all health and nutrition claims that can be used on other foodstuffs can also be used on food supplements. However, the list of nutrients eligible for food supplement status is short.

Only vitamins and minerals are eligible and only those provided for in the original directive or subsequently approved by the EC in additional directives are permitted. Nutrients added to the list of acceptable food supplements must undergo a safety evaluation. This safety evaluation is separate and distinct from novel food registration if novel food registration is deemed necessary. A technical dossier and application must be made to the EFSA and the EFSA will prepare an opinion that the Commission will use to determine whether or not to permit the nutrient as a food supplement (HCDG, 2009).

The 2002 Directive also provides the requirements for labelling food supplements. Labels must include:

- the nature of the nutrients
- the daily recommended serving
- a warning not to exceed the daily recommended serving
- a statement that the food supplement is not a substitute for a varied diet
- a statement that the food supplement should be kept out of reach of children
- the numerical amount of nutrient(s) intended as the supplement is declared (EC, 2002).

In summary, the EU regulates functional food tightly as indicated by the paucity of approved disease risk reduction claims and extensive list of claims denied. The novel food registration procedure is the most stringent of any country examined in this book, imposing additional costs on novel functional food producers. Food supplements are considered food and can use approved claims; however, food supplements are limited to vitamins and minerals, a significantly narrower band of products than is the case for NHPs in Canada or nutraceuticals/supplements in some other countries. Despite this tight regulatory regime, there may be benefits to negotiating harmonization or recognition of equivalence of legislation on functional foods between trading partners, thereby reducing still further the need for firms to adhere to different regulations in different countries in order to market the same products. Given the considerable legislative differences that exist between the EU and other countries, however, this would be a significant challenge.

4.5 JAPAN

The Ministry of Health, Labour and Welfare (MHLW) is responsible for overseeing regulation of the health foods sector in Japan. Japan was one of the first countries to move towards regulating functional foods. Facing an ageing population and rising health care costs, regulation began in earnest in the 1980s.

4.5.1 Health Claims

Japan uses a largely product-specific system for health claims, with a relatively new category for generic claims. Disease risk reduction and structure/function claims are both permitted. Health claims in Japan are divided into two main categories (as well as some subcategories): foods for specified health uses (FOSHU) and foods with nutrient function claims (FNFC). FOSHU is a product-specific health claim system and refers to food with ingredients that affect health and are officially approved to make claims of effects on the human body. Functional foods for which a firm wants to make a health claim need FOSHU approval. Well over 600 different products have been authorized to make Regular FOSHU claims (Hayashi, 2007). If a health claim is not Qualified or Standardized, then it is a Regular FOSHU claim. Regular FOSHU also includes disease risk reduction claims (Hayashi, 2007) of which only two have been approved: calcium and osteoporosis and folic acid and neural tube defects in infants (see Table A1.2 in Appendix 1) (MHLW, n.d.a).

There are four main criteria to obtain Regular FOSHU approval. First, the effect of the functional food on the human body must be clearly proven. Second, there must be no safety issues with the food. Third, the food must not contain an excess of unhealthy ingredients (for example, salt). Fourth, the food must have established quality assurance and control methods. The MHLW decides whether or not to grant FOSHU approval after consulting with the Council on Pharmaceutical Affairs and Sanitation to determine the effectiveness of the food. The Ministry also consults with the Safety Commission to ensure the food is safe for consumption (MHLW, n.d.a).

In an effort to facilitate applications for FOSHU approval, the MHLW introduced two additional categories of FOSHU health claims: Qualified FOSHU and Standardized FOSHU. Qualified FOSHU are for foods that have a function for which there is not conclusive scientific evidence. The wording of Qualified FOSHU claims usually includes the statement that the 'grounds for this effectiveness have not necessarily been established'. Standardized FOSHU is for food processing ingredients that are well established in FOSHU claims. When many products that have these ingredients achieve a certain number of FOSHU claims, then new products seeking to make claims based on those ingredients have a shorter process to achieve approval (MHLW, n.d.a). For example, products that fall under Standardized FOSHU claims regarding maintaining gastrointestinal functioning and health (specifically, these products can claim that they 'maintain a healthy gut') contain:

- 3–8 g/day of indigestible dextrin
- 7–8 g/day of polydextrose
- 1–3 g/day of xylo-oligosaccharide
- 3–8 g/day of fructo-oligosaccharide
- 2–6 g/day of soybean oligosaccharide
- 10 g/day of isomalto oligosaccharide
- 2–8 g/day of lacto-fructo-oligosaccharide
- 2–5 g/day of galacto-oligosaccharide
- 5–12 g/day of partially hydrolyzed guar gum (Hayashi, 2007; Ohama et al., 2008).

FNFC are foods with structure/function claims and are labelled with the nutrient function claims stipulated by the MHLW. These are generic claims that can be made on food without prior approval for that specific product, unlike any FOSHU claims. FNFC indicate evidence of a relationship between a vitamin or mineral and a health function or structure. Food must fall within a certain range of values and must bear a disclosure statement depending on the vitamin or mineral. Approved claims for vitamins (see Table A1.1 in Appendix 1) (MHLW, n.d.b) include:

- niacin and skin or mucous membranes
- pantothenic acid and skin or mucous membranes
- biotin and skin or mucous membranes
- vitamin A and night vision or skin or mucous membranes
- vitamin B_1 and skin or mucous membranes
- vitamin B_2 and skin or mucous membranes
- vitamin B_6 and energy from protein or skin or mucous membranes
- vitamin B_{12} and red blood cell formation
- vitamin C and skin or mucous membranes or antioxidant
- vitamin D and absorption of calcium or bone growth
- vitamin E and prevention of fat oxidation or cell health
- folic acid and red blood cell formation or normal foetus development.

Approved claims for minerals (see Table A1.1 in Appendix 1) (MHLW, n.d.b) include:

- zinc and normal taste or skin or mucous membranes or protein and nucleic acid metabolism
- calcium and bone and teeth development
- iron and red blood cell formation
- copper and red blood cell formation or enzymes function or bone formation
- magnesium and bone and teeth development or enzymes function or energy generation.

Originally, FOSHU claims were only permitted on 'conventional food' and not nutraceuticals/supplements. However, as of 2001, FOSHU approval was extended to products in alternative forms, including tablets and capsules. Some dosage methods are still restricted to drugs only, including ampoules and oral sprays. Most importantly, there is no legal or regulatory distinction in Japan between 'supplements' or 'nutraceuticals' and 'conventional food'. As such, all FOSHU regulations are the same whether or not the product comes in a conventional food format or a nutraceutical/supplement format. Regardless, the vast majority of products (over 700) with FOSHU approval are in conventional food form. Indeed, the fact that Japan does not distinguish between conventional food and supplements may make it challenging for foreign firms accustomed to complying with differing regulations for food and supplements (Ohama et al., 2006, 2008).

4.5.2 Nutrient Content Claims and Nutrition Labelling

Japan has a relatively uncomplicated nutrient content claim system. There are four different kinds of statements (ranked in order from highest to lowest concentration of the nutrient): 'high in' statements, 'contains' statements, 'low' statements and 'does not contain' statements. 'High' and 'contains' statements apply to nutrients that are useful for healthy living. The amount needed to make these claims varies for solid and liquid food and must also meet a minimum per 100 kcal energy requirement. Generally, the minimum amount required for solid food is twice that of liquid food. Similarly, 'high' statements generally require twice the level of the nutrient as 'contains' statements. 'Low' and 'does not contain' statements apply to nutrients that need to be consumed in limited amounts and there is no per 100 kcal requirement in those cases. For 'low' statements, food in liquid form is held to a higher standard (must have less of a nutrient to qualify for the 'low' statement) (see Table A1.3 in Appendix 1) (MHLW, n.d.a).

Nutrition labelling in Japan was initially voluntary unless a claim was made. However, mandatory nutritional labelling came into effect on 1 January 2013, with a five-year grace period (FAS, 2013a). Nutrition labelling information must be provided in the following order: serving size, energy, protein, fat, carbohydrates and sodium. Any other nutrients should be declared after sodium. Vitamins that can be declared in nutrition labelling are: niacin, pantothenic acid, biotin, vitamin A, vitamin B_1, vitamin B_2, vitamin B_6, vitamin B_{12}, vitamin C, vitamin D, vitamin E, vitamin K and folic acid. Minerals that can be declared in nutrition labelling are: zinc, potassium, calcium, chromium, selenium, iron, copper, sodium, magnesium, manganese, iodine and phosphorus (MHLW, n.d.a).

4.5.3 Novel Food

In Japan, novel foods and food additives are defined as products that have been produced through the use of recombinant DNA techniques. The products must undergo examination for safety assessment and their methods of manufacturing should also undergo confirmation of compliance standards for manufacturing established by the Minister for Health and Welfare. Nutrition labelling is mandatory for all novel foods and food additives in Japan. The applicable claims are similar to that of FOSHU products.

Japan currently provides an interesting mix between a purely generic system and a purely product-specific one. Although the system is decidedly more product-specific, Standardized FOSHU lowers the costs to individual firms seeking claims on ingredients with well-established ingredient–health effect relationships. At the same time, there are potentially significant returns to investment for firms wishing to market a new product with health benefits.

4.6 AUSTRALIA AND NEW ZEALAND

Recognizing the benefits of a coordinated regulatory approach, Australia and New Zealand developed a joint policy on nutrition content and health claims and created the Food Standards Australia New Zealand (FSANZ) Agency (Veeman, 2002). Disease risk reduction claims and structure/function claims are permitted but qualified claims are not. No pre-market approval is required for structure/function claims, although firms need to be able to provide substantiation of these claims. Registration is required for novel functional foods. Nutrient content claims are permitted. Nutrition labelling is mandatory and is similar to requirements in the USA and Canada.

4.6.1 Health Claims

A new regulatory standard for health claims, Standard 1.2.7 – Nutrition, Health and Related Claims, came into effect on 1 January 2013 and further refines a set of well-established policies governing the use of health claims on food. Health claims are divided into two groups: high-level claims and general claims. High-level health claims refer to a serious disease or a biomarker of a serious disease and are disease risk reduction claims. They elucidate a relationship between the consumption of a nutrient and the risk of a disease (FSANZ, 2008a). General-level claims are equivalent to structure/function claims in that they describe the relationship between a nutrient and a health function.

FSANZ has evaluated a number of high-level health claims. Approved claims include, for example:

- sodium (with or without potassium) and reduced risk of CHD
- fruits and vegetables and reduced risk of CHD
- saturated and/or trans fat and lower cholesterol
- calcium (with or without vitamin D) and osteoporosis, bone density
- folic acid and reduced risk of foetal neural tube defects
- beta-glucan and reduced cholesterol
- phytosterols, phtyostanols and reduced cholesterol
- diets low in sodium and reduced blood pressure (FSANZ, 2010a, 2013c).

Some proposed health claims have been rejected, for example a proposed claim that sought to establish a relationship between whole grains and heart disease and a proposed claim linking consumption of omega-3 fatty acids and reduced risk of CHD (FSANZ, 2010a).

Before using a new high-level health claim that is not currently approved, the firm must obtain pre-market approval from FSANZ, which evaluates whether there is 'convincing' scientific evidence for the claim. If the evidence is less than convincing (for example, 'probable' or 'insufficient'), then the claim will not be approved. These claims are generic insofar as a successful application means that any firm can use the claims, as long as they meet the conditions prescribed in the standard (including certain nutritional scoring requirements, so that foods that use high-level claims do not contain excessive levels of unhealthy nutrients) (FSANZ, 2008b).

If using an approved general-level health claim, firms do not require pre-market approval of the claim's use but must keep records of the claim's substantiation (FSANZ, 2013b). Firms may also use general-level claims that have not been approved by FSANZ but must notify FSANZ of the claim and certify that the relationship between the food and health has been substantiated according to FSANZ acceptable standards (FSANZ, 2013c). FSANZ has a list of over 200 approved general-level claims that count as scientific substantiation for firms wishing to use those claims. Below is a sampling (but not an exhaustive list) of some of the approved relationships for which general-level health claims can be made:

- vitamin D and calcium for phosphorus utilization and absorption, muscles
- vitamin E as antioxidant
- vitamin K for proper coagulation, normal bone structure
- thiamine and normal metabolism of carbohydrates, neurological function
- riboflavin and metabolism, nervous system, vision
- niacin and metabolism, neurological function, fatigue
- pantothenic acid and metabolism of fat, mental performance, fatigue
- vitamin B_6 and protein metabolism, iron metabolism, energy metabolism
- folate and blood formation, amino acid synthesis
- vitamin B_{12} and blood formation, neurological function, immune system
- biotin and energy metabolism, psychological function, hair and skin
- vitamin C and connective tissue, neurological function, cartilage and bones
- calcium and bones and teeth, metabolism, blood coagulation, digestion
- magnesium and energy metabolism, muscle function, fatigue, psychological function
- iron and blood formation, cognitive function, fatigue
- copper and immune system, neurological function, metabolism
- iodine and thyroid hormones, neurological function, energy metabolism
- zinc and wound healing, cognitive function, hair and nails
- manganese and bone function, energy metabolism

- phosphorus and bones and teeth, energy metabolism
- selenium and immune system function, thyroid hormones
- protein and building and repairing body tissues
- DHA and brain, eyes and neural development
- EPA[12] and DHA (but not omega-3) and heart health
- dietary fibre and normal laxation
- potassium and water and electrolyte balance, nervous system
- chromium and macronutrient metabolism
- fluoride and tooth mineralization
- molybdenum and sulphur and amino acid metabolism, liver function
- choline and homocysteine metabolism, fat metabolism
- vitamin A and vision, iron metabolism, immune system
- folic acid and foetal neural tube development
- beta-glucan and reduced blood cholesterol
- carbohydrate and normal metabolism
- energy and normal metabolism
- live yoghurt cultures and lactose digestion
- phtyosterols, phytostanols and reduced dietary and biliary cholesterol absorption
- fruits and vegetables contribute to heart health
- low sugar (chewing gum) contributes to dental health (FSANZ, 2013a, 2013c).

In addition, firms can use approved high-level health claims as the basis for a general-level claim. A third means of substantiation is based on a declaration made by an 'authoritative source' as determined by FSANZ. A systematic review of the scientific literature indicating significant support for the general-level claim can also be used as substantiation (FSANZ, 2009).

4.6.2 Nutrient Content Claims and Nutrition Labelling

The new standard for the regulation of health and nutrition claims (Standard 1.2.7 – Nutrition, Health and Related Claims) allows for nutrition content claims (in other words, 'good source of calcium') so long as the product meets specified criteria. For example, foods that meet the conditions for an omega-3 fatty acid content claim can make a 'good source' or 'increased' claim depending on the proportions of omega-3 fatty acids in the reference food; in other words, a minimum quantity is required to make a claim regarding omega fatty acid content. Similarly, foods can be labelled as being a 'good source', an 'excellent source' of dietary fibre or a source of 'increased' dietary fibre, depending on the quantities of dietary fibre in a serving. Table A1.3 in Appendix 1 provides examples of allowable nutrient content wording claims. Of the countries examined here, only Australia and New Zealand currently regulate and authorize the use of gluten content claims, with definitions provided for the use of 'low' and 'free'. In general, for nutrients, the 'free' claims in Australia and New Zealand are also much stricter than other countries, requiring no detectable levels of nutrients for those claims (FSANZ, 2010b).

Australia and New Zealand have regulatory requirements for nutrition labelling. The Australia New Zealand Food Standards Code sets out regulations for nutrition information panels in Standard 1.2.8, similar in nature to the nutrition facts tables in other countries examined in this chapter. Nutrition information panels must contain the number of servings of food in the package, the average quantity of food in a serving, the average energy in a serving, the average amounts of protein, fat, saturated fat, carbohydrate and sugar in a serving, the average quantity of sodium in a serving and the amount of a nutrient or biologically active substance that is in a nutrition claim made on the food in a serving. These must be expressed both in per serving and in per 100 g or 100 ml amounts. The panel must include trans-, mono- and polyunsaturated fats when a nutrition claim is made on cholesterol or on unsaturated, trans- or saturated fat. Similarly, dietary fibre must be declared when a claim is made about dietary fibre, sugar or other carbohydrates. Percentage daily intake of the nutrients may also be listed, but it is not necessary (FSANZ, 2010b).

As is the case for other countries, Australia and New Zealand provide a list of exemptions for nutrition information panels. Almost all of the exemptions are based on the type of food sold (for example, tea, coffee, kava, herbs and spices are all exempt from nutrition information table labelling). Other countries tend to have more exemptions based on who is selling or buying the good (for example, farmers' markets in Canada and small businesses in the USA). Australia and New Zealand only exempt food sold at fundraisers from nutrition information tables. However, all exempt food loses its exemption if a nutrition claim is made on the food and the food must either be labelled accordingly or the information must be given to the purchaser on request (FSANZ, 2010b).

4.6.3 Novel Foods

Novel foods are non-traditional foods (without a history of human consumption in Australia or New Zealand) that undergo a safety assessment to determine if they are safe to consume. Novel foods are therefore subject to a registration process. Australia and New Zealand have placed a unique mark on novel food registration. Unlike other countries discussed here, foods that successfully attain novel food status are eligible for exclusive market access to Australia and New Zealand for 15 months, to the exclusion of other products. This unique feature increases the incentive for firms to research novel functional foods and reduces the spillover and free-rider benefits that accrue to other firms when one firm applies for novel food registration in another country. In other countries, once a food receives novel food approval, other firms with products featuring the same novel ingredient can all enter the market at the same time. Only one firm has to apply for and bear the costs of novel food approval and registration. Therefore, there are significant spillover and free-rider benefits that accrue to firms that do not bear the costs of novel food registration. Australia and New Zealand reduce the spillover benefits and increase the benefits for the applicant through the 15 months of exclusive market access.

4.6.4 Dietary Supplements and Complementary Medicines

The new Standard 1.2.7 for health and nutrient content claims applies to food only. This is because of the decision to regulate dietary supplements under a separate regulatory body as of 2003. In 2003, Australia and New Zealand signed a treaty with the intention of establishing the Australia New Zealand Therapeutic Products Authority (ANZTPA), to include authority over complementary and alternative medicines, including dietary supplements. In June 2011, Australia and New Zealand signed an agreement for the joint regulation of therapeutic products. The Australian government's Therapeutic Goods Administration and the New Zealand Medicines and Medical Devices Safety Authority (Medsafe) are currently overseeing the process of regulatory harmonization leading to the creation of an ANZTPA. Regulations on these matters thus remain at the national level, discussed in detail below.

In Australia, the Australian Regulatory Guidelines for Complementary Medicines set out the regulations for registering and selling complementary medicines. Complementary medicines include, but are not limited to, products that have approved vitamins, minerals and amino acids but also homeopathic medicines (TGA, 2006).[13]

Approval is granted on a product-by-product basis. This approval is contingent upon evidence of both the safety and efficacy of the claim because complementary medicines must possess claims. Claims are divided into two types with different levels of evidence for each. One type is traditional use evidence. Among other forms of evidence, written histories of use in traditional or classical medical literature and other countries' acceptance of the claim constitute evidence of traditional use (Williams and Ghosh, 2008). The applicants that seek traditional use regulation can use either 'general-' or 'medium'-level claims. General traditional use claims can be made in relation to health maintenance, vitamin/mineral supplementation or symptom relief (without mention of the disease causing the symptom). Medium-level traditional use claims pertain to health improvement, disease risk reduction, symptom relief of a specific disease or condition or helping manage a specific symptom or disease or condition.

Scientific evidence can also be used to substantiate the same general- and medium-level claims; however, 'high'-level claims are restricted to complementary medicines with the highest quality of scientific evidence. High-level claims include treatment or curing, illness prevention or treatment of specific vitamin/mineral deficiencies. To make a high-level claim, a complementary medicine must be 'registered' as opposed to 'listed'. Listed complementary medicines are considered lower risk than registered medicines. As a result, most complementary medicines are 'listed' rather than 'registered' (and only possess general- or medium-level claims) (Williams and Ghosh, 2008).

Therapeutic Goods Order 69 establishes labelling requirements for therapeutic goods, including complementary medicines. Labels must be in English and use metric units to list the amounts of the active ingredients. All active ingredients must be named and listed with quantities or proportions, but only certain inactive ingredients are required to be listed. The name of the dosage form is also required, as is the quantity of goods in the package and any applicable warning statements deemed necessary. Finally, directions on how to use the goods must also be provided (TGA, 2001).

In New Zealand, recent amendments to the 1985 Dietary Supplements Act clarified the definition of dietary supplement. A dietary supplement is any amino acid, edible substance, herb, mineral, nutrient or vitamin normally available in food that is put into a controlled dosage form and is intended to be taken orally (Medsafe, n.d.).

Besides clearly defining dietary supplements, the 1985 Dietary Supplements Act remains relatively unchanged by the 2010 amendments. The Act permits claims but they cannot be misleading and cannot be therapeutic. Therapeutic claims are ones that claim disease prevention or treatment, disease or disorder or condition diagnosis, body weight or shape or size altering or physiological function modification (Medsafe, n.d.).

New Zealand has a very laissez-faire regulatory system for dietary supplements. Nowhere in the 1985 Dietary Supplements Act and its amendments are pre-market approvals required. The firm still holds responsibility for ensuring the product is safe. The firm must also ensure that if it uses claims, they should not be misleading or therapeutic. Violations of these and other regulations in the Act are met with a fine (Medsafe, n.d).

Dietary supplement labelling in New Zealand includes a consumer information panel. The consumer information panel must declare all active ingredients and their quantities or proportions per dosage unit. Inactive ingredients (but not their quantities or proportions) must also be listed, with either their specific or class names. The permitted class names are antioxidants, artificial sweeteners, colouring or colour, encapsulating aids, flavouring or flavour, minerals, preservatives, tablet aids and vitamins. The consumer information panel must also include any storage instructions where appropriate. Other general labelling requirements include information on daily doses for adults and children, a warning statement in case of overdose and an expiry date (Medsafe, n.d).

4.7 SYNTHESIS

In establishing regulatory frameworks governing the health foods sector, policymakers need to strike a balance between the protection of consumers from false and misleading claims that also weaken consumer confidence in the sector and facilitating R&D leading to new health foods product innovations. Regulation in this sense is a double-edged sword. While governments have moved to establish regulatory frameworks governing the use of health claims and the approval of new products with novel traits, slow and restrictive approval processes and weak protection of intellectual property rights will blunt incentives to innovate. Among ostensibly broadly similar, well-established, developed markets examined in this chapter, significant differences in regulatory approaches still exist. For example, the USA and Canadian markets for health foods products have a number of similarities, yet the Canadian regulatory system has often been criticized for being slow to adapt to the changing nature of technology in the sector.[14]

Most of the disease reduction claims currently permitted in Canada have been available to firms in the USA for a much longer time period and the list of permissible health claims in the USA is more extensive than in Canada. Given the relatively small size of the Canadian domestic market, firms may be deterred from seeking regulatory approval for a new health claim if this is an overly slow and costly procedure compared to the potential payback of targeting a larger market such as the US.

The use of 'qualified' health claims in the USA and Japan stands in stark contrast to the EU, Canada and Australia and New Zealand, which reject the use of lower standards for disease reduction claims because of the risk of misleading consumers. The authorization of qualified health claims requires lower standards of evidence and usually requires the provision of a disclosure statement or less authoritative wording. Qualified structure/function claims may be more palatable. Nevertheless, this must be balanced against the need for consumer protection and the potential for consumer confusion if a health claim is accompanied by a long list of 'small print' qualifiers.

Another notable difference in the approach to health claims among countries is the approach to product-specific health claims. Generic claims create a potential free-rider problem: many firms benefit but only one firm has to go through the application process to obtain approval for a new health claim. Japan allows product-specific health claims for functional food and Canada for NHPs. Nevertheless, the generic health claim systems in use for food in the USA, Canada, EU and Australia and New Zealand have the advantage that more products can use approved health claims with the potential to facilitate improved consumer knowledge of the relationship between diet and health. A middle ground could be to consider a blended approach with both generic and product-specific health claims available.

Some countries make no regulatory distinction between supplements and (functional) food (for example, Japan). In many other countries, the two categories are distinct from a regulatory perspective, as is the case in Canada, where NHPs face a product-specific regulatory system but functional foods utilize generic health claims, and in Australia and New Zealand, where a functional food is subject to a harmonized regulatory system while supplements have been subject to separate national regulatory treatment. While the USA does make a distinction between food and dietary supplements, it does not impose significantly different regulations (the same generic claims are available to both product categories). The EU treats food supplements as a 'food', but restricts the definition of food supplements to vitamins and minerals.

Navigating this complex array of regulatory approaches can be a bureaucratic headache for firms wishing to access international markets; they must attempt to determine which set of regulations apply to their products and the extent to which the same product will be regulated differently in different markets. Disparate regulatory requirements with respect to what constitutes an allowable health claim and whether firms can use an approved generic health claim or must seek approval for a product-specific health claim raise the costs of accessing international markets and are an unintended consequence of regulation.

One implication of treating supplements/nutraceuticals and food as equivalent from a regulatory perspective is that regulation should not factor into a firm's decision about which format to use (food versus pill and so on) when researching and developing a new product. Regulation does not distort the costs or benefits of using food relative to using supplements as the carrier for the functional ingredient. Countries in which foods and supplements are regulated differently, as is the case in Canada and Australia and New Zealand, present a more complex decision environment for firms. For example, in Canada, if firms choose the food route, then the regulation is less stringent but the claim does not belong to that firm on that product alone. If the firm chooses to register the product as an NHP, then a product-specific claim is available (with potential monopoly rents) but the product must meet more stringent approval processes. As a result, a firm's decision to develop and manufacture food or NHPs in Canada is likely to depend on how the firm views these trade-offs, as well as the perceived level of uncertainty in the health claims approval process. This is an example of an unintended consequence of regulation: a 'derived externality', as outlined in Chapter 3.

In some jurisdictions, efforts are being made to harmonize regulations or to recognize equivalence in regulatory standards; Australia and New Zealand and the development of a single regulatory approach across EU member states being prime examples, but, for the most part, regulatory approaches between countries remain quite distinct. Establishing equivalence (for example, recognizing US health claims in Canada and vice versa) is a possible route for functional foods. Indeed, many of the approved health claims in Canada are based on claims already approved in the USA and the Canadian approval process for nutrient function claims specifically references the Institute of Medicine of the US National Academies. The regulatory approaches to dietary supplements in the USA, NHPs in Canada and food supplements in Europe, however, are markedly different; indeed, the categories are not even directly comparable in the sense that not all products classified as NHPs in Canada would be considered dietary supplements in the USA or food supplements in the EU and therefore it seems unlikely that these jurisdictions would recognize the other's regulations as equivalent.

Similar issues arise in emerging markets. This is the focus of the next chapter, which discusses the regulatory approaches within the BRIC countries (Brazil, Russia, India and China) and other emerging markets in Asia.

NOTES

1. Two special categories of foods – medical foods and foods for special dietary uses – are discussed in Appendix 2.
2. Exemptions include food produced by a small business, food served in restaurants and take-out or delivery food intended for immediate consumption, donated food that is given free to the consumer, and fresh produce and seafood (see Appendix 3 for a complete list).
3. Bioengineered food is defined by the FDA as food from new plant varieties that have been developed using recombinant deoxyribonucleic acid (rDNA) technology.
4. The Food and Drugs Act gives Health Canada its mandate, while the FDR are used to implement the goals of the Act.
5. When health claims are generic, manufacturers are not required to prove that their product(s) contain the required amount of ingredient(s) associated with the claim or the truthfulness and efficacy of the health claim (no pre-market approval/notification required), though they should be able to provide the information when requested.
6. Arachidonic acid, an omega-6 fatty acid.
7. Docosahexaenoic acid, an omega-3 fatty acid.
8. There are a variety of exemptions for food, most notably when there is zero for all nutrients required to be listed in a nutrition facts table, when the food is a fresh vegetable or fruit with no added ingredients or when the food is sold by individuals at a farmers' market (see Appendix 3 for a full list of exemptions).
9. See Chapter 2 for a definition of NHPs in Canada, which are somewhat similar to nutraceuticals and supplements in other countries, and Chapter 3 for a discussion of the evolution of the Canadian regulatory system for NHPs.
10. If the food was labelled with one of these optional nutrients, then all nutrients had to be declared. For example, if fibre was labelled on the food, the label had to also include sugar, saturated fat and sodium declarations (FSA, 1999).
11. For a list of rejected health claims see http://ec.europa.eu/food/food/labellingnutrition/claims/community_register/rejected_health_claims_en.htm.
12. Eicosapentaenoic acid, an omega-3 fatty acid.
13. See Williams and Ghosh (2008) for a complete listing.
14. See, for example, Farrell et al. (2009), Herath et al. (2008b), Malla et al. (2007), Veeman (2002).

5. Health claim regulations in emerging markets

This chapter reviews the regulatory environment for the health foods sector in key emerging markets, including Brazil, Russia, India, China, South Korea and Taiwan. As with Chapter 4, a primary focus of the discussion is the regulations surrounding allowable health claims, while nutrient content labelling regulations, nutritional labelling and regulations pertaining to novel functional foods are also discussed. Tables offering country-by-country comparisons of structure/function claims, disease risk reduction claims and nutrient content claims can be found in Appendix 1.

5.1 BRAZIL

In Brazil, the National Health Surveillance Agency (ANVISA in Portuguese) has regulatory responsibility for the health foods sector, including the establishment and enforcement of standards, new product registration and oversight of health claims. Brazil led the way in the development of functional food and health claim regulations in Latin America with the establishment of the Food and Nutrition National Policy in 1999 (Stringueta et al., 2012). Brazilian legislation does not define functional food but defines the basis on which functional and health (disease risk reduction) claims may be made. Therapeutic claims are prohibited. Nutrient content claims are also permitted and nutrition labelling is mandatory. Novel food registration is necessary for novel functional foods.

5.1.1 Health Claims and Structure/Function Claims

Examples of permitted disease risk reduction claims in Brazil include:

- omega-3 fatty acids and triglycerides (heart health)
- beta-glucan (dietary fibre) and cholesterol
- psyllium (dietary fibre) and fat absorption
- chitosan and fat and cholesterol absorption

- phytosterols and cholesterol
- mannitol, xylitol or sorbitol and dental caries
- soy protein and cholesterol (Toledo and Lajolo, 2008).

Permitted structure/function claims include:

- lycopene as an antioxidant
- dietary fibres and normal intestine function
- powdered resistant dextrin (dietary fibre) and normal intestine function
- partially hydrolyzed guar gum (dietary fibre) and normal intestine function
- polydextrose (dietary fibre) and normal intestine function
- fructo-oligosaccharides and gut flora
- inulin and gut flora
- lactulose and normal intestine function
- probiotics and gut flora
- lutein as an antioxidant
- Zeaxan as an antioxidant (Stringueta et al., 2012; Toledo and Lajolo, 2008).

All functional food products must obtain pre-market approval and firms seeking to use a new or existing claim must also obtain pre-market approval for the claim. The food must be both safe and effective before a claim can be used. The extent of required substantiation is contingent upon the kind of claim; in some cases, a single scientific study may be sufficient to qualify use of the claim while in other cases, submitting only a single scientific study may result in the rejection of the claim. Criteria for approval are not necessarily the quantity of studies submitted but the quality of the study design and data (Toledo and Lajolo, 2008).

5.1.2 Nutrient Content Claims and Nutrition Labelling

Nutrient content claims are permitted in Brazil and are subject to regulatory oversight. Values for 'low' and 'free' claims have been established for solid and liquid food and for energy, fat, saturated fat, cholesterol, sugars and sodium. Generally, the maximum level for 'free' claims is half the level of 'low' claims. Cholesterol claims are contingent upon also meeting a certain level of saturated fat (see Table A1.3 in Appendix 1). A 'free' claim is permitted with respect to trans fat and is conditional upon the levels of saturated fat in the food. 'Source' and 'rich' claims are permitted on protein, vitamins and minerals with established daily recommended values. 'Rich' claims require twice the minimum levels of protein, vitamins or minerals in 'source' claims. Only one comparative claim is permitted and that is a 'reduced' energy claim, where the food must have been reduced in energy by at least 30 per cent (CFS, 2008).

Nutrition labelling is mandatory in Brazil for all pre-packaged foods and must include content information on protein, calories, carbohydrates, cholesterol, total fats, saturated fats, trans fat, calcium, iron, sodium and dietary fibre. Should a health or nutrient content claim be made on a nutrient, then that nutrient must be declared (Coitinho et al., 2002; FEHD, 2005).

5.1.3 Novel Foods

Brazil has implemented a novel food registration procedure that applies to foods that do not have a history of consumption in Brazil and foods with substances that do have a history of consumption but that have been augmented to levels beyond that used in other foods. ANVISA oversees the registration procedure; it evaluates whether or not the food is safe for consumption on the basis of scientific studies (in animals and humans, as well as clinical and epidemiological studies). The decision to approve or reject the novel food is also informed by the food's regulatory status in other countries (Toledo and Lajolo, 2008).

5.1.4 Bioactive Substances (Nutraceuticals)

Brazil implemented functional food regulations in the late 1990s, which helped address the confusion surrounding the status of nutraceuticals between food and drugs. ANVISA developed a regulatory framework for nutraceuticals in 2002 based around the concept of 'bioactive substances', which are substances that have a particular physiological or metabolic function and must be extracted and isolated from their original source (Toledo and Lajolo, 2008).

Unlike health claims on conventional food, which are generic, health claims on bioactive substances are product-specific, primarily to address safety concerns over the concentrated nature of the products. Unlike conventional food, bioactive substances must carry an approved health or function claim and the number of approved bioactive substances is quite restrictive. The list of eligible substances is fairly limited and includes, for example, carotenoids, phytosterols, flavonoids, phospholipids, organosulphur compounds, polyphenols and probiotics (Toledo and Lajolo, 2008).

In summary, Brazil's regulatory system is similar to a number of the developed markets discussed in the previous chapter in the sense that generic claims are permitted, pre-market approval is necessary for all claims, nutrition labelling is mandatory, novel functional foods must undergo a registration procedure and qualified claims are not permitted. As is the case elsewhere, bioactive substances occupy a somewhat grey area between medicine and food and are subject to a product-specific regulatory system.

5.2 RUSSIA (THE RUSSIAN FEDERATION)

In Russia, food products with health benefits are known as biologically active food supplements (BAFS), which are nutritive substances and minor food components used to ameliorate deficiencies, decrease the risk of debilitating diseases and improve quality of life. BAFS are categorized into nutraceuticals and parapharmaceuticals. Nutraceuticals refer to biologically active substances, which are basic components of organisms, vitamins or their predecessors, macro- and microelements (iron, calcium, selenium, zinc and so on), dietary fibres and indispensable amino acids used for correction of chemical composition of food. Parapharmaceuticals are biologically active substances with a certain pharmacological activity, which are used for auxiliary therapy and maintaining organs and systems within their normal physiological limits. The compositions of these two categories are different for adults and children under 14 years (Tutelyan and Sukhanov, 2008).

The health foods market in Russia has been experiencing rapid growth in recent years, mirroring consumer interest found in other countries. Estimates valued the Russian BAFS market at over US$2 billion in 2009. However, the sector is also characterized by a significant black market of unregulated products, estimated to be worth an additional US$1 billion in sales. This dichotomy between official and unofficial markets, with reputable firms selling high-quality products while less scrupulous firms market poor or even harmful products, spurred the Russian government to implement stricter regulations in 2010 (Altaffer and Washington-Smith, 2011). Significant restraints have been imposed upon the ability of firms to advertise, promote and distribute nutraceuticals/supplements in Russia; most legitimate products are sold via retail pharmacies, which accounted for 61 per cent of sales in 2009 (AAFC, 2011). Product launches involve registration procedures that include the submission of documents to the Russian authorities for registration, testing and proof of product safety (Altaffer and Washington-Smith, 2011). Popular categories of health and wellness food products include organic food and beverages, fortified/functional food and beverages, better-for-you food and beverages, vitamins and dietary supplements, herbal/traditional products, slimming products and sport nutrition products (AAFC, 2011).

The Health Ministry is responsible for regulation of BAFS. International firms wishing to enter the Russian market face a challenge in navigating an uncertain regulatory environment, such that developing relationships with established Russian partners familiar with the regulatory and operating environment is often seen as a safer market entry strategy (AAFC, 2011; Altaffer and Washington-Smith, 2011).

5.2.1 Claims and Nutrition Labelling

Structure/function health claims and nutrient content claims are permitted on BAFS, nutrition labelling is mandatory but disease risk reduction health claims and therapeutic claims are prohibited. Permitted nutrient content claims are generic, an example of which is 'Additional source of (insert vitamin or mineral)' or if a product is comprised of only herbal components, then an example would be 'source of arbutin'.

Structure/function claims are product-specific, must be scientifically proven and should describe the expected effect of the product on the physiological function of the human body. Products carrying structure/function claims require pre-market approval and a product licence before they can be marketed. Any structure/function claims must be clinically proven, but relatively low levels of substantiation are required for dietary supplement registration. Claims cannot use words that will relate the product to a disease in any way, imply any form of healing or that the product is for any purpose other than a supportive function (Altaffer and Washington-Smith, 2011). Examples of structure/function claims include:

- optimization of carbohydrates, fat, vitamin and other metabolism in various functional conditions
- normalization and/or improvement of the function state of the human organ/system
- decreased morbidity risk
- improvement of the gastrointestinal tract microflora (Tutelyan and Sukhanov, 2008).

Nutritional labelling is mandatory for BAFS in Russia. All labels must meet the required standards before they are allowed into the market. Labelling standards are established in regulation GOST P51074-2003 (2005), which was amended in 2009 and was further superseded by TR

TS 022/2011 'Food Products Labelling' on 1 July 2013 as regulations in Russia synchronized with those of the EU (FAS, 2011). It is an offence to make a false claim on the label. Nutrition labelling standards require labels to include the name of the product, complete listing of the product's ingredients with their respective quantities, all other substances in the product and their quantities, recommendations for use including the dosage, all contradictions or side-effects, a notice indicating the product is not a drug, a 'consult your doctor before use' notice, storage conditions, expiry date, registration number, date of registration and the manufacturer information. The label must not contain information that cannot be scientifically substantiated, for example, terms and phrases, such as 'ecologically clean product' cannot be used on the labels of BAFS (Tutelyan and Sukhanov, 2008).

In summary, in Russia the definition of a functional food is closer to that of a supplement in other countries. A substantial black market in products purporting to offer health benefits prompted a tightening of the regulatory environment. Only product-specific structure/function claims are permissible and the evolving regulatory environment represents a challenge for firms.

5.3 INDIA

Prior to 2006, regulation was piecemeal and no single regulatory authority or body of food law regulated the food sector in India. The government of India responded to pressure from stakeholders and the industry by enacting the Food Safety and Standards Act (FSSA) 2006, transforming the regulation of food in India. The Food Safety and Standards Authority of India (FFSAI), under the Ministry of Health and Family Welfare, now has regulatory responsibility for the health foods sector in India. According to Palthur et al. (2009), the effective implementation of the FSSA faced several challenges, including the inability of small and medium-scale firms to identify and comply with regulations due to lack of capacity and access to information; a regulatory vacuum created between the repealing of the old regime and the implementation of the new FSSA; and education and competency requirements for firms and regulators.

In India, the terms 'functional food', 'health supplements', 'nutraceuticals' and 'food for special dietary use' are used interchangeably and all are referred to as foods that are specially processed or formulated to satisfy particular dietary requirements that exist because of a particular physical or physiological condition. These foods should differ from the composition of ordinary foods of comparable nature. India's FSSA prohibits disease risk reduction health claims but allows structure/function health claims and makes nutrition labelling mandatory. FSSA was updated in 2011 with the Food Safety and Standards (packaging and labelling) Regulations Act, which, effective January 2013, requires the labelling of products containing biotechnology ingredients. In January 2013, India embarked on a process to harmonize its food standards with the Codex standards[1] and other international best practices, with completion and implementation planned for December 2014 (FSSAI, 2013).

The FSSA prohibits any claims that imply medicinal and therapeutic functions but nutrition structure/function claims that are not misleading can generally be used on functional foods/supplements, provided that sufficient scientific evidence to support the claim exists. While there is no pre-market approval for these products, the responsibility lies with the manufacturer to ensure that all claims satisfy the stipulated regulations (FSSA, 2006).

Labelling of these health food products is mandatory; all information on the label should be truthful and must not mislead the consumer. Information about ingredients, nutrients and quantity of the product on the label must not be different from the actual product in the package. Labels that falsely represent the product to promote its sale and give the public any guarantee of effectiveness that is not scientifically justified are not permitted.

In summary, India's health claims and labelling regulations are less restrictive compared to other countries, such as the EU. Health claims are not permitted but nutrition claims are allowed and labelling is mandatory. If disease risk reduction health claims are permitted in the future, with India's status as one of the new emerging economies of the world, it is likely to become an attractive market for further development of the health foods sector.

5.4 CHINA (THE PEOPLE'S REPUBLIC OF CHINA)

China uses the term health foods for functional food. As is the case in Japan and South Korea, China uses a product-specific system of registration to regulate the industry. Both disease risk reduction claims and structure/function claims are permitted. The regulatory process in China for achieving approval of health claims is relatively strict, requiring the applicant to conduct studies through an approved agency, in addition to the regular scientific literature review. Novel food registration requires similar testing. Only recently has China moved to instituting mandatory nutrition labelling and regulating nutrient content claims to address abuses.

5.4.1 Health Claims and Nutrition Labelling

The China Food and Drug Administration (CFDA) is responsible for regulatory oversight of the health foods sector and maintains a list of four permissible disease risk reduction claims that firms can apply to use. Claims can be made between the approved food and/or food constituent and: weight loss, cholesterol (blood lipids) reduction, blood sugar reduction and blood pressure reduction (Yang, 2008).

China also permits the use of product-specific structure/function claims. Firms must apply to the CFDA to use claims that specify a relationship between the food or food constituent and specific health effects (see Table A1.1 in Appendix 1), for example:

- enhances immunity
- antioxidative
- assists in memory improvement
- alleviates eye fatigue
- facilitates lead excretion
- moistens and cleans throat
- improves sleep
- facilitates milk secretion
- alleviates physical fatigue
- enhances anoxia endurance
- assists in irradiation hazard protection
- improves child growth and development
- increases bone density
- improves nutritional anaemia
- assists in protecting against chemical injury to the liver
- eliminates acne
- eliminates skin chloasma
- improves skin's water content
- improves skin's oil content
- regulates gastrointestinal tract flora
- facilitates digestion
- facilitates faeces excretion
- assists in protecting against gastric mucosa damage (Yang, 2008).

The approval process for the use of health food claims is similar for either domestic or foreign applicants. The CFDA requires samples of the food, a scientific evidence literature review and an approved testing agency for evaluation. Testing involves safety and efficacy assessments. If the firm wishes to use a claim not in the approved list of structure/function or disease risk reducing claims, the firm must arrange for testing (human and animal trials) to demonstrate efficacy. The CFDA may also commission an inspection of the manufacturer's facilities to evaluate safety. If the application is approved, then a Domestic Health Food Registration Certificate or an Imported Health Food Approval Certificate is issued. Imported Health Food Approval Certificates are valid for five years (Roberts and Rogerson, 2008).

Similar to Japan, current Chinese regulations do not make a distinction between nutraceuticals/supplements and conventional food and there is confusion regarding the distinction between food and drugs. Yang (2008) reports that less than 0.8 per cent of functional foods in China are in the form of conventional foods, whereas over 60 per cent of functional foods are in the form of tablets or capsules. This also means that firms face the same (stringent) regulatory procedure regardless of whether they choose to format the product as a supplement or as a food (Roberts and Rogerson, 2008).

Nutrition labelling and nutrient content claims regulations lag behind those for functional food and health, as China only recently began to implement significant nutrition-related regulations. New labelling requirements for pre-packaged food products were implemented in January 2013 by the Ministry of Health. Nutrition labelling remains voluntary but must meet mandatory requirements when claims are made. For example, when a nutrient content or nutrient comparative claim is made, nutritional information on protein, fat, carbohydrate and sodium is required, while labels may voluntarily declare cholesterol, sugar and fat content (FAS, 2013b). Nutrition content claims can be made on calcium, iron and fat and require that the food meet certain criteria for these foods. Labels must not be misleading or make claims regarding the curing of illness (Reuters, 2008).

5.4.2 Novel Foods

Health foods that are considered novel are subject to novel foods registration. Novel foods are defined as raw foods or food materials with no history of safe use as a food in China and do not include GM organisms, which are regulated by laws and a different ministry than novel foods. The Ministry of Health evaluates the safety of novel foods (or the demonstration that the novel food is substantially similar to other registered novel foods). Similar to the health food approval process, the Ministry of Health in this case requires samples of the food to be sent to an approved testing facility to determine the food's safety. This testing is conducted at a cost to the applicant. On site examinations may also be conducted before the Ministry of Health makes its final decision on whether to approve the novel food. If the food is evaluated as safe or substantially similar to other novel foods, then it will be permitted as a novel food in the Chinese market (Roberts and Rogerson, 2008).

In summary, product-specific claims regulations have emerged as a regional regulatory preference of several nations in Asia, with South Korea (discussed below), Japan and China all having product-specific systems. China permits a wide list of claims, but has implemented an additional safety assessment, which requires testing by approved agencies as a scientific literature review is insufficient to obtain approval. Novel food registration follows a similar process. The regulatory environment in China continues to develop, with the need for a more cohesive approach to labelling regulations and the use of health claims.

5.5 SOUTH KOREA (THE REPUBLIC OF KOREA)

The Ministry of Food and Drug Safety (MFDS), formerly the Korean Food and Drug Administration (KFDA), has regulatory oversight of the health foods sector in South Korea. The Health Functional Food Act (HFFA), enacted in August 2002 and implemented in 2004, is the primary legislative vehicle governing the sector. The main goal of the HFFA is to improve public health by ensuring the safety of new active ingredients; upon establishment, it created a new category for health and functional foods separate from conventional food.

In a significant departure from other countries, South Korea approves specific individual ingredients to carry health claims and restricts the definition of functional food to nutraceuticals/supplements. Health functional food (HFF) is defined as ingredients manufactured and processed into the form of a tablet, pill, powder or liquid so they can be consumed in measured doses. These ingredients must have some functional importance for the human body (for example, disease risk reduction or normal growth and development) (KFDA, 2006; Kim et al., 2008). Conventional food or food supplemented with vitamins, minerals or nutrients are not considered functional foods and are therefore ineligible to use health claims. In order for a firm to use health claims, the food must come in a medicine-like form, making all functional foods essentially supplements in South Korea. This contrasts sharply with the regulatory stances of the USA, EU and Canada that all allow the use of health claims on food that does not come in pill form (Zawistowski, 2008).

Some generic claims are permitted (and were permitted prior to South Korea's regulation of functional foods), but health claims are primarily a product (ingredient)-specific system. Disease risk reduction, structure/function and 'other function' health claims are allowed in South Korea. Functional foods in South Korea must bear nutrition labelling and have significantly more stringent labelling requirements than in many other countries.

5.5.1 Health Claims

The HFFA references at least 37 generic HFF ingredients including vitamins, minerals, essential amino acids, proteins, dietary fibre and essential fatty acids. Product-specific HFFs refer to all other products not included in the generic category. The HFFA requires these products to be sold in measured doses (for example, pills, tablets, capsules and liquids) to ensure GMP and that claims on nutrients and other functions are compatible with those adopted by the Codex Alimentarius Commission in 2004.

In a more restrictive regulatory approach than is present in other countries, firms wishing to sell health/functional food in South Korea must obtain government permission to do so (KFDA, 2006). The requirement that retailers of health food products be granted official approval to sell functional food treats retailers much more like pharmacies than is the case elsewhere.

Disease risk reduction health claims are divided into generic and product-specific claims. Generic disease risk reduction claims are permitted on a wide range of product ingredients, for example:

- ginseng products
- red ginseng products
- eel oil products
- eicosapentaenoic acid (EPA)/docosahexaenoic acid (DHA)-containing products
- royal jelly products
- yeast products
- pollen products
- squalene-containing products
- yeast-containing products
- chlorella products

- spirulina products
- gamma-linolenic acid-containing products
- embryo bud oil products
- embryo bud products
- lecithin products
- octacosanol-containing products
- alkoxy-glycerol-containing products
- grape seed oil products
- fermented vegetable extract products
- mucopolysaccharide products
- chlorophyll-containing products
- mushroom products
- aloe products
- Japanese apricot extract products
- soft-shelled turtle products
- beta-carotene products
- chitosan-containing products
- chito-oligosaccharide-containing products
- glucosamine-containing products
- propolis extract products
- green tea extract products
- soy protein-containing products
- phytosterol-containing products
- fructo-oligosaccharide-containing products
- red yeast rice products (Kim et al., 2008).

Any ingredients not included on the generic claim list must go through a product-specific approval process. To be eligible to make a product-specific claim, the product's manufacturing process must be sufficiently standardized and the product needs to pass both a safety evaluation and an efficacy evaluation (Kim et al., 2008).

The MFDS evaluates all three of these criteria. Firms rely on toxicity tests and human studies, as well as historical evidence of safe use by humans to demonstrate to the MFDS that the product is safe. The efficacy of the product is demonstrated through the use of scientific studies. No precise formula is used by the MFDS to evaluate the efficacy of health claims, but two major areas are examined when evaluating efficacy. The quality of the individual studies supporting the claim must be high and 'randomized, double-blind, parallel group, placebo controlled intervention study[ies]' (Kim et al., 2008, p. 287) are highly favoured. Additionally, the studies themselves need to be placed into the context of the entire domain of scientific evidence on the subject: a large number of independently conducted high-quality studies bode well for efficacy approval (Kim et al., 2008).

The MFDS has different standards for different health claims. Disease risk reduction claims require the highest level of scientific agreement (many high-quality studies showing a functional relationship between the nutrient and the risk of a disease). As of 2005, only one disease risk reduction claim was approved for use, involving the reduced risk of dental caries (see Table A1.2 in Appendix 1). Therapeutic or disease prevention claims that go one step further than disease risk reduction claims are prohibited in South Korea (Kim et al., 2008).

South Korea also permits nutrient function claims showing a relationship between a nutrient and normal human growth, development or functioning. Tertiary nutrition textbooks can provide evidence for these claims, so long as the nutrients have an established recommended daily allowance (Kim et al., 2008).

Finally, 'other function' claims are also permitted. These claims capture residual claims that are not prohibited and do not fall into either of the other two categories. These claims describe a nutrient's specific beneficial effect on human health (improving it or preserving it). As of 2005, the following claims were permitted on some products:

- reduction of blood pressure
- reduction of cholesterol
- reduction of body fat
- maintenance of good health
- modulation of blood glucose level
- modulation of postprandial glucose level
- maintaining health gastrointestinal conditions
- antioxidant effects
- improvement of memory functions
- improvement of cognitive functions (Kim et al., 2008).

Other function claims have three different levels of scientific evidence. The highest level of evidence would garner a 'convincing' claim with the wording 'Can have a beneficial effect on (function)' (Kim et al., 2008). Lower levels of evidence – for example, the use of *in vitro* or animal studies as opposed to human studies – may qualify the claim for 'probable' claims or 'insufficient' claims. Insufficient claims carry a disclaimer that the claimed effect is not fully verified. Probable claims use the word 'may' instead of the word 'can' used by convincing claims.

Insufficient claims are also accompanied by disclaimers that the effect 'requires verification' or that 'scientific evidence is insufficient' (Kim et al., 2008).

5.5.2 Nutrition Labelling

Health/functional foods in South Korea must bear nutrition labelling. Labels must contain the following information:

- representation (text or symbol) that the supplement is a health/ functional food
- health claim
- list of functional nutrient(s) and amounts as a percentage of recommended daily allowance
- directions for consumption and warnings of excess consumption
- sell-by date and method of storage
- disclaimer that health/functional food does not prevent or cure any diseases
- all requirements for general food labelling (KFDA, 2006; Zawis-towski, 2008).

In summary, South Korea's product-specific claims have likely encouraged innovation in the industry as the use of qualified claims ('other claims' with lower level of evidence) reduces the risks of rejection for firms and encourages them to innovate. However, the restriction of functional food to nutraceuticals/supplements potentially limits choice for both consumers and firms. Additionally, the government's strict control of who can sell these products may be evidence of a proclivity to treat these products more as drugs rather than food. Therefore, while the product-specific regulatory system encourages innovation, incentives for research tend to be constrained both by government regulations over who can sell these products and by the limited definition of HFF.

5.6 TAIWAN

Taiwan has a well-established set of regulations for the health foods sector with the Taiwan Food and Drug Administration within the Ministry of Health and Welfare providing regulatory oversight. In Taiwan, the term used for these products is health foods. The Health Food Control Act (HFCA), enacted in 1999, defines and regulates the production of health foods and related health claims. The HFCA defines health food as food with specific nutrient or health maintenance effects, which is especially labelled or advertised and does not aim at treating or remedying human diseases (HFCA, 2006). The HFCA maintains a list of approved health maintenance claims, which are claims that the product promotes health by reducing the risk of serious illness (structure/function claims). The health maintenance claims are product-specific; each product is individually assessed and evaluated before it can use an approved claim. Therapeutic claims are not permitted under the HFCA. Nutrient content claims are permitted and nutrition labelling is also regulated. All health foods, both locally produced and imported, must undergo a registration process.

5.6.1 Health Maintenance Claims

Examples of approved health maintenance claims include:

- regulate blood lipid
- improve gastrointestinal functions
- alleviate osteoporosis
- maintain dental health
- regulate immune system
- regulate blood sugar level
- protect the liver (Liu and Lee, 2000).

Health maintenance claims must be scientifically substantiated. Where there is insufficient evidence to do so, the ingredients must be identified and supported with literature and submitted to the Ministry of Health and Welfare for assessment and approval. Taiwan is very strict with the registration of health foods. Failure to comply with the registration process is an indictable offence punishable with imprisonment and fines. An initial permit to manufacture or import a health product is valid for a five-year period, which can be extended for another five years provided the renewal application was submitted three months prior to the expiry of the initial permit. The permit is subject to immediate revocation should any doubt about the safety of the product or its ingredients arise (Liu and Lee, 2000).

5.6.2 Nutrient Content Claims and Nutrition Labelling

Nutrient content claims are permitted in Taiwan but are regulated less strenuously than health maintenance claims. Nutrient content claims are generic, although the nutrient levels required to make a claim for

nutrients such as cholesterol, sugar, salt, fat and saturated fat are not
stipulated in the HFCA. Firms are at liberty to make any content claims
about these nutrients in their products. As a result, there have been calls
to amend the HFCA to restrict the amount of these nutrients that can be
used in a health product when related claims are made (Zawistowski,
2008).

Nutrition labelling is required on all foods in Taiwan. Conventional
food labelling is regulated by the Food Administration Act (2007) and
health food labelling is regulated by both the Food Administration Act
and the HFCA (FAA, 2007). Taiwan's labelling standard is reminiscent
of international standards stipulated in the Codex Alimentarius. All
labelling should be in Chinese and should be easily noticeable on the
product. Information required on the product includes the following
(FAS, 2012b):

- product name
- name, weight or volume of the contents; separate labelling is
  required if there is a mixture of two or more ingredients in the food
  composition
- names of food additives
- expiry date, methods and conditions of preservation
- manufacturer's information and if imported, name and address of
  the local business operator
- all approved health claims
- permit number and standard logo of the health food
- nutrient composition and their contents
- other material facts designated by the Health Department by way of
  public notice
- intake amount and important messages and other necessary warnings
- country of origin
- country of origin of beef and/or beef cattle offal.

The regulatory system regarding nutrient content claims in Taiwan is
more relaxed compared to that of other countries examined here. Firms
are at liberty to make any content claims about some nutrients. This
flexibility may encourage more investment in a wider range of claims but
runs the risk of consumers being misinformed or misled.

5.7 SYNTHESIS

The approach to regulating the health foods sector and the status of regulatory development across the countries examined in this chapter is somewhat more disparate than is the case for the countries discussed in the previous chapter. To some extent, this reflects the emerging nature of these markets and the greater degree of regulatory development that is occurring in general across these countries. A marked difference between several of the countries discussed here lies in the definition of what constitutes a functional food, a health food, a supplement or a nutraceutical. It is also difficult to find a common theme with respect to the treatment of health claims, with disease risk reduction claims permitted by some jurisdictions but specifically prohibited by others and, with widely differing standards of evidence to substantiate a health claim or a structure/function claim. There exists a greater degree of concordance with respect to nutrition labelling, which in most cases countries have moved to make a mandatory requirement, particularly in the presence of a health claim.

Differences in new product approval processes, allowable health claims and labelling requirements create a complex environment for firms wishing to market these products internationally. Navigating the complex array of regulations raises transaction costs for firms and inhibits investment in R&D. This can be a particular challenge in smaller markets where the payoff to achieving a new product or health claim approval may be relatively small compared to a large market such as the USA, EU or China. Harmonizing regulations or establishing equivalence would help reduce these transaction costs and organizations such as the Codex Alimentarius Commission provide a forum through which consensus can be built. Nevertheless, this remains a challenging – and not particularly realistic – prospect given the substantial differences that currently exist in regulatory frameworks in just the small sampling of countries examined in this book.

In some respects, differences in the regulatory treatment of the health foods sector should not be surprising. Different consumer preferences and priorities, agricultural and food sectors characterized by different base commodities and technologies, and very different cultural contexts influence the regulatory trajectory and priorities within a country. While a policy priority for one country might be to facilitate innovation and new product development in the health foods sector, another country may be motivated by consumer scepticism over label information and the need for rigorous and credible approval processes for new products and new health claims. Differences in regulatory approach can also reflect disagreements over the standards of scientific evidence necessary to validate a health claim. Indeed, many of these factors underlie the different regulatory trajectories taken by countries with respect to food products derived from the use of agricultural biotechnology.[2] While the health foods sector has not been plagued to the same extent by the vastly different philosophical approaches to product approvals and new technology that has dogged the biotechnology sector, there appears to be considerable room for the establishment of a stronger scientific consensus surrounding the functional properties of foods and supplements and their efficacy. Meanwhile, governments continue to balance the regulatory objectives of facilitating innovation and growth while protecting consumers from misleading or fraudulent health claims.

NOTES

1. For a discussion of Codex Alimentarius guidelines see Appendix 4.
2. The regulation of biotechnology is beyond the scope of this book; interested readers are referred to Isaac and Hobbs (2002) and Hobbs et al. (2004).

6. Industry and market trends

This chapter provides an overview of developments within the health foods sector in the USA, EU, Japan and Canada. The discussion of the regulatory frameworks governing the health foods sector in these markets is provided in Chapter 4 and provides a backdrop to the industry analysis presented in this chapter. The size of the sector, market trends and the research landscape in each of these markets are discussed.

6.1 THE GLOBAL PICTURE

The challenges in defining what constitutes the 'health foods sector' in different countries complicate obtaining consistent estimates of the size of the industry globally and the relative importance of different markets.[1] Nevertheless, while still a relatively small component of the global food market, it is clear that the sector has exhibited strong growth in recent years. In 2004, the World Bank estimated the global health foods product market to range between US$30 to US$60 billion, depending on which definition of functional food was used, which at the time represented between 1 and 3 per cent of the global food market (Kotilainen et al., 2006). With the caveat that accurate estimates are notoriously difficult to generate and are usually 'best guess' estimates, more recent estimates put the global market for functional food, beverages and supplements in 2011 at US$151 billion, with the sector forecast to grow to around US$207 billion by 2016, assuming a 6.5 per cent compound annual growth rate (BCC, 2011).

Major markets for the industry include Japan, the USA and Europe (Klimas et al., 2008; LFI, 2011; NBJ, 2007a). Table 6.1 provides estimated market shares for these three regions and illustrates an industry in transition, with the USA estimated to be the single largest market for functional foods in 1997 and 2000, the EU in 2005 and Japan in 2011. Again, this data should be treated with caution as discrepancies exist over global market shares. Nevertheless, a number of market analysts now place Japan as the largest market for functional food and supplements, followed by the USA (AAFC, 2009; LFI, 2011; Malla et al., 2013b; NZTE, 2007).

Regulating health foods

Table 6.1   Estimated global market shares for health foods

	1997		2000		2005		2011	
	US$ billion	%	US$ billion	%	US$ billion	%	US$ billion	%
USA	13.6	35.0	17.4	34	25.7	28.7	47.0	31.1
Japan	9.6	24.7	12.8	25	22.6	25.2	58.0	38.4
EU	12.3	31.6	16.4	32	34.4	38.4	43.6	28.9
Rest of the world	3.0	7.7	4.1	8	5.9	6.6	2.42	1.6
Total	38.9	100	51.3	100	89.6	100	151.0	100

Note: Data for 1997, 2000 and 2005 data are derived from NBJ (2007a). Data for 2011 are the authors' estimates based on BCC (2011) and LFI (2011).

Source: Derived from NBJ (2007a), BCC (2011), LFI (2011) and authors' estimates.

These apparent inconsistencies can be explained by two factors: differences in the terminology used to define functional food, supplements and nutraceuticals (see Chapter 2) and a sector experiencing rapid growth combined with a shifting landscape of new product development. Regardless, the fact remains that Japan, the USA and EU are the dominant global markets for the health food category. New emerging economies such as Brazil, Russia, India, China, Mexico and other Asia-Pacific countries are expected to become more significant markets in the future (Klimas et al., 2008; NBJ, 2007a).

The structure of the functional food industry, its market development and research trends in the USA, Europe and Japan are presented in the following sections, followed by Canada, which is included as a case study of developments in a smaller but growing market.

6.2   THE UNITED STATES OF AMERICA

The health foods sector in the USA has been experiencing significant growth. Recognition by consumers of the link between diet and health, the increasing cost of health care, the ageing US population and the challenges faced by consumers in meeting their daily nutritional needs through conventional food have all contributed to the industry's growth (AAFC, 2009). It is estimated that the US functional food and beverage market accounted for approximately 8.6 per cent of the total US food and beverage market in 2007 and that the number of functional food introductions in the North American market grew from approximately 200 in 2006 to over 800 in 2008 (Evani, 2009; Klimas et al., 2008; NBJ, 2007a).

Analysts estimate that roughly 8 per cent of the population are heavy consumers of functional foods and dietary supplements in the USA, 17 per cent are regular consumers, 48 per cent occasional consumers and 31 per cent rarely or never consume these products (Klimas et al., 2008; NBJ, 2007b). In 2005, total annual expenditure in the 'occasional consumers' category was the highest, consistent with a category typified by relatively new products and a high proportion of experimental consumers who are relatively new users of these products on an occasional basis. Average monthly expenditure on functional food is estimated to range between US$50 for heavy consumers and US$3 for those who rarely purchase the products (Klimas et al., 2008; NBJ, 2007b).

In the case of dietary supplements, it is estimated that heavy users constitute roughly 4 per cent of the total population, while 31 per cent are regular users, 22 per cent occasional users, 18 per cent rare users and 25 per cent are non-users (Klimas et al., 2008; NBJ, 2007a). Dietary supplements contributed 26.4 per cent to total US health food industry sales in 2006. The most common supplements in the USA ranked by consumer sales in 2006 included: multivitamins, meal replacements, sports nutrition, calcium, B vitamins, vitamin C, glucosamine/chondroitin, homeopathics, vitamins D and H, others and fish/animal oil (Klimas et al., 2008; NBJ, 2007a). The same studies argue that consumption of dietary supplements is being negatively affected by consumer confusion regarding the number and broad selection of products in the US market combined with a lack of product education (Klimas et al., 2008; NBJ, 2007a).

Broadly speaking, three types of firms participate in the US health foods sector. Mainstream food and drink companies such as Danone, PepsiCo and Quaker dominate the industry, followed by pharmaceutical companies such as Johnson & Johnson, then smaller single-product companies (LFI, 2006). Multinational corporations dominate, as illustrated by Table 6.2. In 2005, PepsiCo had approximately a 16 per cent share of the US market for functional food, followed by Kellogg Co., Coca-Cola Co. and General Mills with approximately 14, 11 and 11 per cent, respectively. Examples of major firms in the US dietary supplements sector include NBTY, Leiner Health Products (purchased by NBTY in 2008), Pharmavite, Wyeth (purchased by Pfizer in 2009), Unilever and Abbott Labs/Ross Products (Klimas et al., 2008; NBJ 2007a).

Table 6.2   Major functional food firms in the USA (2005)

Manufacturer	Sales (million US$)	Share (%)
PepsiCo	2397	16.3
Kellogg Co.	2100	14.3
Coca-Cola Co.	1591	10.8
General Mills	1558	10.6
Kraft Foods, Inc.	847	5.8
Group Danone	643	4.4
Nestle USA, Inc.	545	3.7
Ocean Spray	427	2.9
Welch Foods, Inc.	330	2.2
Dean Foods	292	2.0
Ferolito Vultaggio & Sons	241	1.6
Red Bull North America, Inc.	226	1.5

Source: Derived from Mintel (2006).

Functional food ingredients most commonly used in the US market include low-calorie sweeteners, fibre, probiotics, omega fatty acids, antioxidants and sodium substitutes. Functional foods exist across a broad range of categories, including dairy products, bakery products, cereal products, soy products, beverage products and meat, fish and egg products (Table 6.3).[2] The dairy functional product market in the USA is relatively small, with cereals, soy and beverages being far larger and dominating the sector (LFI, 2006). Functional dairy products include probiotics and cholesterol-lowering yoghurts, while bakery products consist primarily of bread and cookies fortified with fibre and omega-3 fatty acids for heart health. The functional properties of cereal products include calcium fortification, fibre fortification and wholegrain cereals, while soy products are dominated by soy milk for reducing the risk of CHD. Beverage products feature calcium fortification, extra fibre properties and enhanced waters. Finally, meat, fish and eggs are mainly fortified with omega-3 and fish oil supplements (LFI, 2006).

The US health foods industry is primarily domestically driven, with exports representing a relatively small proportion of production (Mintel, 2006). The sheer size of the US domestic market can absorb most of its domestic production; however, another potential reason for the limited foray into export markets is the lack of global uniformity surrounding health claims. While most countries are able to export their products to

Table 6.3   Examples of functional foods and beverages in the USA

Functional food area	Functional food product	Company	Brands
dairy products	probiotic yoghurt/kefir	Dannon (Stonyfield Farms)	DanActive (marketed as Actimel outside the US); Activia; YoBaby; All Natural Fruit Blends; YoSelf
		Lifeway Foods	Lifeway Organic ProBugs Milk Drinks
	cholesterol-lowering yoghurt	General Mills	Yoplait Healthy Heart
		Dannon	Light'n Fit with Fiber
	active health drinks	Dannon	Actimel
	fortified milk	Deans; Borden Dairy Farmers; Mayfield Farms; Kemps; Suiza	None are major, market shares distributed among these
bakery products	wholegrain (heart healthy) and fortified breads	Sara Lee	Heart healthy Plus; Soft & Smooth
	breads with omega-3 fatty acids	Wegmans Food Markets; The Baker	None are major, market shares distributed among these
		Arnold Foods	Arnold Smart & Healthy
	high-fibre cookies	RD Foods	Right Direction Cookies
		Quaker	Quaker Breakfast Cookies
		Nabisco	Wholegrain Chips Ahoy!, Wheat Thins and Fig Newtons
cereal products	heart health cereals	Quaker	Take Heart Instant Oatmeal
		General Mills	Cheerios; All Big G brands
		Kraft's Post	Grape Nuts; Raisin Bran; Shredded Wheat; Toasties; Bran Flakes
		Kellogg's	Smart Start brands; Heart to Heart (under Kashi, Kellogg subsidiary)
	calcium fortified cereal bars	Quaker	Chewy
		Kellogg's	Cereal and Milk Bars
	high-fibre cereal bars	Kellogg's	All Bran
	heart healthy cereal bars	Nature Valley	Health Heart
	wholegrain pasta	Barilla	Barilla Plus
		Kraft	Supermac & Cheese Pasta and Sauce

Table 6.3   (continued)

Functional food area	Functional food product	Company	Brands
soy products	soy milk	White Wave	Silk
		Odwalla	Odwalla soymilk
beverages	fruit juices and juice blends	Tropicana (PepsiCo)	Pure Premium Orange Juice with Calcium and Extra Fiber; Pure Premium Essentials (Immunity Defence, Healthy Heart, Healthy Kids, Light & Healthy)
		Minute Maid (Coca-Cola)	Heartwise; Minute Maid Extra
		Ocean Spray	Cranberry Juice Cocktails
		POM Wonderful	POM Wonderful
	enhanced waters	Gatorade (PepsiCo)	Propel Fitness Water
		SmartWater (Coca-Cola)	Glaceau VitaminWater
		PepsiCo	Aquafina flavoured water; SoBe Life Water
		Coca-Cola	Dasani
meat, fish and eggs	canned fish with omega-3	Star Kist	None are major, market shares distributed among these
		Chicken of the Sea	
	fish oil supplements	Bumble Bee and Leiner Health	
	omega-3 (DHA)-enriched eggs	Gold Circle Farms	
		Eggland's Best	

Source: Derived from LFI (2006), pp. 135–53 and Klimas et al. (2008).

the US market due to a relatively open US health claim regime (see Chapter 4), US products often struggle to access international markets due to more stringent health claim regulations in other markets (Mintel, 2006). The FDA's approval of a number of SSA health claims as well as qualified health claims[3] has been credited with enabling the rapid development of the US functional food market (FDA, 2009b).

US functional food manufacturers are heavily engaged in R&D (PWC, 2009). It is estimated that US-based researchers accounted for 24 per cent of the identified total global functional food-related publications in 2006[4] indicating high levels of research activity (Stein and Rodríguez-Cerezo, 2008). Recent areas of research include technologies that should lead to the development of more stable functional food formulations, improve the taste and smell of the products, remove grainy textures of fibres added to beverages and technologies that include the use of probiotics in beverages and baked goods as well as healthy oils in dairy products (PWC, 2009).

The patenting of functional foods in the USA has been on the rise and has been attributed to the regulatory approval of many health claims (Klimas et al., 2008). Between 1994 and 2001, the USA had over 28 per cent of global patent applications or pending patents (Stein and Rodríguez-Cerezo, 2008), mainly in the areas of extraction and purification, rather than end-products (Lloyd and Leber, 2008). In order to patent a product with the United States Patent and Trademark Office (USPTO), an inventor has to show only that the invention is 'useful' and 'new' and not necessarily that it will meet operational or functional goals, which makes the patent process somewhat easier to undertake (Trueman, 2009). Contrast this with the patent process in Canada, for example, where an inventor must provide information on the 'novelty' (be the first in the world), 'utility' (functional and operative) and show inventive 'ingenuity' on the product before it can be patented with the Canadian Intellectual Property Office (CIPO, 2010). The additional requirement of functional utility may be one reason why patenting of functional foods is less common in Canada than in the USA (as discussed in Section 6.5).

The IFT (2005) examines the opportunities and challenges facing the functional food sector in the USA using an expert panel chosen for their scientific, medical and legal expertise. The study asserts that food technology and nutrition have improved life expectancy over the last 200 years and that the impact of diet on health extends far beyond basic nutrition. Growth of consumer interest in healthier food products, the availability of food technology and scientific evidence of a correlation between diet and disease prevention all provide opportunities for enormous growth in the functional food industry. However, the lack of exclusivity of health claims discourages companies from investing in functional food research and the absence of a well-established property rights system to provide effective patent protection are identified as major challenges facing the industry. This study also confirms a common finding that the high cost of developing new functional food is a major challenge for the industry.

The IFT (2005) makes a number of recommendations regarding the opportunities and challenges facing the functional food sector, including that government should invest in basic and applied research to promote product development. It suggests tax incentives for companies that pursue research in the industry and recommends the granting of periods of exclusivity with respect to health claims and patents to encourage food companies to pursue functional food development by providing them greater periods to recoup their costs and generate a reasonable profit for their investment. The panel concludes that success in the industry will require contributions from academia, government and industry and necessary steps to ensure product safety. As health claims help increase consumer confidence and enable consumers to select products that satisfy their desire to promote self-care and improve health, the report recommends the establishment of scientific, regulatory and business frameworks in order to facilitate the review of new functional ingredients and their health claims for efficacy and safety. Communicating the findings of regulators will ensure informed decision-making on the part of consumers, which is important for the success of the functional food sector. Finally, the study suggests that even though the sector is growing, research must identify bioactive compounds and determine their mechanisms of action and effects on health. This knowledge must then be verified through well-designed pre-clinical and clinical studies.

In summary, the functional food and dietary supplement industry in the USA has been growing for reasons similar to those in other countries, but is also further driven by a less restrictive regulatory structure for approval of health claims than is the case elsewhere, particularly in the EU and Canada. Challenges to the industry include the credibility of health claims associated with products, which may deter some consumers from purchasing these products. Further discussion of consumer acceptance is provided in Chapter 7.

6.3 THE EUROPEAN UNION

While estimates of actual value vary, the EU remains a dominant market for the health foods sector but is highly segmented by country-specific health and dietary patterns. The European health food market is very much concentrated in northern Europe, with the UK leading in terms of per capita expenditure and overall volume (Table 6.4). In 2006, the UK functional food market was estimated to be valued at US$1998 million, with a per capita spending on functional food of US$33; the UK and Germany represent almost half of the total European functional food market (NZTE, 2007). It is estimated that the EU market grew by 36 per cent between 2001 and 2006, with Italy and Sweden having the highest growth rates (54 per cent), followed by Spain (49 per cent), Germany (38 per cent), the UK (28 per cent) and France (28 per cent). As Table 6.4 indicates, forecasted growth rates in 2006 for continued expansion of the

Table 6.4   EU functional food market trends

Country	2001		2006		Per capita expenditure (2006)	Growth (2001–2006)
	US$ million	%	US$ million	%	$	%
UK	1565	26.7	1998	24.9	33.0	+28
Germany	1375	23.4	1890	23.6	23.0	+38
Italy	677	11.5	1042	13.0	18.0	+54
France	599	10.2	764	9.5	12.7	+28
Spain	401	6.8	598	7.5	15.0	+49
Netherlands	216	3.7	272	3.4	17.0	+26
Sweden	140	2.4	215	2.7	23.9	+54
Rest of EU	893	15.2	1235	15.4	N/A	+10
EU	5865	N/A	8013	N/A	N/A	+36

Source: Adapted by authors from NZTE (2007).

market were bullish; however, the reality has likely been tempered by the subsequent economic slowdown in Europe following the 2008 financial crisis.

An estimated 168 companies market at least one functional food in the EU. However, the European functional food industry is dominated by a relatively small number of large multinational companies including, for example, PepsiCo, GSK, Danone, Nestle and Unilever (NZTE, 2007) (Table 6.5). Dairy products (including yoghurt drinks) have the biggest market share in the EU functional food sector followed by beverages, cereals, confectionary, fats and fat supplements, infant foods, bakery, convenience and miscellaneous products (Stein and Rodríguez-Cerezo, 2008).

The primary distribution channel for functional foods in the EU is retail food outlets, while for food supplements, health food stores dominate. Food service outlets are growing in importance as a distribution channel for health food options and are beginning to include functional food ingredients on their menus (NZTE, 2007).

One study identified 385 functional food products in the EU market in 2004, utilizing 503 different ingredients, the most common of which were probiotics, prebiotics and plant extracts (Stein and Rodríguez-Cerezo, 2008) (Table 6.6). Almost 30 per cent of the functional foods

Table 6.5   Examples of EU functional food and beverage companies and products

Company	Product(s)
PepsiCo	Quaker Oats, Gatorade, Tropicana
GSK	Lucozade, Ribena
Danone	Actimel, Activa, Essensis, Senja
Nestle	Calcium Milk, beta glucans
Unilever	Slim Fast
Muller	Vitality prebiotics and probiotics yoghurt
Yakult	*Lactobacillus*-based drinking yoghurt
Innocent	Fruit Smoothie

Source: Derived from NZTE (2007).

contained more than one functional ingredient. Bacteria cultures (primarily probiotics) were used in nearly 45 per cent of all functional food products. Saccharides (mostly prebiotics) were the next most commonly used ingredient, contained in 20 per cent of all products, followed by plant extracts, terpenes, fibres, phenols, peptides and lipids. Weight loss and weight management products, those that improve digestion, support women's health and enhance immunity are those experiencing high demand (Stein and Rodríguez-Cerezo, 2008).

Analysts suggest that there is a dominance of already well-established conventional agri-food product companies in the EU functional food sector, which may indicate the existence of barriers to entry (Stein and Rodríguez-Cerezo, 2008). Moreover, the withdrawal rate of functional food products from the EU market is roughly 75 per cent within the first two years.

The EU has supported R&D in the health foods sector, often through fairly large cooperative research projects, for example, the Co-operative Research Action for Technology (CRAFT) and Collective Research programmes for small and medium-sized firms, specific support actions such as the Functional Food Net (FFNet) and Specific Targeted Research Projects (STREPs). In the EU, research output on functional foods (as measured by academic publications and patents) has been larger than that of the other major markets (USA and Japan). Between 1994 and 2003, for example, 1.5 times more functional foods-related academic publications were published from EU sources than from the USA, including 387

Table 6.6　Functional products on the European market in 2004, by ingredient

Ingredient type	Number of products	% of all products
bacteria cultures (mostly probiotics)	173	44.9
saccharides (mostly prebiotics)	78	20.3
plant extracts	53	13.8
terpenes	41	10.6
fibres	35	9.1
phenols	33	8.6
peptides	30	7.8
lipids	23	6.0
miscellaneous	37	9.6
Total	503	130.6[a]

Note:　a. Total greater than 100 per cent due to products that contain two or more bioactive ingredients being listed under each ingredient type.

Source:　Derived from Stein and Rodríguez-Cerezo (2008), p. 18.

functional food-related publications; the EU was the source of an estimated 39 per cent of global functional food-related publications in 2006. EU funding for functional food research was approximately 10–20 per cent of the total EU food and nutrition R&D budget; between 2002 and 2006, the EU spent €753 million on food quality and safety R&D and €73 million on functional food R&D (Stein and Rodríguez-Cerezo, 2008).

As might be expected of a rapidly evolving sector utilizing new materials, processes and methods, patenting activity for functional foods is more dynamic than is the case in the EU's general food sector. The volume of R&D activities is evident in the number of innovations and new products that are introduced into the market. The number of European patent applications or pending patents for functional foods grew from 3.2 per cent to approximately 7.7 per cent of total food sector applications between 1994 and 2001. Patent applications or pending patents in the general food sector grew from 500 in 1994 to 1200 in 2001. During this same period, there were 554 patents within the EU for functional foods, comprising over 41 per cent of the global patent applications or pending patents on functional foods (Stein and Rodríguez-Cerezo, 2008).

In summary, as is the case in the USA, the health foods sector in the EU has experienced considerable growth in terms of number of establishments, sales and new product development, with early growth concentrated in the markets of northern European countries. While the economic downturn following 2008 slowed market growth, investment in R&D has continued and Europe is well placed to be an important source of new product development, as well as an important market for functional food and supplements.

6.4 JAPAN

Japan was the first country to introduce government approved health claims for functional foods and various estimates place Japan among the three largest markets for health foods. The growth of the health foods sector in Japan is attributed to similar factors as in other countries, including increasing incomes, increased consumer awareness of the correlation between food and health in an ageing society and a rise in lifestyle-related diseases (Heasman, 2004; NBJ, 2007a).

As explained in Chapter 2, health foods in Japan are classified into four different categories. 'Food for specified health use' (FOSHU) includes foods with specified health benefits for which health claims can be made; both functional foods and supplements can be FOSHU. The classification of 'food with nutrient function claims' (FNFC) is restricted to approved vitamins, minerals and nutrients not requiring pre-market approval; FNFCs in Japan roughly equate to nutraceuticals/dietary supplements in other countries. The final two categories are 'medical drugs' and all other foods or general foods. Medical drugs require prior approval and the general food category includes nutritional supplements (NZTE, 2009).

There were roughly 755 FOSHU approved products in 2007, with an estimated retail value of US$6.5 billion. FOSHU products can be marketed in many forms including capsules, tablets or conventional food, although the majority are in conventional food form (Ohama et al., 2006). Dietary fibre is the most commonly used ingredient in FOSHU products followed by probiotics with soy peptides, green tea catechin and gamma amino butyric acid gaining in popularity (LFI, 2006). Flax seed oil and processed seed fraction products are also gaining popularity in the Japanese market.

FOSHU in Japan are mainly produced to help in the control and reduction of disease related to digestive health, weight management, dental health and metabolic syndrome risk factors (Figure 6.1). The

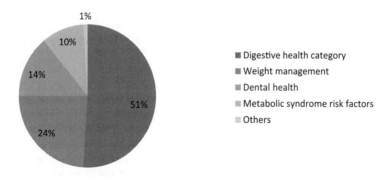

Sales

1%
10%
14%
51%
24%

- Digestive health category
- Weight management
- Dental health
- Metabolic syndrome risk factors
- Others

Source: Adapted from Bailey (2008).

Figure 6.1   Health categories of FOSHU in Japan

control and reduction of disease related to digestive system health is the focus of an estimated 51 per cent of FOSHU products, while 24 per cent target weight management; dental health control and management account for about 14 per cent. This stands in contrast to the emphasis in other markets on products addressing cardiovascular health.

Ingredients used in FOSHU production vary according to the purpose of the product (Table 6.7). For example, in 2006 the principal ingredients used in 254 approved FOSHU products addressing gastrointestinal health included oligosaccharides, *Lactobacillus*, *Bifidobacterium*, psyllium husk, indigestible dextrin and partially hydrolyzed guar gum. In the same year, 117 high cholesterol/triglyceride and body fat FOSHU products were approved for use in Japan, with major ingredients that included soy protein, low molecular sodium alginate, peptides, plant sterol/stanol and degradation products of globin protein. Table 6.7 provides further examples of approved products by category and key ingredients.

Japan's FOSHU market is supplied by a large number of companies, making it difficult to clearly identify the industry's major players. The majority of FOSHU products in the Japanese market are local brands with a few foreign brands sold under licence. Distribution channels include drug stores (17 per cent) and health food stores (9 per cent), but direct sales (network/multi-level marketing, mail order and internet channels) account for by far the largest sales channel, accounting for an estimated 74 per cent of sales (NZTE, 2009).

Japan has become a hub in the international market for health foods. As a dominant global market for these products, Japan relies on international trade to sustain the sector. Most of the ingredients used in

Table 6.7   Examples of FOSHU functions and functional components
(2006)

FOSHU function	Number of approved products	Principal functional ingredients
gastrointestinal health	254	oligosaccharides, *Lactobacillus*, *Bifidobacterium*, psyllium husk, indigestible dextrin, wheat bran, low molecular sodium alginate, partially hydrolyzed guar gum
high cholesterol/ triglyceride level and body fat	117	soy protein, chitosan, low molecular sodium alginate, peptides, diacylglycerol, plant sterol/stanol (esters), green tea catechin, middle chain fatty acids, psyllium husk, degradation products of globin protein
high blood glucose	71	indigestible dextrin, L-arabinose, h-wheat albumin
high blood pressure	64	gamma amino butyric acid (GABA), peptides
dental health	34	xylitol, polyols, tea polyphenols, casein phosphopeptide and amorphous calcium phosphate (CPP-ACP)
bone health	26	soy isoflavone
anaemia	3	haem iron

Source: Derived from Ohama et al. (2006).

these products are sourced internationally and Japan also exports functional foods and supplements globally (Bailey, 2007b).

The Japanese government collaborates with the private sector in conducting R&D on new health food technologies. Between 1990 and 2002, the Japanese Ministry of Agriculture, Forestry and Fisheries (MAFF) funded cost-share programmes for the industry (Klimas et al., 2008), particularly towards the development of new technologies in ingredient component isolation and purification. The MHLW also provided financial support to functional food-related research while non-profit organizations such as the Japan Functional Food Research Association (JAFRA) also undertake research. A study by Bailey (2007a) suggests that many food and beverage firms in Japan have been developing innovative functional food, nutraceuticals or ingredients. As a proxy measure of research activity, Stein and Rodríguez-Cerezo (2008) report that Japan had 42 functional food-related publications or 4 per cent of the global functional food-related publications identified in their database search. As in other countries, the time and costs involved in obtaining regulatory approvals for new products have been identified as the primary challenges to commercializing R&D in the sector (Bailey, 2007b).

The patent law in Japan is based on the 'first-to-file principle' as is the case in the USA and Canada, implying that the first person to file a patent application for an invention obtains the registered patent, irrespective of the number of applicants (JPO, 2010). Over 22 per cent of the global patent applications or pending patents related to functional food and nutraceuticals/supplements between 1994 and 2001 were filed in Japan, with a higher number of patents filed for dairy-based functional foods compared to other functional foods (Stein and Rodríguez-Cerezo, 2008; Trueman, 2009). It is reported that Japan's patent office has more applications for functional food than any other jurisdiction, receiving approximately 1000 applications between 2001 and 2009 (Trueman, 2009). The greater number of patent filings/applications has been attributed to differences in the patent process in Japan compared to other countries, including fewer claims in Japanese patents than is the case in the USA where it is possible to claim the rights to a process and a formulation within the same patent. This means that it may take two or more Japanese patent applications to cover the same innovation claimed in a single US patent (Trueman, 2009).

Japan represents a significant portion of the global health foods sector, one relatively dependent on imported ingredients. The number of approved FOSHU products and the interest of the government in collaborating with the private sector, providing financial support and facilitating R&D in technological innovation in the industry are indications of continued growth in the sector, as is a high degree of patent application activity. The size and growth potential of the Japanese market presents significant opportunities for exporters, both in terms of market opportunities for value-added health food products and in the provision of key ingredients to the Japanese sector.

6.5 UNDER THE MICROSCOPE: A CASE STUDY OF THE CANADIAN HEALTH FOODS SECTOR

On a global scale, Canada represents a relatively small market, but is illustrative of market developments outside the 'big three' markets considered above. This section presents a detailed case study of the

Canadian health foods sector as well as a series of metrics that are used to assess the development of the sector over the past 15 years. In Canada, the health foods sector is generally referred to as the functional food and natural health product (FFNHP) industry and is broadly diverse, with the number of firms involved in both functional food and NHPs increasing dramatically over time.[5] Growth in the Canadian sector can be attributed to similar factors as in other countries related to recognition among consumers of the link between diet and health and ageing populations (Malla et al., 2013b).

Health Canada groups functional food/components into six categories: carotenoids; dietary fibre; fatty acids; soy phytoestrogens; phenolics; prebiotics; and probiotics, examples of which are provided in Table 6.8.

Natural health products are further categorized in numerous ways by Health Canada including by product name, product licence holder, NHP number or homeopathic medicine number, medicinal ingredients, non-medicinal ingredients, dosage form, recommended use, risk information associated with the product's use and companies that are involved in production. Table 6.9 provides examples of NHPs available in Canada.

The Canadian industry most commonly develops products relating to sleep, gut health, eye health, stress, weight control, anti-ageing and skin health, with claims for health and wellbeing most often made in these areas. The majority of Canadian functional food firms are involved in the development of food and beverage products that contain added active ingredients other than vitamins and minerals, examples of which include drinks with herb blends, foods that include phytosterols, soluble fibre or probiotics. NHP firms tend to focus on supplements produced or sourced from plants, animals or microorganisms, marine sources or vitamins and minerals as evidenced by a large product ranges of vitamins, minerals and amino acids. Both NHP and functional food firms commonly use reduction of disease risk claims that focus upon cardiovascular, cancer, diabetes and arthritis health benefits (Khamphoune, 2013).

Failure in new product development and commercialization, particularly for novel functional foods and NHPs, is common. As is likely the case elsewhere, the reasons for these failures include a poor matching between a product's attributes and those sought by consumers, resulting in lack of market acceptance and clinical trial failures because of the difficulty in proving product efficacy and/or gaining regulatory approval. Some researchers have suggested that regulatory reform, including the harmonization of compositional and labelling regulations with those of the USA, may encourage product innovation by Canadian firms, particularly given the relatively small size of the Canadian market (Herath et al., 2008b).

Table 6.8   Examples of functional foods in Canada

Functional components	Source/food	Potential health benefits
carotenoids		
alpha-carotene/ beta-carotene	carrots, fruits, vegetables	Neutralize free radicals, which may cause damage to cells
lutein	green vegetables	Reduce the risk of macular degeneration
lycopene	tomato products	Reduce the risk of prostate cancer
dietary fibre		
insoluble fibre	wheat bran	Reduce risk of breast or colon cancer
beta-glucan	oats, barley	Reduce risk of cardiovascular disease, protect against heart disease and some cancers, lower LDL and total cholesterol
soluble fibre	psyllium	Reduce risk of cardiovascular disease, protect against heart disease and some cancers, lower LDL and total cholesterol
fatty acids		
long chain omega-3 fatty acids – DHA, EPA, CLA	salmon and other fish oils	Reduce risk of cardiovascular disease, improve mental, visual functions
	cheese, meat products	Improve body composition, decrease risk of certain cancers
high oleic canola oil	nexera	Reduces the risk of CHD
prebiotics/probiotics		
fructo-oligosaccharides (FOS)	Jerusalem artichokes, shallots, onion powder	Improve quality of intestinal microflora, gastrointestinal health
Lactobacillus	yoghurt, other dairy	Improve quality of intestinal microflora, gastrointestinal health
soy progesterones		
isoflavones: daidzein genistein	soybeans and soy-based foods	Menopausal symptoms, such as hot flushes, protection against heart disease and some cancers, lower LDL and total cholesterol
phenolics		
lignans	flax, rye, vegetables	Prevention of cancer, renal failure
flavones	fruits/vegetables	Neutralize free radicals, reduce risk of cancer

Note: CLA – conjugated linoleic acid; DHA – docosahexaenoic acid; EPA – eicosapentaenoic acid; LDL – low density lipoprotein.

Source: Derived from Health Canada (2010).

Table 6.9   Examples of natural health products in Canada

Product/ ingredient name	Source material	Uses	Selected companies or organizations
conjugated linoleic acid (CLA)	in triacylglycerol form and free fatty acid form, CLA is derived from processed safflower or sunflower oil	May help to support a modest improvement to body composition and a modest reduction of fat mass when used with a programme of reduced intake of dietary calories and increased physical activity.	Herbal Magic Inc. Jamieson Lab. Ltd
folate	folic acid/folacin/ folate	General: helps in the maintenance of good health. Specific: helps the body to metabolize proteins, helps to form red blood cells.	Nature's Sunshine Products of Canada Ltd
selenium	monohydrate selenium dioxide, selenium hydrolyzed animal protein chelate, selenium citrate, selenium yeast, sodium selenate	General: a factor in the maintenance of good health. Specific: an antioxidant for the maintenance of good health.	Flora Distributing and Manufacturing Ltd Pegasus Pharmaceuticals Group Inc.
pantothenic acid	calcium DL-pantothenate. D-panthenol/ dexpanthenol, Solaray® Pantothenic Acid	General: maintenance of good health. Specific: helps the body to metabolize carbohydrates, fats and proteins, helps in tissue formation, prevents pantothenic acid deficiency.	Au Naturel Inc.

Source: Derived from Health Canada (2010).

Hobbs (2002) discusses factors that influence the evolution of supply chains in the health foods sector in Canada. The health foods sector is characterized as resource-intensive in terms of financial resources, the time required for research, technological development and commercialization; moreover, institutional failures, such as an under-developed property rights system that provides weak patent protection, may discourage investment in R&D by both new entrants and existing enterprises. Many firms enter into some form of partnership arrangement in order to raise the necessary resources, as discussed below, but this can create issues regarding contractual rights. Disputes over property rights are common, which limits the ability of firms to capture rents. More closely coordinated supply chains could reduce trans-action costs and assist in the provision of credible quality assurances; however, the concentrated nature of the downstream food processing sector and, to some extent, the industry's upstream raw materials supply create challenges in this regard.

A later analysis by AAFC (2009) highlights similar challenges with respect to the resource-intensive nature of the sector, both in terms of financial resources and the lengthy time lags between initial R&D and product commercialization. New entrants struggle to gain market share and customer loyalty as the industry is highly concentrated, dominated by a few large companies. Successful commercialization is a challenge for most firms, such that targeting products for niche markets is often a successful market entry strategy.

Laeeque et al. (2006) explore firms' motivations for complying with the new NHPR in Canada, interviewing, either in person or by telephone, the person responsible for regulatory affairs in 20 companies selected from across the country. The motivations for regulatory compliance differ, based on the size of the firm (large or small) but four main motivations dominate. The main motivation behind regulatory compli-ance, for both large and small firms, is fear. Large firms fear the negative publicity associated with regulatory non-compliance. Small and medium-size firms are fearful of punitive actions for non-compliance. The next most important motivators for compliance with the regulations are legal responsibility and civic duty. Social motivation, where firms perceive that compliance will enhance public perception of NHPs, is also relevant and is more prevalent among large firms than small and medium-size firms. The fourth motivation for compliance is the sheer ability of the firms to comply: large firms are better able to undertake regulatory compliance because they have the resources and capacity to do so. Enforcement activities such as premises inspection, though strict and likely effective, are expensive and time consuming for regulatory bodies and other strategies to encourage compliance can complement direct inspection activities. Potential strategies include publishing the names of products that have gained approvals or companies that have licensed sites.

A series of industry surveys by Statistics Canada charts the develop-ment of the FFNHP sector in Canada in recent years (Cinnamon, 2009;

Khamphoune, 2013; Palinic, 2007; Tebbens, 2005). In 2002, there were 294 companies involved in the production of functional food and NHPs (Tebbens, 2005); by 2005 this had grown to 389 companies (4.6 per cent of all Canadian food companies) (Palinic, 2007) and to 689 companies (8.1 per cent of the Canadian food industry) by 2007 (Cinnamon, 2009). The growth has continued, with 750 firms documented in the sector in 2011, of which 117 are involved with functional foods while 422 focus on NHPs and 144 produce both functional food and NHPs; many of these firms are also involved with conventional food product development and production (Khamphoune, 2013).

For the purposes of this analysis the Canadian FFNHP industry is divided into subsectors according to type of activity: (1) firms producing functional food; (2) firms producing NHPs; (3) firms producing both functional food and NHPs; and (4) firms engaged in service-only activities for either sector. These categories are shown in Table 6.10. Firms that specialize in NHPs have continued to dominate the Canadian industry in terms of number of firms. The share of firms focusing on NHPs has grown 10 per cent while the share of functional food firms has declined by over 13 per cent between 2002 and 2011.

The FFNHP sector in Canada experienced growth through the mid to late 2000s with respect to product range and offerings, number of establishments and revenues. In 2011, total functional food and NHP revenues (CDN$11.3 billion) accounted for just over 70 per cent of the total revenue from all sources for firms in the sector, which was CDN$16.4 billion (Khamphoune, 2013). This stands in stark contrast to 2004, when FFNHP revenues at CDN$2.9 billion represented just 11 per cent of the total revenue of firms engaged in the sector (Palinic, 2007) and reflects a significant structural change within the sector with the growth of firms more heavily specialized in functional food and/or NHP production. As can be seen from Table 6.11, functional foods and NHPs were of relatively equal importance with respect to the source of FFNHP revenues in 2011; revenue from functional food product lines accounting for a slightly higher share of FFNHP revenues (53 per cent).

Table 6.12 takes a closer look at the 2011 revenue data and is broken down into the four categories of firm type. As the table shows, revenue from all sources (in other words, not just FFNHP production) totalled nearly CDN$16.4 billion. Revenue sourced directly from functional food and NHP products accounted for CDN$11.2 billion or 69 per cent of the firms' total revenue, with firms' activities in areas such as conventional food processing and manufacturing, R&D or chemical or pharmaceutical wholesale distribution accounting for the remaining CDN$5.1 billion.

Table 6.10   Distribution of firms in the functional food and NHP industry in Canada (2002, 2005, 2007, 2011)

	Functional food firms (%)[a]	NHP firms (%)[a]	Firms producing both (%)[a]	Service-only firms (%)[b]
2002	28.0	46.0	26.0	N/A
2005	30.3	44.7	25.0	N/A
2007	25.3	42.1	25.7	6.9
2011	15.6	56.2	19.2	8.8

	Type of activity, by number of firms 2011			
	Functional food	NHP[a]	Both	All
R&D	63	222	109	394
Product development	75	234	116	425
Extraction of bioactive or medicinal ingredients	X	42	X	68
Manufacturer – ingredients, raw materials to be used in FFNHP	17	78	45	140
Manufacturer – semi-finished FFNHP for further processing	11	73	32	115
Manufacturer – consumer-ready products	88	180	72	340
Wholesaler	55	293	82	429
Retailer	24	133	45	202
Other	X	16	X	23

Notes:

a. Includes firms with or without service contracts.

b. Service only refers to firms that do not exclusively develop, produce or sell functional food or NHPs, but specialize in quality control services like claims verification or patent registration.

X data not available (supressed to meet the confidentiality requirements of the Statistics Act).

Source: Derived from Cinnamon (2009), Khamphoune (2013), Palinic (2007) and Tebbens (2005).

Table 6.11   Industry growth

	2004	2007	2011
Number of firms	389	680	750
Number of product lines	9715	22 000	32 266
Total FFNHP revenue (CDN$)	2.9 billion	3.7 billion	11.3 billion
Total functional food revenues[a]			6 billion
Total NHP revenues[a]			5.3 billion

Note: a. Including firms active in both categories and category-specific firms.

Source: Derived from Cinnamon (2009), Khamphoune (2013) and Palinic (2007).

Table 6.12   Revenue for firms in the functional food and NHP industry in Canada, by subsector in 2011 (thousands of CDN$)

	Functional food firms	NHP firms	Firms producing both	Service-only firms	All firms
Total revenues (all sources)	7 735 118	3 858 791	4 496 778	266 517	16 357 203
From FF and NHP	4 453 928	3 281 776	3 313 073	215 893	11 264 670
From FF products	4 453 928	–	1 536 034	12 069	6 002 031
From NHP products	–	3 281 776	1 777 039	203 824	5 262 639

Source: Derived from Khamphoune (2013).

Across the four types of firms, total functional food-related activity accounted for just over CDN$6 billion in revenues (53 per cent) while NHP-related activity accounted for over CDN$5.2 billion in revenues (47 per cent). A marked contrast exists in the structure of revenues across the firm types. Of total revenue generated by firms specializing in functional food (CDN$7.7 billion), 58 per cent (CDN$4.45 million) is attributed directly to functional food-related activities; in other words, many of these firms are engaged in other activities outside the health foods sector. Natural health product firms, however, tend to be more specialized, reporting a significantly larger share of revenue directly attributable to specific NHP activities, 85 per cent or CDN$3.9 million. The difference in revenue is less sharp for firms that are active in both areas, where functional foods account for 34 per cent of total revenue and NHPs 40 per cent. For service-only firms, NHP-related activities are the major source of revenue, earning nearly 17 times more revenue than those of functional foods (Khamphoune, 2013).

In terms of number of products, 32 266 FFNHP product lines were sold in Canada in 2011, with over half of the product lines sold exclusively to the domestic market and an additional 40 per cent sold both domestically and internationally. Of the total product lines sold in Canada, NHPs easily dominate, accounting for 85 per cent while over 75 per cent of products in development were also NHP product lines (Khamphoune, 2013). As Table 6.11 shows, there has been a significant expansion in the number of product lines since 2004.

The majority of firms in the Canadian FFNHP sector are privately owned with most being structured as private corporations; for example, in 2011, 660 Canadian FFNHP firms were private corporations compared to only 38 publicly traded firms; furthermore, 732 maintained head offices in Canada while 109 were subsidiaries of multinationals (Khamphoune, 2013). Of the 110 firms indicating in 2011 that they were seeking to raise capital, almost 60 per cent were NHP firms, of which 29 (45 per cent) were successful in their efforts. No functional food firms sought to raise capital in 2011. A total of CDN$42 million was reported as raised by the FFNHP sector in 2011, with half raised from foreign capital, followed by government funding (11 per cent) and conventional funds (banks, credit unions, initial and secondary public offerings) (7 per cent) (Khamphoune, 2013).

Most Canadian functional food firms also produce conventional food and beverage products and of the total staff employed by FFNHP firms in 2011, 44 per cent (or 16 259 employees) performed duties directly related to functional food and NHPs. Of the employees engaged in FFNHP-related activities, 38 per cent worked in NHP firms (these firms tend to be specialized in direct NHP-related activities), while 29 per cent were employed in functional food firms and another 29 per cent in firms active in both fields. Service-only firms account for just 4 per cent of employees engaged in FFNHP activities. Sales, marketing or advertising and R&D were the most highly sought after skills by FFNHP firms in 2011, with NHP firms accounting for 58 per cent of all vacancies (Khamphoune, 2013).

The Canadian FFNHP sector is a net exporter, shipping CDN$1.7 billion of exports to Canada's trading partners in 2011, compared to total imports by FFNHP establishments of CDN$670 million. The USA is the industry's largest export market as well as its largest supplier. Table 6.13

Table 6.13   Exports and imports, functional food and NHP industry in Canada (2011)

	Functional food firms[b]	NHP firms[b]	Firms producing both[b]	All firms
	(thousands of CDN$)			
Total exports (all sources)[a]	507 135	780 556	983 258	2 270 950
Functional foods and NHP	269 062 ^{E}	735 421	685 723 ^{E}	1 690 206
Functional foods	269 062 ^{E}	–	84 047 ^{E}	353 109^E
USA	X	–	X	194 499 ^{E}
EU	X	–	0	X
Japan	X	–	0	X
China	X	–	F	X
Others	X	–	X	X
NHP	–	735 421	601 676	1 337 097
USA	–	487 122	186 777 ^{E}	673 899
EU	–	X	X	280 700
Japan	–	X	X	78 476 ^{E}
China	–	X	X	175 504 ^{E}
Others	–	74 573	53 945	128 518

FFNHP imports

	Functional food firms[b]	NHP firms[b]	Firms producing both[b]	All firms
Total imports (all sources)	33 356	303 332	336 688	670 260
USA	32 939	200 131		
EU	X	83 243 ^{E}		
Japan	0	X		
China	243	14 838		
Others	X	X		

Notes:

a. Total exports/imports from all sources means those by all establishments active in FFNHP and include products not specifically related to FFNHP produced by those establishments.
b. Includes establishments with or without a service providing component.
0 true zero.
E use with caution.
X suppressed to meet confidentiality requirements of the Statistics Act.

F too unreliable to be published.
– not applicable.
Source: Derived from Khamphoune (2013).

summarizes key trade indicators for 2011. Exports of NHPs, both from firms specializing in the production of NHPs and those producing both NHPs and functional food, accounted for 79 per cent of export revenue derived from the FFNHP sector, while exports of functional food accounted for the remaining 21 per cent. Firms focusing on the production of NHPs accounted for about 44 per cent of FFNHP export revenue, closely followed by firms engaged in both product specializations at 41 per cent. Firms specializing in functional food generate a far smaller portion of export revenues, accounting for only 16 per cent of the FFNHP export revenues.

By far the most common distribution channel for the Canadian FFNHP industry is selling direct to a retailer. For NHP firms, direct distribution to other manufacturers and wholesalers is the second most preferred means of distribution, while functional food firms also use direct selling and other forms of distribution, as illustrated by Table 6.14

These differences are a reflection of the food distribution system in Canada, where supermarkets dominate the food retailing sector and are vertically integrated into the wholesaling function; therefore, functional foods reach consumers directly at the retail supermarket level. In contrast, NHPs are presented in pill/capsule/tablet/powder form and while they are also available at mainstream retail outlets such as major supermarkets, they often require intermediaries to educate consumers about any health benefits; therefore NHPs are also marketed through wholesalers prior to reaching a retail outlet (Cinnamon, 2009).

In 2011, 368 firms reported providing services to the Canadian FFNHP sector, offering accounting, insurance, extraction, custom manufacturing, scientific R&D as well as technical, engineering or mechanical services, sales and marketing or advertising, market research or other services. Of firms offering services, half (49 per cent) were FFNHP firms of which just over a half were NHP firms. Custom manufacturing, production or formulation is the most popular service, comprising 60 per cent of all services provided, with two-thirds of NHP firms and three-quarters of functional food firms undertaking such activities. R&D accounted for 36 per cent of services sought as did sales, marketing or advertising. Very few firms (less than 10 per cent) involved in services for the FFNHP sector are service only, most of these provide regulatory services, scientific R&D or quality control services to other firms within the sector (Khamphoune, 2013).

Table 6.14   *Distribution methods, functional food and NHP industry in Canada, by subsector, in 2011 (%)*

	Functional food firms[a]	NHP firms[a]	Firms producing both[b]	Service-only firms	All firms
All revenue	100	100	100	100	100
Direct selling	23.1	14.4	3.5	0	14.3
Internet/mail order	–	10.8	0.3	0	2.5
Wholesaler	3.8	19.2	16.0	70.4	12
Direct to retailer	30.3	27.9	51.9	8.8	36.9
Direct to other manufacturer	6.7	20.6	6.9	20.8	10
Multi-level/ network marketing	0	0.3	0.8	0	0.3
Broker/third party distributor	6.3	6.1	19.2	0	10.5
Other	29.7	0.7	1.3	0	13.4

Notes:

a. Includes firms with or without a service providing component.
b. Includes firms involved in both functional foods and NHPs, with or without a service providing component.

Source: Derived from Khamphoune (2013).

Just over 20 per cent of Canadian FFNHP firms are involved in cooperative or collaborative arrangements with other domestic or foreign business units or firms. The arrangements focus on developing or improving products through scientific expertise, regulatory affairs, training, marketing, distribution and clinical trials. The most common collaboration was with other business units, followed by universities (30 per cent) and federal and provincial government agencies (Khamphoune, 2013). In 2011, 43 per cent of Canadian FFNHP firms contracted out FFNHP-related activities where another business unit performed services contractually on their behalf. Nearly 70 per cent of these were NHP firms utilizing the services of others for custom manufacturing, production or formulation as well as quality control activities; few service-only and functional food firms contracted out work (Khamphoune, 2013).

The R&D activities of Canadian FFNHP firms focus on nutritive value and the functional properties of plant and animal products, an example of which is the development of technologies for the processing of raw materials such as soy, oats and other cereals. Technology and expertise in the extraction, characterization, modification, stabilization and enhancement of products in Canada are also well developed (Cinnamon, 2009). Support for R&D in the sector has also been trending upwards, with R&D focusing on vascular health, weight control, energy, immune system and overall health and wellbeing (Cinnamon, 2009; Palinic, 2007).

Table 6.15 charts R&D spending by Canadian functional food and NHP firms for 2004, 2007 and 2011. Total expenditure on R&D (all sources) by these firms was estimated to be approximately CDN$320 million in 2011, an increase from CDN$209 million in 2007 with roughly 74 per cent (CDN$238 million) directly invested in FFNHP R&D (Cinnamon, 2009; Khamphoune, 2013). Nevertheless, this represents just 2.1 per cent of FFNHP product revenue, down from 4 per cent in 2007 and signals a sector with an increasing focus on commercialization of existing innovations. In terms of the direction of R&D expenditure towards functional foods versus NHPs, the data show that NHP R&D expenditures far outstripped spending on functional foods in 2011, with 69 per cent of all FFNHP-focused R&D expenditures devoted to NHP R&D. This may reflect changes in the regulatory environment, including the establishment of a clearer regulatory framework for NHPs in Canada, as discussed in Chapter 3, as well as different stages of development of these two sectors.

Firms active in both product areas accounted for 45 per cent of total FFNHP R&D spending, split nearly evenly between functional foods and NHPs. Firms producing only NHPs invested nearly CDN$100 million in NHP R&D spending (60 per cent of all R&D spent on NHPs) while functional food-specific firms accounted for a 25 per cent share of total functional food R&D spending (Khamphoune, 2013).

In summary, R&D expenditures exhibit an upward trend in absolute terms in total and with respect to R&D on both types of product. Although based on only three sets of observations over a seven-year period, the marginal rate of increase in R&D expenditures was positive; in other words, the increase in expenditures for the 2007 to 2011 period is larger than the increase between 2007 and 2004, suggesting continued industry growth. The dip in the share of FFNHP revenues devoted to R&D expenditures in 2011 may signal a stronger focus on commercialization as the industry matures.

Table 6.15   Research and development expenditures by functional food and NHP firms (2004, 2007, 2011)^a (thousands of CDN$)

	Functional food firms[b]	NHP firms[b]	Firms producing both[b]	Service only firms	All firms
2004					
Total R&D spending	45 612	76 190	41 063	–	162 865
FF R&D	21 186	29 831	23 537	–	74 554
NHP R&D					
2007					
Total R&D spending	98 894	64 601	41 527	4284[E]	209 305
FF R&D	62 018	9890	16 266	1723[E]	89 897
NHP R&D	628[E]	40 749	14 702	1979[E]	58 058
2011					
Total R&D spending	45 716	114 358	145 615	14 126	319 815
FF R&D	18 345	–	54 952[E]	236[E]	73 534
NHP R&D	–	98 130[E]	52 611[E]	13 820	164 560

Notes:

a. Totals may not add up due to rounding.
b. Includes firms with or without a service providing component.
E   use with caution.
–   not applicable.

Source: Derived from Cinnamon (2009), Khamphoune (2013) and Palinic (2007).

Firms in Canada have the option of protecting their intellectual property (IP) through the registration of either a patent or trademark with IP agencies in Canada and in other countries, but most choose to protect their IP via trade secrets; thus, firms in the sector have tended not to register their patents and trademarks (Krakar and Gao, 2006). This remained the case in 2011 where almost 25 per cent of FFNHP firms used trade secrets to protect their IP, followed by 23 per cent using registered trademarks and 13 per cent using FFNHP licences. Patents remain under-used as a form of IP protection, used by only 13 per cent of firms in the sector (Khamphoune, 2013).

The choice of IP strategy differs somewhat depending on the main focus of activity, with NHP and dual activity firms the most active in IP protection. Firms specializing in functional food production mostly tend to prefer trade secrets (23 per cent of firms), followed distantly by registered trademarks (8 per cent) as a means of IP protection; no patents were registered by functional food firms according to the 2011 Statistics Canada survey data. In contrast, NHP firms used the full spectrum of IP protection methods available, with the largest percentage (19 per cent) of these firms using registered trademarks, followed by trade secrets and licensing. Unlike functional food firms, firms focusing on NHP production did engage in patent protection of IP; nevertheless, patents were used by only 12 per cent of these firms. Firms active in both functional and NHP production primarily use trade secrets (54 per cent of firms) and trademarks (53 per cent), followed by licensing (23 per cent). Data on patent use by these firms were not available (Khamphoune, 2013).

Firms active in both product fields held nearly all pending patents (96 per cent) as well as existing patents (91 per cent) in 2011 (Khamphoune, 2013). Those Canadian firms with registered patents tended to register them mostly with the USPTO, some with the CIPO and/or the European Union patent office (Cinnamon, 2009; Palinic, 2007).[6] In an analysis using the same 2003 Statistics Canada data used by Tebbens (2005), Herath et al. (2008b) examine the factors affecting innovation in the Canadian sector. Their analysis suggests that firms holding patents are likely to have significantly fewer functional food and NHP product lines. Acquiring IP from other firms also negatively affects the number of product lines under development, indicating that firms who are focused on product development tend to acquire products from other developers rather than developing their own technology. Herath et al. (2008b) conclude that the focus of Canadian firms tends to be more on the commercialization of existing products with health attributes than the development of new products, suggesting that fewer product lines are important for successful new product development.

Tables 6.16 and 6.17 provide a summary of key indicators for the Canadian FFNHP sector and offer a basis of comparison of industry activities related to the production of functional food versus NHPs (Table 6.16), as well as across type of firm, that is, firms producing only functional food, producing only NHPs, firms involved in the production of both functional food and NHPs and firms providing services only to either field (Table 6.17).

A number of observations emerge from these comparisons and from the analysis presented in this section. First, while both functional foods and NHPs account for similar proportions of industry revenue, the NHP

Table 6.16   *Comparison of functional foods versus NHP activity, in 2011*
             (% share)

	Functional foods	NHPs
Share of FFNHP revenue	53	47
Share of product lines	15	85
Share of products in development	25	75
Share of export revenues	21	79
Share of imports (costs)	10	90
Share of FFNHP R&D expenditures	31	69

Source: Derived from Khamphoune (2013).

Table 6.17   *Comparison of activities by firm type (2011)*

	Functional food firms (%)	NHP firms (%)	Firms producing both (%)	Service firms (%)
Number of firms	16	56	19	9
Share of FFNHP revenue	40	29	29	2
Share of product lines	11	61	28	–
Share of products in development	7	41	51	–
Share of attempts to raise capital	0	59	N/A	N/A
Share of FFNHP employees	29	38	29	4
Share of FFNHP staffing vacancies	0	58	31	N/A
Share of export revenues	16	44	41	–
Share of FFNHP R&D expenditures	8	41	45	6
Share of contracting out	5	70	21	3

Source: Derived from Khamphoune (2013).

sector is characterized by a substantially larger range of product lines, more products in development, a considerably larger share of export revenues and of R&D expenditures, all of which suggests a sector undergoing a substantial growth phase. Indeed, when examined from a firm-type perspective (Table 6.17), it is clear that there are a considerably larger number of firms engaged in NHP activities (both individually and alongside functional food activities) than firms solely involved in the production of functional food, indicating that the NHP sector is characterized by a large number of small firms. Firms producing NHPs are actively seeking financing and employees and are extensively engaged in contracting out activities, usually in their pursuit of R&D, all of which are also indicators of investment in future growth and a relatively young sector. In comparison, the functional foods category exhibits fewer signs of long-term growth, particularly with respect to new product development and R&D expenditures, suggesting stagnation in the sector.

While the reasons for the above are not entirely clear, it is possible that the overhaul of the NHP regulatory framework in the mid 2000s provided a stronger stimulus to the NHP sector than was the case for the more incremental changes that have occurred in the regulatory environment governing new product approvals and allowable health claims for functional foods. The differences may also be due to the nature of technological change in these sectors, with a greater potential to incorporate functional health ingredients in an NHP formulation versus within a food. Finally, differences in consumer preferences for product type, acceptance of health claims and the willingness to pay for functional food versus NHPs may also factor into the perceived market potential of these product categories. These issues are addressed in Chapter 7.

6.6 SYNTHESIS

Sections 6.1 through 6.5 have provided a detailed overview of key industry and market trends in the USA, EU, Japan and Canada. A summary of literature charting industry and market developments is also available in Table A5.2 in Appendix 5. The analysis presented in this chapter demonstrates the diversity of the sector in terms of products, utilization, applications and ingredients. The health food industry exhibits a strongly upward trajectory across the globe. Growth can be attributed to a number of factors including consumer demand, scientific discovery and regulatory developments to facilitate new product approvals and the making of health claims. Recognition of the relationship between diet and disease prevention/health has increased the interest of consumers in health-enhancing products. Concurrently, developments in food technology have enabled the creation of healthier food products to meet this increasing consumer interest. In most major markets, the functional food market is dominated by established and internationally active firms. Even though there are greater numbers of small firms in the global health foods sector, the dominance of large, established firms in the industry limits the long-run ability of small firms to gain significant market share. Nevertheless, many of these small firms are the source of innovations that are subsequently adopted by larger firms through licensing agreements, contracts or outright purchase of the technology.

Challenges faced by the sector include constraints on resources, lack of effective IPR protection and under-investment in R&D. The health foods sector is particularly resource-intensive with respect to R&D, both in terms of financial capital requirements and also in terms of the lengthy time lags from initial R&D to commercialization. The absence of a well-established IPR system for effective patent protection in some jurisdictions increases the risk of free-ridership and limits the ability of firms to capture rents. In this environment, firms have stronger incentives to seek innovative ways of undertaking product-oriented R&D (private and public) as well as to make use of inter-firm collaborative agreements for research and in the development of new distribution and ingredient supply channels. The creation of networks of relationships among stakeholders has proven important to generating innovations in the sector. Nevertheless, IP protection remains important and obtaining IPR protection through patenting key ingredients or products is a means of ensuring firms protect their investment and capture rents.

The case study of the Canadian functional food and NHP sector presented in this chapter provides a window into many of these issues. While differences do exist across the three major markets – the USA, EU and Japan – particularly with respect to the IPR regimes in place, in general these markets exhibit broadly similar patterns of development and growth. Continued growth is contingent upon consumer demand for health food products, which is the topic of the next chapter.

NOTES

1. In addition, as Kotilainen et al. (2006) indicate, 'Statistics on international trade of functional foods are not directly available because functional foods are traded in the tariff code categories of "among other foods". Similarly, a large portion of botanical ingredients are funnelled into the pharmaceutical, natural medicine or dietary supplement markets, along with the portion used in the production of functional foods making commodity trade figures of limited informational value' (p. 11).
2. The products, companies and brands listed in Table 6.3 are intended to illustrate the types of products that are or have been available in the US market and are by no means an exhaustive list.

3. Recall that health claims are based upon SSA standards; qualified health claims are supported by credible scientific evidence that is inconclusive.
4. To identify publications, Stein and Rodríguez-Cerezo (2008) conducted a comprehensive search of two databases: the Food Science and Technology Abstracts and MEDLINE (the Medical Literature Analysis and Retrieval System Online).
5. As explained in Chapter 2, Canada defines functional food as a food similar in appearance or substance to conventional food, consumed as a normal and regular part of the diet, with demonstrable health benefits. Natural health products (NHPs) include most nutraceuticals but also homeopathic and traditional medicines.
6. Specifically, in 2005, 30 per cent of patents were registered with the USPTO, 16 per cent with CIPO, 11 per cent with the EU patent office and the rest were registered with other jurisdictions (Palinic, 2007). Data are not available for 2011.

7. Consumer responses to health foods

The growth of the health foods sector is dependent on continued consumer demand for these products. A growing literature charts consumer awareness and acceptance of health foods and assesses consumer willingness to pay (WTP) for health benefits. This chapter summarizes key insights from this literature. A brief overview of the primary methodological approaches used in the consumer literature is provided in Section 7.1 as a precursor to the discussion of the literature in section 7.2.[1] Section 7.3 concludes the chapter with an assessment of the key messages arising from this body of research.

7.1 CONSUMER RESEARCH METHODOLOGIES

Researchers interested in examining consumer awareness of health food products, their acceptance of new functional ingredients and their WTP for these products usually turn to survey methodologies to gather data for their analyses. Surveys enable researchers to gather data on consumers' attitudes and preferences, the factors shaping attitudes and in particular, are useful in exploring the market potential for new functional foods or ingredients that may not yet be available commercially.

A considerable number of the consumer research studies summarized in Section 7.2 use Stated Preference survey techniques. This encompasses a family of methodologies in which consumer preferences are elicited through requesting that respondents indicate their preferences for a product or product attribute in a survey. This differs from Revealed Preference data in which preferences are inferred from real market data reflecting actual purchases. Stated Preference approaches have a number of advantages, including the ability to examine products or product attributes not yet currently available in the marketplace and can be combined with other data measuring respondents' risk preferences, health status, food purchasing habits and so on to explore socio-demographic and psychographic influences on consumer attitudes. Critics of Stated Preference approaches point to the problem of hypothetical bias – the extent to which consumers' preferences elicited from a survey are a true reflection of their actual purchase behaviour in a real market environment. These limitations are well known and methods to reduce the problems of hypothetical bias have been developed, including the use of so-called 'cheap talk' scripts in which survey respondents read a script explicitly highlighting the problem of hypothetical bias before indicating their preferences (Lusk, 2003).

Various permutations of Stated Preference methodologies appear in the literature summarized in the next section, including Conjoint analysis, Discrete Choice Experiments (DCE) and Contingent Valuation (CV). In Conjoint analysis, the products of interest are described by a series of product attributes (for example, functional ingredient, product format, health claim and price). The attributes are further defined with respect to levels, for example: omega-3, probiotic, plant sterols for the functional ingredient; available as a food versus a pill for the product format attribute; with and without a verified health claim and various price levels. In Conjoint analysis, respondents are presented with a series of product profiles described as bundles of attribute levels and indicate their preferences by ranking or rating the product profiles. This enables an assessment of the implicit relative importance given to the individual attributes and is considered more reliable than asking respondents to provide an explicit assessment of the importance of an individual attribute on an attribute-by-attribute basis.[2] In addition to evaluating the relative importance of product attributes, Conjoint analysis also allows an assessment of the extent to which consumers would be willing to trade off between attributes.

In a similar fashion, a DCE is an attribute-based Stated Preference methodology in which products are described as bundles of attribute levels. Rather than rate or rank product profiles, however, respondents are presented with a series of repeated choice sets and asked to indicate which product they would purchase. Often a 'no purchase option' is included in each choice set to increase the realism of the choice scenario, since in a real purchase environment, consumers can elect not to purchase a product. Regression analysis is used to measure the extent to which individual attributes have a significant influence on consumers' choices. Since price is almost always included as an attribute in a DCE, the regression coefficients are used to derive WTP estimates for specific attributes using the estimated coefficient for the price attribute.[3] DCEs are useful for measuring the WTP for product attributes and therefore the relative importance of attributes as reflected in monetary WTP measures.

More common in the environmental economics literature, but still occasionally used in consumer preference analysis, is Contingent Valuation. This method involves direct elicitation of a respondent's WTP for a product or product attribute. Various methods are used to elicit WTP estimates; for example, respondents could be presented with a description of a functional food product incorporating a series of attributes and a health claim and asked to indicate whether they would be willing to pay a fixed sum of money ($X) for the product, with yes/no responses. Prices may be varied over respondents and double-dichotomous choice questions are often used, wherein respondents are asked a follow-up question, for example, if yes to the first price, would you pay a higher price ($X+10 per cent) or if no, would you pay a lower price ($X–10 per cent). The yes/no responses are combined with socio-economic variables in a regression model to estimate the probability of purchase intentions at different price levels.

Other survey and data analysis techniques that feature in the next section include techniques from the marketing literature, such as Means– End Chain analysis. This research method explores the connection between a consumer and a product through the construction of an associate network between product attributes, consequences and the consumer's core or terminal values. For example, a means–end chain for organic egg purchases could be as follows: Attributes: 'I like this egg because it is organic'; Consequences: 'I feel I am behaving responsibly when I purchase this egg'; Core values: 'Behaving responsibly makes me feel more ethical'.

Other studies feature the use of multivariate data analysis techniques such as Factor analysis and Cluster analysis. Factor analysis is a data reduction technique that summarizes a number of variables into a smaller set of composite dimensions, or factors. For example, survey responses may be used to identify a set of factors capturing consumers' risk preferences whereby a number of survey variables measuring risk preferences are coalesced into a single factor. Cluster analysis groups individuals into clusters where there is homogeneity within clusters and heterogeneity across clusters. As such, it is often used to identify consumer segments with similar preferences within the cluster but whose preferences differ across clusters.[4]

7.2 CONSUMER AWARENESS AND ACCEPTANCE: INSIGHTS FROM THE LITERATURE

The emergence of the health foods sector has stimulated a great deal of consumer research across a number of countries. While much of the research focuses on consumers in a specific country, a number of studies feature multi-country analyses and comparisons of consumer attitudes.

Research on European consumer attitudes features prominently in the literature, as does research examining consumer preferences in North America. The studies that follow offer a sampling of consumer research across countries, across themes and across methods. Common themes include consumer awareness and responses to new health foods, acceptance of new functional ingredients, factors affecting either willingness or reluctance to try new health foods, the credibility of health claims and information sources and estimates of the WTP for new health foods.

Consumer acceptance is the primary focus of Verbeke (2005), who interviewed 215 grocery shoppers in Belgian households. The major determinants of consumer acceptance of functional foods are assessed using a Multivariate Probit model, enabling the researchers to simulate probabilities of events occurring over a range of explanatory variables. Socio-demographic factors such as age, income, literacy and location, and attitudinal and cognitive factors such as beliefs and knowledge affect consumers' acceptance of functional foods; nevertheless, the health benefit is the paramount factor in the acceptance of functional foods. Interestingly, Belgian households with higher education levels are less likely to accept functional food, whereas high-income households have a positive attitude towards functional food.

In an exploratory study to determine the factors that influence the acceptance of functional food as well as to determine the variation in acceptance across cultures, Labrecque et al. (2006) surveyed students from France (170 respondents), the USA (161 respondents) and Québec, Canada (280 respondents) using a self-administered questionnaire. Using regression analysis, the study assesses the effect of beliefs about health benefits, knowledge, information credibility and gender on attitudes towards functional foods. The researchers determine that there is very little difference between Canadian and American consumer attitudes towards functional food. The major determinants of acceptance are health and product-related benefits, credible information and knowledge about the products. The results also indicate that the promotion of other product benefits, in addition to health attributes (such as high quality), will be important to market development. Finally, the study reveals that the French respondents had less knowledge of the term functional food relative to respondents in Canada or the USA. The French students reported a less favourable attitude towards functional food than the French Canadian and US students, however, the attitude differences were very small. Hence, the authors conclude that market development should be approached from a global perspective.

In a study for the EC, Stein and Rodríguez-Cerezo (2008) interviewed 116 consumers in Germany, 110 in Poland, 279 in Spain and 121 in the

UK. The objective of the study was to determine consumer awareness, attitudes and WTP for functional food. These countries were chosen strategically to represent diverse market segments in the EU. Germany was chosen as a continental European country characterized by its size, the competitive nature of its food market and a history of sceptical consumers. Poland was chosen as an eastern European country reflective of the development of the functional food market in a new member state. Spain was chosen as a Mediterranean country with a high volume food market and the UK was chosen as a western European country with a high-profile food retailing industry.

Based on descriptive statistics of the survey data, the study concludes that the consistent reason for buying functional food was to stay healthy, although it is acknowledged that there is not a single unique determinant of consumer acceptance of functional food. Indeed, taste, convenience, a reasonable price, an attractive design and practical packaging are also widely held consumer expectations. Functional food awareness and understanding among consumers depends on mediated information, which hinges on the credibility that consumers attach to this information. The authors also note that the food industry's communication policy is weak and food retailers appear to have limited knowledge about the functional food products that they sell. Regional differences are apparent in the reasons for avoiding functional food. In Poland and Spain, the predominant deterrent to purchasing was the price of functional products, which is less of an issue in Germany or the UK. The fear of side-effects is more important among Polish consumers than among consumers in the other countries, while for UK and German consumers, taste is the primary concern. The authors recommend further research into functional food as a potential cost-effective means of addressing health problems in Europe.

In another pan-European study, Dean et al. (2007) evaluate how consumer perceptions of healthy cereal products are influenced by production methods, gender, nationality, base product (staple versus fun food) and health claims (generic versus specific). The study uses a survey with a sample size of over 2000 consumers responsible for family grocery purchasing from the UK, Italy, Finland and Germany, which is then analysed using analysis of variance (ANOVA) methods. The authors define functional cereal products as grains, such as wheat, maize, rice and oats that have been modified to provide health benefits over and above basic nutrition. The products selected are bread, pasta and biscuits (cookies). Bread and pasta represent staple grain foods, while cookies are an 'occasional' food. The health claims specifically selected are 'choles-terol lowering' and 'added fibre'. The results indicate that British,

Finnish and Italian consumers perceive bread that lowers cholesterol as being more beneficial than do German consumers. Cholesterol-lowering pasta is perceived to be more beneficial by British and Italian consumers than by Finnish and German consumers. Finnish consumers perceive bread with added fibre as being more beneficial than do consumers in the other countries. Overall, among the selected products, bread with fibre added on average is regarded as the most beneficial, with cholesterol-lowering cookies the least.

The results also illustrate that consumers prefer modified base products, that is, staple foods such as bread and pasta, over modified occasional foods such as cookies. Consumers also show preferences for production methods such as fortification and traditional cross-breeding over genetic modification. Finally, men value products with specific health claims, while women perceive more benefits in products with general health claims. The study confirms the findings of others in the area of functional food regarding the importance of gender, health claims, nationality, base products and consumer perceptions and attitudes.

Further evidence that credible health benefits as a determinant of acceptance is similar across the globe and across cultures is provided by Bech-Larsen and Grunert (2003). The effect of cultural values on the demand for functional foods was explored using a sample of American, Danish and Finnish consumers. Specifically, the study assesses the extent to which consumers' perceptions of the healthiness of a food depend on different types of health claims, functional enrichments (omega-3 versus oligosaccharides), base products (juice, yoghurt, spread) and processing methods (organic, not organic) and price. A survey of the primary grocery purchasers in 500 randomly selected households in each country used Conjoint analysis to evaluate the relative importance of these attributes.

The researchers determine that a consumer's perception of functional food is dependent on the initial healthiness of the base product to a greater extent than the health claim or functional properties. Functional enhancements of base products for which consumers already have positive views about the nutritional content or healthiness are most likely to be accepted and generate a higher WTP. This perception is consistent across the three countries; the sample populations show only minor differences with respect to the perceived healthiness of functional food. Some cultural differences are apparent, however: Finnish respondents were generally more positive towards functional food than American or Danish respondents, while Danish and Finnish consumers have a more negative attitude towards GM products relative to American consumers. Bech-Larsen and Grunert (2003) recommend that further studies focus on

cross-cultural segments among consumers rather than on the identification of international differences at a broad level.

In another Scandinavian study, Urala and Lahteenmaki (2004) examine
Finnish consumers' attitudes towards functional foods and factors that
predict willingness to consume these foods. Survey data from 1158
respondents are used to analyse a number of factors affecting consumer
attitudes towards many aspects of functional foods, including perceived
reward from consumption, possible role as medicines, absence of nutritional risks, consumption as part of a healthy diet and the health effects
of functional foods relative to their taste. Factor analysis is used to group
the attitudinal statements. Consistent with other studies, the reward
(health benefits) associated with consumption of functional food is a
major determinant of WTP. The reward from consumption also overshadows any perceived risks associated with consumption. Contrary to
the findings of Tuorila and Cardello (2002) and Verbeke (2006) (discussed below), the study asserts that consumers will compromise on taste
if there is a clear promise of lowering the risk of commonly recognized
diseases such as CVD.

Staying in Scandinavia, Mark-Herbert (2003) examines strategies for
the development and marketing of functional foods in Sweden. Three
strategies by which individual firms can achieve sustainable competitive
advantages are recommended, including the need to acquire proprietary
rights to ingredients that have undergone independent clinical studies, to
develop brand recognition among consumers and to utilize health experts
in product testing to build credibility among consumers. The study
identifies three consumer market segments in Sweden, the first being
consumers who already suffer from a disease: for this group, the author
suggests targeting health professionals as a means to convey information
to consumers. The second segment is an 'at risk group' of consumers:
health-related news and talk shows are recommended vehicles to reach
this group. The last group is the 'prevention and mass market segment' of
consumers: members of this group may already be taking vitamins and
minerals. Using the print media and radio to create awareness is
recommended to convey information to this third group.

Information features prominently in many studies of consumer attitudes towards functional food, with clear and credible messages about
health benefits deemed a prerequisite for consumer acceptance. In an
Australian study, Cox et al. (2004) examine the specific characteristics of
messages that would motivate consumers to buy functional foods and
supplements aimed at preventing memory loss. A survey was administered to 290 consumers between the ages of 40 and 60, describing a

range of products including natural functional foods, sweetened functional foods, GM functional foods and supplements. An adaptation of Protection Motivation Theory[5] forms the theoretical basis to the analysis. Respondents made no clear distinction between functional foods and supplements and, consistent with studies in other countries, the health benefit is the major predictor of consumer intentions to purchase these products. However, improving health benefits by genetic modification is not acceptable to most respondents. Women are found to have a less favourable attitude towards genetic modification. Respondents are cautious about attempts to improve the palatability of functional foods: even though the study did not involve a sensory analysis, the suggestion, for example, that functional foods could be sweetened to offset any bitterness was not acceptable (Cox et al., 2004).

More generally, numerous studies across a range of countries find that tangible health benefits, communicated through credible health claims, is a critical requirement for consumer acceptance of functional foods. In the USA, Teratanavat and Hooker (2006) sampled over 3000 Ohio consumers to explore consumer valuation and preference heterogeneity for novel functional food attributes. The effect on consumer preferences of health benefits, organic ingredients, source of nutrients and price are examined. Using a DCE, WTP for functional health attributes is derived. Sources of heterogeneity in consumer responses include previous purchase experience with health foods and organic foods. For example, consumers who regularly purchase functional foods, organic foods and food with natural ingredients tend to react more positively to novel functional foods. The maintenance of good health and disease prevention are strong motivators contributing towards receptiveness to functional and novel foods with health claims.

In another US study, Markosyan et al. (2009) measure consumers' responses to a specific functional food (apples with enriched antioxidant coatings). Antioxidants may protect cells from damage from free radicals, which are believed to lead to cancer. A CV survey instrument was administered in face-to-face interviews with 730 US consumers, using a dichotomous choice model to elicit individual WTP estimates. The analysis finds that consumers value and are willing to pay for health attributes embedded in functional foods. Consumers are responsive towards health claims, underlining the importance of credible information dissemination. Anxiety over the utilization of a new technology that is considered unnatural and risky is the primary reason that some respondents reject the prospect of apples with enriched antioxidant coatings.

In a relatively early study focusing on US consumers and, with further evidence that the base product matters, Marshall et al. (1994) examine

US consumers' willingness to purchase speciality functional eggs, finding that 65 per cent of respondents in five major Texas cities were willing to purchase n-3 fatty acid-enriched table eggs, of which 75 per cent were willing to pay an additional US$0.50 per dozen. As Surai and Sparks (2001) note, however, perceptions that egg consumption may lead to a rise in blood cholesterol levels with negative health consequences is a potential barrier to increased consumption of such so-called 'designer' eggs. While this perception may be changing as expert opinion on the role of dietary cholesterol in the development of heart disease continues to evolve, understanding consumer attitudes towards the base product remains of critical importance to the development of new functional foods.

While health benefits are clearly the dominant motivator for consumer interest in functional food, other factors have also been found to affect consumer acceptance. In another Belgian study, Verbeke (2006) investigates consumers' willingness to compromise on taste for health benefits in functional foods. Using two surveys conducted in 2001 (255 respondents) and in 2004 (205 respondents), Verbeke (2006) finds that Belgian consumers have developed a somewhat critical attitude towards functional foods. This attitude is evident in their stated unwillingness to compromise on taste for health. Specifically, the results show that the gap between willingness to accept functional foods that taste good and those with a poorer taste relative to conventional food widened across the intervening years between the two surveys. Perhaps unsurprisingly, taste is seen as a precondition for the acceptance of functional food. Given that the study was not product-specific, the authors recommend further research focusing on specific functional foods rather than functional food as an abstract category.

The extent to which consumers are willing to compromise on taste in exchange for a health benefit is also examined by Tuorila and Cardello (2002), but they use real products rather than a hypothetical survey instrument. Fruit juice was chosen as the product of interest, based on the expectation that consumers perceive juice to have healthy attributes, as well as the ease with which fruit juice can be enriched; 78 civilian employees of the US army tasted different formulations of fruit juice with functional attributes. Analysis of variance is used to assess the preference ratings. The results indicate that the presence of off-flavours in a functional food has a negative effect on the likelihood of consumption, regardless of the type of health benefit the product offers. The study also shows that consumer acceptance of functional food based on health benefits depends upon the specific expected health benefit. The study finds that improvements in physical and cognitive performance are more likely to motivate consumer acceptance than simply emotional wellbeing. To clarify the factors determining long-run purchasing behaviour, the study recommends further research on actual consumer usage of functional foods in the context of taste variations, as well as research on the benefits of labelling claims.

Commercialization failure is common for new functional food products and Bleiel (2010) shows that functional foods fail more often than succeed in the commercial marketplace. Product failures are related to consumer rejection as firms often ignore consumer insights at the innovation stage and it is necessary for firms to understand the drivers of consumer purchasing behaviour. Consumers may be more willing to pay for the wellness benefit rather than the ingredient used in producing a functional food. As an example, the claim 'added probiotics' may have less meaning to consumers compared to 'stronger defences' or 'better immunity'. The author concludes that firms should communicate the benefits of consuming the product and not emphasize the ingredients used in making the product, while a solid understanding of consumer behaviour should inform new product development.

Evani (2009) makes similar observations for the US market, suggesting that most US consumers are turning to functional foods due to time constraints and convenience as a means to meet their nutritional needs and therefore firms should consider consumer demographics and lifestyle trends when developing new functional foods and beverages. Younger consumers and time-pressed consumers represent important market segments, as consumers are seeking out functional products that provide quick health solutions in a convenient format. Evani (2009) argues that new products need to be easy to understand and communication of the benefits of these products should avoid over-use of scientific jargon.

In another country-specific study, Arnoult et al. (2007) examine UK consumers' WTP for enhanced foods, conducting face-to-face interviews with 200 consumers. Attitudes towards a number of potential products are examined, including strawberries and lettuce with higher antioxidant levels and lamb chops with higher levels of unsaturated fatty acids. The results indicate a viable market for functional foods, balanced with a strong polarization of opinion against anything that is perceived to be artificial or GM. Highly skilled professionals in urban areas, women and smaller households on lower incomes are more likely to be willing to pay for enhanced products. Supplements in the form of pills are most likely to be rejected by women, white collar workers and households with children under 18. However, larger households with higher incomes or higher education levels tend to exhibit a positive WTP for supplements. Finally, the study concludes, somewhat surprisingly, that UK consumers tend to have a stronger WTP for enhanced animal than for enhanced plant products.

In a Swiss study, Siegrist et al. (2008) examine the factors that influence consumers' willingness to buy functional foods. Using data from a mail survey of 249 respondents conducted in the German-speaking part of Switzerland, the study uses regression analysis to test the significance of factors such as physiological benefits, the carrier or base product of the functional food, as well as socio-economic factors including age and social trust on a consumer's WTP. The results reinforce the findings of other studies: physiological/health benefits are a major determinant of consumer acceptance and willingness to purchase. Consistent with research in other countries, the study also finds that the consumer's prior attitude towards the base product is significant in the sense that consumers are more willing to buy functional food that is derived from an already accepted conventional food with a positive health image. A consumer's perception of functional food is not independent from the base product. Trust is also important. Consumers with higher levels of trust in the food industry are more likely to buy functional food compared to those who do not trust the food industry. Finally, the researchers find that older Swiss consumers are more interested in functional foods than younger consumers.

The motivations and cognitive processes of Greek consumers in purchasing functional foods are explored by Krystallis et al. (2008). The study examines the most frequently purchased functional food products, provides insights into consumers' motives for buying functional foods and attempts to model the cognitive structures explaining consumers' functional food choices, as the authors explain: 'the way that functional food consumption-relevant knowledge is stored and organized in consumers' memories' (Krystallis et al., 2008, p. 527). Using Means–End Chain analysis, a pilot study with 60 consumers is used to develop the Means–End Chain framework, which is subsequently applied in the main study to a sample of 40 consumers. The respondents are homogeneous with at least a university education and are grouped into young adults (25–34 years) and an older group (34–44 years).

Two functional foods are used in the study, a functional juice with enhanced vitamins and a functional spread with reduced cholesterol risk. The young adult group generally preferred the functional food juice, while the older group preferred the functional spread. According to the authors, this result indicates the possibility of a fragmented functional food market. Nevertheless, both groups share similar preferences with respect to the attributes deemed the most important, including those pertaining to quality (in other words, purity, safety, healthy), label information (in other words, best before and packaging dates, nutritional value and health/functional claim), price and brand name. In terms of the motives for buying functional foods, the young adults tend to be concerned about enhancing their health status through functional foods that improve their physical condition and energy levels, while the older group is concerned about prevention or reduction of disease risks. The authors conclude, unsurprisingly, that the success of functional foods depends on how well these products satisfy consumer needs, thus in developing functional foods a solid understanding of consumer expectations is critical.

As is apparent from many of the studies discussed here, consumers are not homogenous in their preferences and distinct consumer segments with different preferences exist. Sometimes these segments are identified by socio-demographic characteristics, as in the UK study discussed above, while other studies also recognize the importance of psychographic or attitudinal factors in segmenting a consumer population. Herath et al. (2008a) survey over 1700 Canadian consumers to identify consumer segments in the health food market. Cluster analysis and ANOVA are applied to data capturing attitudes, motivations and knowledge. The researchers find that factors such as age, location, education and income are prominent determinants of functional food and NHP consumption in Canada. The most receptive groups for functional food and NHPs are the elderly, the less educated and low-income households who tend to be more concerned about a wide range of health issues/ diseases and indicate greater willingness to learn about foods with potential health benefits. These consumer segments also tend to make more use of what are arguably more credible sources of information, such as health professionals. Receptive consumers were more interested in knowing the health benefits of these products before making a purchase decision. The less receptive group consists of younger consumers with higher education and incomes, mostly living in urban areas, who tend to be less concerned about a wide range of potential health issues/diseases, perhaps reflecting the fact that they are younger. This group of consumers is also characterized by higher levels of knowledge about specific diseases (Herath et al., 2008a).

In an earlier Canadian study, West et al. (2002) examine consumers' valuations of functional properties in food, comparing functional organic and GM foods to functional conventional foods. Tomato sauce described as having 'anti-cancer' properties, 'heart-healthy' potato chips and 'heart-healthy' chicken breast were incorporated into a stated choice experiment administered via telephone survey to 1008 Canadian household food shoppers. The study finds that Canadian consumers generally have a positive attitude towards functional foods and are willing to pay a premium, especially when the added functional property is derived from plants (but are less receptive if derived from meat). Use of vitamins or herbal supplements is commonplace and Canadians view positively the potential illness prevention role of food. The researchers find that credible information about the safety and benefits of these products from reliable sources outside the food industry is needed and, to that end, government experts and health care experts are identified as the preferred information sources. The study concludes that although the probability of purchasing both GM and organic products increases with the addition of a functional attribute, the increase is relatively small (West et al., 2002).

Using the same set of respondents, West and Larue (2004) identify the factors that influence Canadian consumers' desires to be among the first to try (early adopters) innovative functional foods. Using an Ordered Probit model, the researchers show that those consumers who strongly believe in the link between food and health and already believe in the current nutritional content claims on food are among the first to try new functional foods. Older consumers and consumers with negative attitudes towards GM foods are not early adopters of new functional foods. Demographically, the study shows that men, metropolitan consumers, consumers with children present in the household and consumers residing in the province of Québec are the most willing to be innovative in the nutritionally enhanced food market. Women are seen to be hesitant when faced with novel foods. Finally, the study also shows that consumers of all ages will accept these products if there is continuous assurance that the diet-related health claims are credible, valid and not compromised in any way.

The study examines the implications for both public and private sector efforts to provide information to consumers, arguing that there is a strong role for government regulatory oversight of health claims to reassure consumers that health claims are not false but are scientifically proven. The authors recommend that firms exhibit caution in the development and marketing process since consumer confidence can easily be undermined with claims that lack sufficient scientific evidence.

In another Canadian study, Peng et al. (2006) examine consumer attitudes towards (hypothetical) dairy products enriched with conjugated linoleic acid (CLA). Using data from a telephone survey of 803 consumers, a maximum likelihood Ordered Probit model is used to estimate the probability of purchasing CLA-enriched milk products. Belief that conventional milk is healthy is the main determinant of the acceptance of CLA-enriched dairy products among survey respondents, again highlighting the importance of attitudes towards the base product. The authors argue that the target consumer segment for this product should be health conscious, middle-aged consumers who believe conventional milk products are healthy.

Dairy products enriched with CLA are also the focus of a study by Maynard and Franklin (2003), who estimate US consumers' WTP for cancer-fighting dairy products. A CV survey, administered to 111 respondents, is used to estimate WTP for hypothetical dairy products. The results suggest consumers are willing to pay more for dairy products enriched with CLA, for example, on average an additional US$0.41 per US gallon for high-CLA milk, an additional US$0.38 per pound for high-CLA butter and US$0.15 per 8-ounce cup more for high-CLA yoghurt; 80 per cent of respondents were willing to pay at least US$0.20 more per gallon for milk with the purported cancer-fighting benefits of CLA. The study suggests that commercial prospects for high-CLA dairy products exist but cautions the need for additional evidence of health benefits and the support of the medical community for the development of robust market opportunities. The paucity of information and scientific evidence available to consumers concerning CLA-enriched products limits their current potential.

Turning to South America, Nepote et al. (2009) examine the relationship between overall acceptance and chemical indicators in roasted peanuts harvested from high-oleic peanut genotypes in Argentina. High-oleic oils can protect against CVD by lowering low density lipoprotein cholesterol. The study uses a panel of 100 consumers between the ages of 18 and 65 with the shared characteristics of being non-smokers, not suffering from allergies and being regular consumers of peanuts. Samples of peanuts with and without high oleic acid were roasted under similar conditions and packaged in identical bags. Chemical analysis was conducted on 20 g of peanut oil that was cold pressed from each sample. The results indicate that conventional peanuts are more susceptible to lipid oxidation compared to high-oleic acid peanuts. A low level of lipid oxidation is desirable as it reduces the risk of CVD. Overall consumer acceptance for the high-oleic peanuts is higher than that of conventional peanuts. The study recommends the replacement of conventional peanut cultivars with high-oleic acid peanut lines to gain the advantage of high stability against the lipid oxidation process without negative effects on consumer acceptance, leading to potential health benefits such as the reduction in the risk of cardiovascular diseases among consumers of peanuts.

In a Uruguayan study, Ares et al. (2010) examine the effect of price, brand and health claim on consumer choice of functional over regular yoghurt using Conjoint analysis. Cluster analysis of the Conjoint model results enables the authors to identify consumers with similar attitudes, while a Multinomial Logit model is used to estimate the utilities of each of the identified clusters. All four of the attributes – the type of yoghurt, brand, price and health claim – influence consumers' yoghurt choices; however, the effect of each of these attributes depends on attitudes towards health issues. Adding a functional ingredient such as fibre or antioxidants to the product increases the probability of consumers choosing functional yoghurt. Brands are important: consumers are more likely to choose a familiar brand of yoghurt with functional ingredients over unfamiliar brands. There are mixed reactions to price. In general, the probability of choosing a specific yoghurt decreases with an increase in the price, but the Cluster analysis shows that price sensitivity varies across consumers, with some consumers less concerned about price due to their interest in health issues. Finally, and in contrast to the findings from other countries, the presence of health claims on functional yoghurt appears to have little effect on consumers, emerging as the least important of the four attributes. Consumers exhibited a willingness to purchase functional yoghurt over regular yoghurt even in the absence of health claims.

In contrast, health claims are found to have a strongly positive effect on WTP in a survey of French consumers by Marette et al. (2010). These researchers also use yoghurt as the base product, which is functionally enriched with plant sterols to lower cholesterol, which in turn could lead to a reduction in the risk of CHD. Using 107 respondents, with a mix between those suffering from cholesterol problems and non-sufferers, the study combines a survey with a lab experiment to elicit attitudes and purchase intentions. The researchers find that WTP increases as a result of information being provided about the cholesterol-reducing properties of plant sterols. Both types of respondents (with and without cholesterol problems) indicated a higher WTP for the enriched yoghurt. The study therefore asserts that positive health information matters in the case of cholesterol. Preferences for this potential health benefit were very robust as, for example, provision of information regarding the lack of proof in the functional ingredient's efficacy and possible side-effects from the intake of plant sterols (for example, low absorption of vitamins A and E) did not significantly reduce consumers' WTP for the functional yoghurt. Thus, the study concludes that scientific uncertainties do not appear to have a significant impact on intentions to purchase, potentially leading to the proliferation of products with unsubstantiated claims. The authors argue that the process of approving health claims on food should be stringent to prevent the entry of these types of products into the market.

The issue of unsubstantiated or implied health claims is explored by Zou and Hobbs (2010) and Zou (2011), who examine the use of visual imagery to imply a health claim, for example, the picture of a red heart on a food package. These implied health claims are referred to as 'partial labelling', while 'full labelling' refers to the use of formal structure– function claims, disease risk reduction or disease prevention claims on food labels. The analyses use data from a survey of 740 Canadian consumers to examine consumer reactions to partial versus full labelling claims on omega-3-enhanced dairy products. Using a DCE, the authors also examine the credibility of health claims endorsed by different agencies, including a government agency (Health Canada) or a third party (Heart and Stroke Foundation).

The results indicate that full labelling is preferred to implied health claims but primarily for risk reduction claims. There is no significant difference between a function claim, such as 'good for your heart' and partial labelling in the form of a red heart image. While consumers respond positively to the verification of health claims, a Latent Class model reveals distinct consumer segments with considerable hetero- geneity in attitudes towards the source of verification. The research highlights the need for policymakers to ensure effective regulation of health claims to avoid misleading inferences through implied health claims and shows that verification of health claims remains an important means of reducing consumer uncertainty and boosting the credibility of approved health claims.

While the majority of studies have focused on attitudes towards functional foods, in 2005 a random telephone survey of over 2000 Canadians was conducted for Health Canada to determine awareness, attitudes and consumption behaviours with respect to NHPs (Ipsos Reid, 2005). The results of the national survey reveal low levels of familiarity with NHPs but a cautious willingness to use them. For example, more Canadians were unfamiliar (45 per cent) than familiar (36 per cent) with NHPs, with more women unfamiliar (41 per cent) relative to men (30 per cent). Nevertheless, a very slight majority of respondents (52 per cent) indicated a willingness to use NHPs to control or influence their personal health, with 20 per cent of the respondents having used NHPs due to a recommendation from a friend or a health professional. Only 29 per cent of respondents were of the belief that NHPs were safer than conventional medication. The primary reason for non-use of NHPs was lack of information. The key recommendations emerging from the study pertain to education and the regulatory environment; the study recommends that the government focus on the dissemination of NHP information to educate Canadians about choosing NHPs to manage their health, as well as informing the public about the role of NHPs regulations in safeguarding consumers.

Attitudes towards NHPs also feature in a Canadian study by Hailu et al. (2009). Using a mall intercept survey of over 200 Canadian consumers, the researchers use Conjoint analysis to examine consumers' preferences for probiotics. Mode of delivery or carrier of the functional ingredient (pill versus food) was a primary focus of the study. In the Conjoint analysis, probiotic products were described in terms of four attributes: mode of delivery; the existence of a health claim; health claim source; and cost. Cluster analysis was used to segment the sample into distinct groups linking consumer characteristics to their preferences for product attributes. The sample was segmented based on attitudes towards the mode of delivery or carriers of the functional food ingredient since this was the most important attribute across the sample. Three segments were identified: 'the pill lovers'; 'yoghurt lovers'; and 'the pill loathers'.

In a common theme across many of these studies, credible health claims are a major determinant of consumers' acceptance of these products. Hailu et al. (2009) suggest that, in general, consumers prefer claims verified by government over those from manufacturers; however, as with Zou (2011), there exists considerable heterogeneity in attitudes. Hailu et al. (2009) find that the consumer segments defined by their attitudes towards mode of delivery (the pill lovers, yoghurt lovers and pill loathers) also differ significantly in the value they place on the source of the health claim. The value placed on the source of the health claim is the strongest for 'pill lovers' and weakest for 'pill loathers'. Moreover, the study also confirms other consumer research where the base product for a functional food plays an important role in consumers' valuations of the enhanced food. It recommends that future research takes into account the potential substitution effects between functional foods and NHPs with attention to specific product or specific health benefits.

In another Canadian study focused on NHPs, Henson et al. (2010) investigate consumers' willingness to purchase food and/or non-prescription pills that contain phytosterols as a means to reduce the risk of CVD. The study uses an adaptation of Protection Motivation Theory to model consumer decision-making, focusing on the tendency of consumers to behave (consume food and/or pills) in a way that is aimed at reducing blood cholesterol, an important risk factor for CVD. The study is based on a mall intercept survey involving 446 respondents, approximately representative of the Canadian population demographically. The products used in the survey included a non-prescription pill, margarine, low-fat milk and bread, all containing phytosterols.

Determinants of purchase intentions are broadly grouped into 'response efficacy' and 'self-efficacy'. Response efficacy refers to the effectiveness of the product, or if consumers believe in the efficacy of the product. Self-efficacy refers to the ability to consume the products in the prescribed manner. Thus, consumers are more likely to use these products if they believe that these products work and that they are able to use the products in the prescribed manner. Perhaps surprisingly, personal fear of CVD does not appear to significantly affect consumers' purchasing intentions. Thus, consumers with a low fear of developing CVD are as likely to signal a willingness to use products containing phytosterols as consumers with high levels of fear. Furthermore, the study suggests that biomarkers, such as blood cholesterol tests indicating the risk of CVD, do not significantly affect consumers' willingness to purchase food and/or non-prescription pills that contain phytosterols. The results raise doubts about the effect of biomarkers on consumers' food purchasing behaviour.

The study concludes that health foods should be promoted as part of strategies to reduce the incidence of CVD. In addition, communication efforts should focus on the efficacy of the products and on the ease with which the product can be used, with communication directed at the general population rather than paying specific attention to the high risk segment. Finally, the form and type of products also deserve attention because health foods must be presented to consumers in a manner that they perceive to be easy to use in order for the desired level of the functional ingredient to be delivered (Henson et al., 2010).

The potential for consumer confusion and scepticism is a common theme in much of the literature. In an examination of the new EU regulatory framework for health foods, Mariotti et al. (2010) identify six sources of potential consumer confusion, all based upon discrepancies in consumer interpretations of a health claim and what the health claim is actually trying to communicate. The first is a wording issue where the use of jargon and terminology, both scientific and/or industry-specific, may be difficult for consumers to understand. The second highlights the discrepancies between consumers' interpretation of a claim and the scientific evidence assessed by experts. An example is the claim 'lipids provide energy to the body', where an expert assessment would interpret this claim as focusing on caloric provision but among consumers, the tendency is to perceive the concept of energy as being energizing and not to do with calorie provision.

The third issue is confusion between food and diet, where consumers may interpret the health claim in the context of overall diets but the claim focuses on a specific foodstuff, hence consumer understanding and scientific reality are misaligned. The fourth incongruity arises when consumers apply the concept of 'more is better' in their perception of a linear relationship between a nutrient/substance/food and the related effect in the claim; in reality, 'more is better' is often not the case. A fifth inconsistency arises when consumers assume that intake of a nutrient/ substance guarantees the associated health effect without considering other factors that may influence the health outcome stated in the health claim. The final discrepancy is confusion regarding target populations. This source of confusion arises when the health effects are only beneficial for a target population but the health claim does not identify a target population, leading consumers to assume that the specific claim is applicable to the general population. Recommendations to address these incongruities include banning or limiting certain claims, restriction on wording of claims and the inclusion of general disclaimer statements in health claims (Mariotti et al., 2010).

Given the ever-increasing number and variety of health food products, Spence (2006) also addresses the topic of consumer confusion, discussing the challenges faced by consumers in interpreting the particular health benefits of different products produced by different firms, all of which can foster negative attitudes towards functional food products. The study asserts that maintaining accurate information about functional food composition is a difficult task because firms must strike a balance between variety and nutrients, observing that despite scientific advancement the roles of dietary ingredients, particularly the non-traditional or emerging ingredients, may be difficult to determine with accuracy. Accurate information about functional food composition and health outcomes is critical to maintain the credibility of the industry.

While a great deal of consumer research has examined consumers' motivations for purchasing health foods, it is also instructive to consider the reasons consumers choose not to consume these products. Drawn from a US market research survey by Mintel (2006), Table 7.1 summarizes the reasons given by US consumers for not consuming functional foods, including the belief that products are overpriced, scepticism regarding health claims, the use of alternative means to boost health (in other words, vitamins, diet, lifestyle) and insufficient information.

As the discussion in this section has illustrated, a rich literature examining consumer attitudes towards the health foods sector has emerged across numerous countries, products and contexts, using a wide range of methodologies. Table A5.3 in Appendix 5 summarizes the literature presented in this chapter. The final section of this chapter offers a synthesis of the key messages arising from this literature.

Table 7.1 Reasons for not purchasing functional foods (US consumers)

Reasons	Per cent[a]
I think they are overpriced	43
I don't believe the claims they make	35
I take vitamin and mineral supplements instead	32
I already maintain a healthy diet and lifestyle	30
I don't know enough about them	29
They cost more than regular versions	28
Regular food or drinks already give me what I need	17
My prescription medication already gives me what I need	11
They could be bad for me	8
Other	7

Note: a. Total may not sum to 100 because respondents could choose more than one reason.

Source: Derived from Mintel (2006).

7.3 KEY MESSAGES

A great many factors affect consumer attitudes towards and WTP for health foods but the most important determinant is the perceived health benefit. A large number of studies conclude that, generally speaking, consumers have a positive attitude towards health foods, for which they are willing to pay a premium. The literature illustrates that consumer responses to these products depend on a variety of factors, including the belief in the correlation between diet and health or the health benefits derived from consumption of these products, socio-economic factors such as age, location, education and income levels, functional properties, acceptance of the base product, taste, price and potential side-effects, health claims and the credibility of these claims.

Consumers have become conscious of the correlation between diet and health and this trend is evident globally. Health benefits are paramount to consumer acceptance of health foods, even overshadowing many socio-economic determinants. Some studies show that consumer acceptance of health-enhancing products is conditional on the specific health benefit claimed by manufacturers; for example, reduced risk of CVD is of primary importance to some consumers, while others are enticed by potential physical and cognitive (mental) health benefits. Thus, the personal health status of the consumer (and his or her family) is likely to be a significant driver of health food demand by category.

In as much as consumer acceptance of health foods is widely evident in the literature, the attitudes of consumers differ among countries as well as within specific countries. For example, surveys suggest that North American consumers generally have a more positive attitude towards functional foods compared to consumers in France, while French consumers tended to be somewhat less knowledgeable about the functional food category (Labrecque et al., 2006). In other cross-country comparisons, Finnish consumers had a more positive attitude towards functional food than consumers in the USA and Denmark (Bech-Larsen and Grunert, 2003). Nevertheless, broad-brush national stereotyping is dangerous and runs the risk of glossing over more nuanced consumer attitudes within a population. Indeed, a number of studies have shown that, even within a specific country, consumer segments with distinct attitudes towards health foods can be identified based on a range of socio-economic factors including age, education, gender, family status, incomes, region, profession and also prior beliefs.

Many of the profiled studies gauge consumer acceptance of health foods through estimating WTP as a measure of the marginal utility gained from consumption of these products, often finding that WTP is moderated by the underlying technology embedded in the product. The use of genetic modification or additives tends to decrease acceptance and enthusiasm for new health food products.

A recurrent theme in the literature is the need to consider the nature of the underlying food product and its primary function as a foodstuff first, with its role as a vehicle for delivery of health benefits a secondary consideration. In other words, existing attitudes towards the base product, as well as the taste of the functional food, remain very relevant determinants of consumer acceptance. Base products that are already perceived to be healthy have a higher likelihood of acceptance as carriers of a functional component. Although there are some discrepancies across the profiled studies, research generally suggests that consumers are not willing to compromise on taste when purchasing functional food, therefore, taste and base products remain important considerations for manufacturers when developing new health food products.

The credibility of information pertaining to these products and their health claims is a leading determinant of acceptance and WTP. Surveys suggest that consumers in many countries generally believe in the safety of health foods but require more credible information, with a heavy emphasis on 'credible'. Although information dissemination is vital for the growth of the industry, the potential for consumers to be misled by unsubstantiated health claims supports the need for the verification of health claims by government agencies, stringent approval processes and communication through trusted sources.

A host of socio-demographic variables influence attitudes towards functional foods, while pricing and potential side-effects also have an influence on attitudes. Nevertheless, there exists little consensus regarding the direction of many of these effects. With respect to age, some Canadian studies have shown that older consumers are more receptive to health foods than younger consumers (for example, Herath et al., 2008a; West and Larue, 2004), while another study suggests that middle-aged consumers are more likely to buy functional food (Peng et al., 2006). In total contrast, studies from Europe seem to show that younger consumers have a more favourable attitude towards health foods compared to older consumers (for example, in the UK and Belgium), while the reverse is true in other countries (for example, Switzerland). In Canadian studies, consumers with children and teenagers in their household were more likely to buy health-enhancing (functional food) products, while in UK studies, health-enhancing products (supplements) were rejected by families with children under the age of 18. General conclusions regarding the effect of age on consumer attitudes towards health foods are therefore difficult to infer, except to note that the effect of variables such as age must be interpreted within the context of the study (type of product, health issue being addressed).

The same observation pertains to the effect of other socio-demographic variables such as income and education. Some Canadian studies suggest that lower-income households and the less educated appeared to be more receptive to health foods compared to the higher-income and highly educated people from urban areas (Herath et al., 2008a). However, a UK study found that it was households with higher incomes and higher education levels that were more receptive to functional food (Arnoult et al., 2007), while in Belgium, households with higher levels of education are less likely to be accepting of functional food but high-income households view these products positively (Verbeke, 2005).

Results for gender also differ, with one UK study indicating that women were willing to pay a premium for functional food but mostly rejected supplements (Arnoult et al., 2007), whereas some Canadian studies have shown that it was men who were more receptive to functional food (West and Larue, 2004), despite the finding that women were more familiar with NHPs than men (Ipsos Reid, 2005).

Geographic location also produced mixed results in the literature. Contradicting studies in Canada find urban consumers are both more and less receptive to functional foods (Herath et al., 2008a; West and Larue,

2004), while a UK study characterized urban consumers as being more receptive to functional food (Arnoult et al., 2007). These comparisons suggest that demographic profiling of consumer segments, while helpful in building a general picture of a market, is too broad an approach to yield productive insights that can be extrapolated successfully across markets and contexts. Indeed, the consumer context is critical; for example, health issues may well have different priority levels across different age profiles. As such, it remains important for researchers to consider psychographic variables capturing individual attitudes towards food and health as well as determinants of trust in information sources.

While the bulk of the literature in this area pertains to functional foods, a number of studies examine supplements. The health benefit derived from supplements is important, but many consumers also appear to use supplements based upon the recommendations of friends and health professionals. Common reasons for consumer reticence towards supplements include lack of information, lack of believability in health claims, inability to distinguish between supplements and functional foods and a fear of negative side-effects.

A number of recommendations emerge from the literature. There is the need for credible information about the benefits of these products and their safety and this information should come from reliable sources outside the food industry, with government experts and health care experts as the preferred choices. Efficacy is critical. If consumers do not believe the products are effective, they will not buy them. The form in which the product is delivered is a component of efficacy; people will not consume a functional food or a supplement if it is too inconvenient to do so. The need for stringent approval processes for health claims is emphasized across numerous studies, as is the need for dissemination of information about health foods from credible sources.

The literature highlights a host of factors that influence consumer attitudes towards health foods. Many of the products examined in these studies were new or even hypothetical – an inevitability given the nascent state of the market for the health foods sector. Over time, Revealed Preference market data on established products will enable longer-term studies of the growth (or demise) of products with specific health benefits. As these markets continue to evolve and new scientific advances deliver novel products with new health benefits spurring new health claims, there will be a continued need for research – using both Revealed Preference and Stated Preference techniques – that helps us understand consumers' responses to new foods with health benefits.

NOTES

1. A summary of this literature is available in Table A5.3 in Appendix 5.
2. For more information on the use of Conjoint analysis see Hair et al. (2006).
3. For more information on the use of Discrete Choice Experiments see Train (2003).
4. For more information on the use of Factor analysis and Cluster analysis see Hair et al. (2006).
5. Protection Motivation Theory posits that when making protection decisions individuals undertake an implicit threat appraisal (how severe is the threat, how likely is it to occur) and an implicit coping appraisal (the extent to which measures can be taken to remove the threat and their perceived ability to undertake these measures).

8. Through the looking glass

The health foods sector continues to evolve as scientific discoveries lead to the creation of innovative products, consumers are motivated to pursue healthier diets and new market opportunities arise in established and emerging markets. It is a fiercely competitive sector in which the pressure for new product formulations offering verifiable health benefits constantly pushes the boundaries of the regulatory environment governing new product approvals and allowable health claims.

This book began with three broad objectives: the primary objective has been to present an in-depth analysis of health claims policies and regulatory frameworks governing the health foods sector internationally. Against this backdrop, the second objective has been to present an overview of the industry and market trends in major international markets including the USA, EU and Japan, as well as a detailed case study analysis of a smaller but growing market – Canada. Ultimately, the long-run growth and sustainability of the health foods sector internationally is dependent upon consumers: the extent to which products purporting to offer health benefits are attractive to consumers and whether the health claims accompanying these products are credible. The third objective, therefore, has been to provide a detailed examination of the growing body of literature exploring consumer responses to health foods and the role of health claims. While this can never be a comprehensive consideration of all the literature examining consumer attitudes towards health foods, the intent has been to capture a broad sampling of relevant socio-economic studies. In examining the consumer behaviour literature, the regulatory landscape governing allowable health claims again provides essential context.

In this final chapter, we draw together insights from the preceding chapters to identify common themes in regulatory approaches and discuss ongoing policy challenges. Section 8.1 identifies the primary sources of market failure that provide the motivations for policy intervention and discusses several policy priorities. Section 8.2 highlights points of similarity and divergence among international regulatory frameworks and discusses the implications for firms, consumers and policymakers. Section 8.3 concludes the chapter with a forward-looking view of the opportunities that lie ahead.

8.1 THE MOTIVATIONS FOR POLICY INTERVENTION

As the discussion in Chapter 3 indicates, two rationales exist for policies to correct demand side market failures in the health foods sector. The first, and primary, motive for regulatory oversight is asymmetric information. In the absence of credible labelling information, consumers may under-consume healthy foods or over-consume unhealthy foods. Health claims that are later shown to be false or misleading can also undermine consumer confidence in the product category in general, weakening demand and damaging the collective reputation of firms in the sector. Potential welfare gains therefore exist for (honest) firms and consumers in resolving the information problems in this market through the establishment of agreed-upon rules of scientific evidence and a common basis upon which to make health claims.

A second type of market failure – externalities from the under-consumption of healthier food (or over-consumption of unhealthy food), which create a long-run cost burden for society – is not likely to be addressed simply through improved information and labelling. Policies that encourage innovations and facilitate approval of foods with health benefits should assist in addressing this market failure to a degree but are unlikely to solve it entirely: ultimately, people must still choose to consume these products. Finally, markets may produce suboptimal levels of investment in foods with health benefits if there are significant positive spillovers (free-riding) that reduce the incentive to innovate.

Regulation in this sense is a double-edged sword. While governments have moved to establish regulatory frameworks governing the use of health claims and the approval of new products with novel traits to protect consumers, overly slow and restrictive approval processes and weak protection of IPR will blunt firms' incentives to innovate.

The proliferation of health claims and the variety in terminology has been the source of confusion and mistrust among health professionals and consumers. Discrepancies between the actual scientific meaning of a claim and consumer perceptions of the meaning can be a problem and associative discrepancies also cause confusion. Examples include interchanging the words 'food' (product-specific) and 'diet' (generalized), a belief that consuming 'more is better' contrary to actual product usage, or attaching the concept of 'energizing' to the word 'energy' rather than caloric provision.

Several steps could be taken if the goal is to improve the information available to consumers to facilitate better choices and to provide consumers with healthier food options. Countries could permit 'qualified' health claims, as is the case in the USA and Japan. The authorization of these claims requires lower standards of evidence and usually requires the provision of a disclosure statement or less authoritative wording. Some countries reject the use of lower standards for disease reduction claims because of the risk of misleading consumers. Qualified structure/function claims may be more palatable. Nevertheless, this must be balanced against the need for consumer protection and the potential for consumer confusion if a health claim is accompanied by a long list of 'small print' caveats. To that end, does a health claim with significant caveats actually reduce information asymmetry or does it merely add noise to the quality signals available to consumers? This question is a fruitful area for future consumer research.

Despite information provision and attempts to foster informed choice among consumers, the use of regulatory measures alone may not be sufficient. If the objective of encouraging healthier diets is a healthier population, labelling alone may not be sufficient to change consumption behaviour if consumers do not directly bear the full consequences of their choices. If the consequence of choosing a less healthy diet is the risk of illness and its associated costs, consumers should logically choose a healthier diet. However, when the consequences of poor decisions (in other words, illness) are borne in part by a third party (in other words, public health care or private health insurance), their ability to act as a motivator for socially optimal choices is diluted. Other barriers to the adoption of healthier diets exist, including access, income, habit, uncertainty and time preferences (in other words, trading off current certain gains for future uncertain health losses) and the disutility arising from having to make adjustments to lifestyles. Thus, the establishment of regulatory frameworks governing health claims and new product approvals are pieces of a larger policy puzzle.[1]

The protection of IP is another piece of the policy puzzle. A potential step to encourage private sector R&D would be to allow product-specific health claims. Generic claims create a free-rider problem because many firms benefit but only one firm has to go through the application process to obtain approval for a new health claim. Allowing product-specific claims (as is the case in Japan, South Korea and China) reduces spillover benefits that would otherwise accrue to other firms producing similar products. Nevertheless, the generic health claim system has the advantage that more products can use approved health claims with the potential to facilitate improved consumer knowledge of the relationship between diet and health. A middle ground could be to consider a blended approach with both generic and product-specific health claims available in different contexts.

8.2 POLICIES IN CONFLICT?

A salient lesson from the review of policies towards health claims and product approvals in various countries presented in Chapters 4 and 5 is the notable differences in regulatory approaches, despite being based on the same underlying science. Indeed, as the discussion in Chapter 2 illustrates, there is no common international definition of functional food, of supplements or of nutraceuticals, and while definitions of functional food at least tend to have a common basis, 'supplements' and 'nutraceuticals' receive somewhat more diverse treatment. Overlapping terminology is common: in South Korea, Taiwan and Russia, for example, the definition of functional food is equivalent to a supplement/nutraceutical, whereas a nutraceutical is now defined as an NHP in Canada and as a dietary supplement in the USA.

Some countries do not make a regulatory distinction between supplements and (functional) food (Japan and China, for example). In other countries, the two categories are distinct from a regulatory perspective, as is the case in Canada where NHPs face a product-specific regulatory system but functional foods utilize generic health claims. Brazil and Australia also regulate supplements differently from food, using a product-specific system with a more substantial level of evidence required. South Korea is the primary example of this category, restricting functional foods to supplements and requiring licences, even for vendors of the products, not just the manufacturers. While the USA does distinguish between food and dietary supplements, it does not impose significantly different regulations (the same generic claims are available to both product categories). New Zealand treats dietary supplements like food, but does not permit certain claims (including disease risk reduction claims) on supplements. However, the regulatory requirements for dietary supplements are more relaxed. The EU treats food supplements as a 'food', but restricts the definition of food supplements to vitamins and minerals.

Navigating this complex array of regulatory approaches can be a bureaucratic nightmare for firms wishing to access international markets who must attempt to determine which set of regulations apply to their products and the extent to which the same product faces different regulatory requirements in different markets. Disparate regulatory requirements with respect to what constitutes an allowable health claim and whether firms can use an approved generic health claim or must seek approval for a product-specific health claim raise the costs of accessing international markets and are an unintended consequence of regulation.

One implication of treating supplements and food as equivalent from a regulatory perspective is that regulation does not factor into a firm's decision about which format to use (food versus pill and so on) when researching and developing a new product. Regulation does not distort the costs or benefits of using food relative to supplements as the carrier for the functional ingredient. Countries that impose quite different sets of regulations on foods versus supplements, as is the case in Canada, create a more complex decision environment for firms. Often in these countries if firms choose the food route, although the regulation may be less stringent, the (generic) health claim does not belong to that firm on that product alone. If the firm chooses to register the product as a supplement, then a product-specific claim is available (with potential monopoly rents) but the product must meet more stringent approval processes. As a result, a firm's decision to develop and manufacture food or supplements is likely to depend on how the firm views these trade-offs, as well as the perceived level of uncertainty in the health claims approval process.

In some jurisdictions, efforts are being made to harmonize regulations or to recognize equivalence in regulatory standards but, for the most part, regulatory approaches between countries remain quite distinct. This can be particularly important in relatively small markets such as Australia, New Zealand or Canada, where firms may be deterred from seeking approvals for new products or new health claims if the process is perceived as overly slow or costly given the relatively limited market potential compared to, say, the US or EU markets with their considerably larger population bases. Examples of harmonized health claims regulations exist, for example, between Australia and New Zealand, as well as across the member states of the EU. The development of new EU-wide regulations and enforcement mechanisms is expected to reduce confusion and remove inconsistencies across member states. The existence of Codex Alimentarius guidelines also provides a common basis on which countries can align their regulatory frameworks. Nevertheless, the prospects for widespread international harmonization seem remote. Establishing equivalence (for example, recognizing another country's health claims) is a possible route for functional foods. Indeed, in some countries, many of the approved health claims are based on claims already approved in another country; this is true to some extent for

Canada with respect to health claims already approved in the US market, although a separate assessment is made of the same evidence. For the most part, however, substantial differences remain in product approval processes and the means by which health claims are substantiated.

The regulatory system for health claims on functional foods and supplements continues to evolve. As ever, the policy challenge for regulators is to find the right balance between the protection of consumers from fraudulent or misleading health claims while creating a regulatory environment that facilitates scientific discovery and the development and commercialization of products with tangible health benefits.

Similar challenges arise in the development of policies governing novel food registration, which balances the requirements to protect consumers and ensure food safety while at the same time avoiding draconian rules that deter or displace R&D activities to other less restrictive markets. The US system for novel food registration is relatively favourable towards encouraging research, but has fairly loose oversight of novel foods. On the other hand, the EU imposes extremely strict requirements on novel food approvals and has not been particularly conducive to the development and introduction of GM food products, regardless of whether these are also functional foods with health benefits.

The joint Australia and New Zealand policy is an interesting approach, offering a potential middle ground. In Australia and New Zealand, novel food must undergo a rigorous safety evaluation process, but approved novel foods are eligible for exclusive market access to Australia and New Zealand for 15 months, to the exclusion of other products. The 15-month exemption provides incentives for novel functional food research by reducing the spillover benefits that accrue to other firms when one firm applies for novel food registration. In other countries, once a food product receives novel food approval, other firms producing similar products can all enter the market simultaneously without bearing the costs of novel food approval and registration.

Nutrition and nutrient labelling elicits far more consensus internationally. Generally speaking, nutrition labels are required when nutrient claims are made and a number of countries have mandatory nutrition labelling requirements. Differences exist, however, with respect to which nutrients must be included on labels, requiring firms to adjust their labelling profiles depending on the market of interest.

8.3   A BRIGHT FUTURE

The policy challenges notwithstanding, the health foods sector remains a vibrant and growing component of the global food industry. With ageing populations, increasing incomes and changing lifestyles, consumer interest in health foods looks set to continue. Scientific innovations in the isolation, purification and enhancement of food attributes continue to reveal new possibilities for delivering health benefits. For firms, this creates new market opportunities and pathways for product differentiation within a dynamic, highly competitive sector. At the same time, policymakers face the need for ongoing evaluation of regulatory landscapes to ensure that policies meet the twin objectives of ensuring consumer protection and facilitating beneficial innovations. Credible communication of health benefits to consumers remains important, both to the industry and to regulators. The means by which consumers access and process health information, and the extent to which labelling or other forms of information elicit a change in consumption behaviour, remain rich areas for further research.

This book set out to explore and document the regulatory frameworks governing the health foods sector from a social science perspective and to consider key industry, market and consumer trends in the context of the regulatory analysis. While every effort has been taken to make this assessment as comprehensive as possible, inevitably gaps remain, circumstances change, industries and policies evolve. As such, the topics explored in this book will continue to be relevant subjects for further social science analysis in the years to come. We hope that the lens through which industry and policy landscapes have been explored within this book provides a useful basis upon which to build.

NOTE

1.   A full consideration of these policies is beyond the scope of this book. Interested readers are referred to the growing behavioural economics literature examining 'nudging' and the effectiveness of policies to promote healthier food consumption decisions in, for example, Galizzi (2014), Liu et al. (2014) and Thaler and Sunstein (2008).

Appendix 1: Summary of labelling claims by country

This appendix contains tables summarizing allowable health claims in various countries, including structure/function claims (Table A1.1) disease risk reduction claims (Table A1.2) and nutrient content claims (Table A1.3).

Table A1.1 Examples of structure/function claims

United States of America

FDA does not evaluate or regulate structure/function claims for food. FDA does have minimal regulation for dietary supplement structure/function claims, but does not evaluate the claims.

Canada

Food (generic claims)

Food or food constituent

- coarse wheat bran and regularity
- green tea and antioxidant effect on blood
- psyllium and regularity

Nutrients, vitamins and minerals (nutrient function claims)

- protein and body tissues or antibodies or strong muscles
- fat and energy or absorption of fat-soluble vitamins
- ARA[a] and development of brain, eyes and nerves in young children
- DHA[b] and development of brain, eyes and nerves in young children
- carbohydrates and energy or utilization of fat
- vitamin A and bones and teeth or night vision or healthy skin and membranes
- vitamin D and bones and teeth or calcium and phosphorus utilization
- vitamin E as antioxidant or oxidation of fatty tissues

- vitamin C as antioxidant or bones and cartilage or teeth and gums or protection against free radicals
- thiamine (vitamin B$_1$) and carbohydrates or normal growth
- riboflavin (vitamin B$_2$) and metabolism or tissue formation
- niacin and growth and development or metabolism or tissue formation
- vitamin B$_6$ and energy metabolism or tissue formation
- folate and red blood cell formation or foetal neural development
- vitamin B$_{12}$ and red blood cell formation
- pantothenic acid and metabolism and tissue formation
- calcium and bones and teeth
- phosphorus and bones and teeth
- magnesium and metabolism and tissue formation and bone development
- iron and red blood cell formation
- zinc and metabolism and tissue formation
- iodine and thyroid gland function
- selenium as antioxidant or protection against oxidative stress

Nutraceuticals/supplements

Called natural health products (NHPs) and subject to product-specific registration. While the same claims that are used on food could be used on nutraceuticals, each firm desiring to make a product with the claim must receive approval individually. No list of claims available.

European Union

General Structure/Function (Article 13(1)(a)) claims

Food and food supplements (generic claims)

In EU Regulation 1924/2006, no structure/function claims were initially provided for. Member states and other stakeholders have provided the European Food Safety Authority (EFSA) and the EU Commission with thousands of structure/function ('general function' health) claims. The European Health Claims Regulation (EHCR) initially allowed 222 approved generic health claims for use on food, with new claims approved by EFSA on an ongoing basis.

Children's Growth and Development (Article 14(1)(b)) claims

- α-linolenic acid (ALA) and linoleic acid (LA) and normal growth/development of children

- docosahexaenoic acid (DHA) and normal visual, brain development in foetus and infants
- calcium and vitamin D and normal growth and development of bone in children
- phosphorus and growth and development of bone in children
- protein and growth and development of bone in children
- iron contributes to normal cognitive development of children
- vitamin D and normal growth and development of bone in children

Emerging Scientific Evidence/Request for Proprietary Information (Article 13(5)) claims

- Water-soluble tomato concentrate and blood flow

Japan

Food and nutraceuticals (generic claims)

Vitamin claims

- niacin and skin or mucous membranes
- pantothenic acid and skin or mucous membranes
- biotin and skin or mucous membranes
- vitamin A and night vision or skin or mucous membranes
- vitamin B_1 and skin or mucous membranes
- vitamin B_2 and skin or mucous membranes
- vitamin B_6 and energy from protein or skin or mucous membranes
- vitamin B_{12} and red blood cell formation
- vitamin C and skin or mucous membranes or antioxidant
- vitamin D and absorption of calcium or bone growth
- vitamin E and prevention of fat oxidation or cell health
- folic acid and red blood cell formation or normal foetus development

Mineral claims

- zinc and normal taste or skin or mucous membranes or protein and nucleic acid metabolism
- calcium and bone and teeth development
- iron and red blood cell formation
- copper and red blood cell formation or enzymes function or bone formation
- magnesium and bone and teeth development or enzymes function or energy generation

Regular/Specific, Standardized and Qualified FOSHU (product-specific)

No list of FOSHU products and effects are available. Well over 600 products possess FOSHU registration.

Australia and New Zealand

Food (generic claims)

FSANZ list of pre-approved general-level claims (not exhaustive)

- vitamin D and calcium for phosphorus utilization and absorption
- vitamin E as antioxidant
- vitamin K for proper coagulation
- thiamine and normal metabolism of carbohydrates, neurological function
- riboflavin and metabolism, nervous system, vision
- niacin and metabolism, neurological function, fatigue
- pantothenic acid and metabolism of fat, mental performance, fatigue
- vitamin B_6 and protein metabolism, iron metabolism, energy metabolism
- folate and blood formation, amino acid synthesis
- vitamin B_{12} and blood formation
- biotin and energy metabolism, psychological function, hair and skin
- vitamin C and connective tissue
- calcium and bones and teeth, metabolism, blood coagulation, digestion
- magnesium and energy metabolism, muscle function, fatigue, psychological function
- iron and blood formation, cognitive function, fatigue
- copper and immune system, neurological function, metabolism
- iodine and thyroid hormones, neurological function, energy metabolism
- zinc and wound healing, cognitive function, hair and nails
- manganese and bone function, energy metabolism
- phosphorus and bones and teeth, energy metabolism
- selenium and immune system function, thyroid hormones
- protein and building and repairing body tissues
- DHA and brain, eyes and neural development
- dietary fibre and normal laxation
- potassium
- chromium and macronutrient metabolism
- fluoride and tooth mineralization
- molybdenum and sulphur amino acid metabolism, liver function
- choline and homocysteine metabolism, fat metabolism
- vitamin A and vision, iron metabolism, immune system

- folic acid and foetal neural tube development
- beta-glucan and reduced blood cholesterol
- carbohydrate and normal metabolism
- energy and normal metabolism

Nutraceuticals/supplements

In Australia, regulated as complementary medicines (claims are product-specific). In New Zealand, regulated as dietary supplements, no pre-market approval required for claims.

Brazil

Food (generic claims)
- lycopene as antioxidant
- dietary fibres and normal intestine function
- powdered resistant dextrin (dietary fibre) and normal intestine function
- partially hydrolyzed guar gum (dietary fibre) and normal intestine function
- polydextrose (dietary fibre) and normal intestine function
- fructo-oligosaccharides and gut flora
- inulin and gut flora
- lactulose and normal intestine function
- probiotics and gut flora
- lutein as an antioxidant
- Zeaxan as an antioxidant

Nutraceuticals/supplements

Called bioactive substances and subject to product-specific regulations and approval.

Russia

Nutraceuticals/supplements (biologically active food supplements or BAFS) (product-specific) examples

- optimization of carbohydrates, fat, vitamins and other metabolism in various functional conditions
- normalization and/or improvement of the function state of the human organ/system
- decrease morbidity risk
- improvement of the gastrointestinal tract microflora

India

Food and nutraceuticals/supplements (generic)
No list of claims available.

China

Food and nutraceuticals/supplements are called health foods (product-specific claims).
- enhances immunity
- antioxidative
- assists in memory improvement
- alleviates eye fatigue
- facilitates lead excretion
- moistens and cleans throat
- improves sleep
- facilitates milk secretion
- alleviates physical fatigue
- enhances anoxia endurance
- assists in irradiation hazard protection
- improves child growth and development
- increases bone density
- improves nutritional anaemia
- assists in protecting against chemical injury to the liver
- eliminates acne
- eliminates skin chloasma
- improves skin's water content
- improves skin's oil content
- regulates gastrointestinal tract flora
- facilitates digestion
- facilitates faeces excretion
- assists in protecting against gastric mucosa damage

South Korea

Nutraceuticals/supplements

Generic and product-specific claims available. Generic claims available on a wide range of product ingredients where no pre-market approval is required as long as the nutrients have an established recommended daily allowance. No list of claims available.

There are qualified claims ('other function' claims with lower level of evidence) that do not fall into either of the two categories of claims

- reduction of blood pressure
- reduction of cholesterol
- reduction of body fat
- maintenance of good health
- modulation of blood glucose level
- modulation of postprandial glucose level
- maintaining health gastrointestinal conditions
- antioxidant effects
- improvement of memory functions
- improvement of cognitive functions

Taiwan

Food and nutraceuticals/supplements called health foods(product-specific claims)

Health maintenance claims include

- regulates blood lipid
- improves gastrointestinal functions
- alleviates osteoporosis
- maintains dental health
- regulates immune system
- regulates blood sugar level
- protects the liver

Notes:

a. Arachidonic acid, an omega-6 fatty acid.
b. Docosahexaenoic, an omega-3 fatty acid.

Source: Derived from CFIA and Health Canada (2009), CFS (2008), EC (2013a), FAO (2004), FDA (2009c), FSANZ (2008b, 2013a), FSSA (2006), Kim et al. (2008), Liu and Lee (2000), MHLW (n.d.b), Toledo and Lajolo (2008), Tutelyan and Sukhanov (2008), Stringueta et al. (2012), Yang (2008), Zawistowski (2008).

Table A1.2   Examples of disease risk reduction claims

United States of America

Food and dietary supplements (generic claims)

Claims meeting Significant Scientific Agreement (SSA)

- calcium, vitamin D and osteoporosis
- dietary lipids (fats) and cancer

- dietary saturated fat and cholesterol and risk of coronary heart disease
- dietary non-cariogenic carbohydrate sweeteners and dental caries
- fibre-containing grain products and cancer
- folate and neural tube defects (in infants)
- fruits and vegetables and cancer
- fruits, vegetables and grain products high in fibre, particularly soluble fibre and risk of coronary heart disease
- sodium and hypertension
- soluble fibre from certain foods and risk of coronary heart disease
- soy protein and risk of coronary heart disease
- plant sterol/stanol esters and risk of coronary heart disease
- potassium and the risk of high blood pressure and strokes
- wholegrain foods and risk of heart disease and certain cancers
- fluoridated water and reduced risk of dental caries
- saturated fat, cholesterol and trans fat and reduced risk of heart disease
- substitution of saturated fat with unsaturated fatty acids and heart disease

Qualified health claims

- tomatoes and/or tomato sauce and prostate cancer
- tomato sauce and ovarian cancer
- tomatoes and gastric cancer
- tomatoes and pancreatic cancer
- calcium and colon/rectal cancer
- calcium and recurrent colon polyps
- green tea and cancer
- selenium and cancer
- antioxidant vitamins and cancer
- nuts and heart disease
- walnuts and heart disease
- omega-3 fatty acids and coronary heart disease
- B vitamins and vascular disease
- monounsaturated fatty acids from olive oil and heart disease
- unsaturated fats from canola oil and heart disease
- corn oil and heart disease
- phosphatidylserine and dementia
- phosphatidylserine and cognitive dysfunction
- chromium picolinate and diabetes

- folic acid and neural tube defects (claim recommends twice the intake of approved SSA claim)
- calcium and hypertension
- calcium and pregnancy-induced hypertension or pre-eclampsia

Canada

Food (generic claims)

- low sodium intake and reduced risk of high blood pressure
- calcium and reduced risk of osteoporosis
- a diet low in saturated fat, cholesterol and trans fatty acids and reduced risk of CHD
- consumption of fruit and vegetables and reduced risk of some kinds of cancer
- psyllium products and blood cholesterol lowering
- plant sterols (phytosterols) and blood cholesterol lowering
- oat products and blood cholesterol lowering
- barley products and blood cholesterol lowering
- unsaturated fat and blood cholesterol lowering
- sugar-free chewing gum and dental caries risk reduction
- ground whole flaxseed and blood cholesterol lowering

Natural health products (NHPs)

Require product-specific registration. While the same claims that are used on food could be used on NHPs, each firm desiring to make a product with the claim must receive approval individually. No list of claims available.

European Union

Food and food supplements (generic claims) (Article 14(1)(a): disease risk reduction claims)

Food supplements and are eligible to bear the same claims as food, for example

- plant sterol esters and reduced blood cholesterol, lower CHD risk
- plant stanol esters and reduced blood cholesterol, lower CHD risk
- chewing gum sweetened with 100 per cent xylitol and reduced dental plaque
- barley beta-glucans and reduced blood cholesterol, lower CHD risk
- oat beta-glucans and reduced blood cholesterol, lower CHD risk
- sugar-free chewing gum and reduced risk of dental caries

Japan

Food and nutraceuticals/supplements

Regular/Specific FOSHU (product-specific)

- calcium and osteoporosis
- folic acid and neural tube defects in infants

Standardized and Qualified FOSHU (product-specific)

No list of Standardized and Qualified FOSHU claims and products available. Well over 600 products have FOSHU approval.

Standardized FOSHU example: claims about maintaining gastrointestinal functioning and health.

Australia and New Zealand

Food (generic claims): high-level claims

- folate and neural tube defects in infants
- sodium (with or without potassium) and hypertension, reduced risk of CHD
- fruits and vegetables and reduced risk of CHD
- saturated fat and/or trans fat and lower cholesterol, reduced risk of heart disease
- calcium (with or without vitamin D) and osteoporosis, bone density
- beta-glucan and reduced cholesterol
- phytosterols, phytostanols and reduced cholesterol

Nutraceuticals/supplements

In Australia, regulated as complementary medicines (claims are product-specific). In New Zealand, regulated as dietary supplements, no pre-market approval required for claims (generic claims). Moves underway to harmonize regulations.

Brazil

Food (generic claims)

- omega-3 fatty acids and triglycerides (heart health)
- beta-glucan (dietary fibre) and cholesterol
- psyllium (dietary fibre) and fat absorption
- chitosan and fat and cholesterol absorption
- phytosterols and cholesterol
- mannitol, xylitol or sorbitol and dental caries
- soy protein and cholesterol

Nutraceuticals/supplements

Called bioactive substances and subject to product-specific regulations and approval.

Russia

Nutraceuticals (biologically active food supplements or BAFS)

Disease risk reduction claims not permitted.

India

Food and nutraceuticals/supplements

Disease risk reduction claims not permitted.

China

Food and nutraceuticals are called health foods (product-specific)

Approved functions:

- weight loss
- cholesterol (blood lipids) reduction
- assists in blood sugar reduction
- assists in blood pressure reduction

South Korea

Nutraceuticals/supplements (product-specific)

- reduction of dental caries

There are specified products (supplements and ginseng) and ingredients on which generic claims can be made.

Taiwan

Food and nutraceuticals called health foods

Health Food Control Act health claims must be proven for health and/or disease risk.

Source: Derived from CFIA and Health Canada (2009), EAS (2009), EC (2013a), FAO (2004), FDA (2009a, 2009d), FSANZ (2010a, 2010c, 2013a), FSSA (2006), Health Canada (2010), Kim et al. (2008), Liu and Lee (2000), MHLW (n.d.a), NZTE (2009), Toledo and Lajolo (2008), Yang (2008), Zawistowski (2008).

Table A1.3   Examples of nutrient content claims, by select country

United States of America	
Claim	*Applicable nutrient*
Free	Calories, fat, saturated fat, sodium, sugars
Low	Calories, fat, saturated fat, sodium
Reduced/less	Calories, fat, saturated fat, sodium, sugars

Special claims	*Claim example*
Comparative claims	Light, Reduced or added, More or less
Nutrients with daily recommended values	High, Good source, Fortified[a] High potency[b]
Seafood and game meat fat content	Lean, Extra lean
Other	Healthy, Antioxidant claims, Fibre claims, Modified

Canada	
Claim	*Applicable nutrient*
Free, Low, Reduced/light, Lower source, More Representation that food is for use in 'reduced energy' diet, Representation that food is for 'special dietary use' vis-à-vis energy value, 'Diet' food	Energy
Low, Source, Excellent source, More	Protein
Free/100 per cent fat free, Low, Reduced, Lower (percentage), Fat free, No added fat, Light, Lean, Extra lean	Fat
Free, Low, Reduced, Lower	Saturated fat

Free, Reduced, Lower	Trans fat
Source of omega-3, Source of omega-6	Polyunsaturated fat
Free, Low, Reduced, Lower	Cholesterol
Free, Low, Reduced, Lower, No added sodium/salt, Lightly salted Representation that food is for use in 'sodium-restricted diets' Representation that food is 'for special dietary use' with respect to sodium content	Sodium/salt
Source, Good source, Excellent source	Potassium
Free, Reduced, Lower, No added sugars	Sugars
Source, High source, Very high source, More	Fibre
Contains, Good source/high, Excellent source/very rich/rich, Added/fortified, Higher	Vitamin/mineral

European Union

Claim	*Applicable nutrient*
Low, Reduced, Free	Energy
Low, Free	Fat
Low, Free	Saturated fat
Low, Free, None added	Sugars
Low, Very low, Free	Sodium/salt
Source, High	Fibre
Source, High	Protein
Source, High	Vitamins/minerals
Contains [name of nutrient], Increased [name of nutrient], Reduced [name of nutrient]	Generic[c]
Source of omega-3 fatty acids, High in omega-3 fatty acids,	Unsaturated fat[d]

High monounsaturated fat, High
polyunsaturated fat, High
unsaturated fat

Light/lite, Natural/naturally	Other

Japan	
Claim	*Applicable nutrient*
High	Protein (15 g/100 g solid food, or 7.5 g/100 ml liquid food and 7.5 g/100 kcal)
	Dietary fibre (6g /100 g, or 3 g/100 ml and 3 g/100 kcal)
	Zinc (2.10 mg/100 g, or 1.05 mg/ml and 0.70 mg/100 kcal)
	Calcium (210 mg/100 g, or 105 mg/ml and 70 mg/100 kcal)
	Iron (2.25 mg/100 g, or 1.13 mg/100 ml and 0.75 mg/100 kcal)
	Copper (0.18 mg/100 g, or 0.09 mg/100 ml and 0.06 mg/100 kcal)
	Magnesium (75 mg/100 g, or 38 mg/100 ml and 25 mg/100 kcal)
	Niacin (3.3 mg/100 g, or 1.7 mg/100 ml and 1.1 mg/100 kcal)
	Pantothenic acid (1.65 mg/ 100g, or 0.83 mg/100 ml and 0.55 mg/100 kcal)
	Biotin (14 micrograms/100 g, or 6.8 micrograms/100 ml and 4.5 micrograms/100 kcal)
	Vitamin A (135 micrograms/100 g, or 68 micrograms/100 ml and 45 micrograms/100 kcal)
	Vitamin B_1 (0.30 mg/100 g, or 0.15 mg/100 ml and 0.10 mg/100 kcal)
	Vitamin B_2 (0.33 mg/100 g, or 0.17 mg/100 ml and 0.11 mg/100 kcal)

Vitamin B$_6$ (0.30 mg/100 g, or
0.15 mg/100 ml and 0.10 mg/
100 kcal)
Vitamin B$_{12}$ (0.60 micrograms/
100 g, or 0.30 micrograms/100 ml
and 0.20 micrograms/100 kcal)
Vitamin C (24 mg/100 g, or 12 mg/
100 ml and 8 mg/100 kcal)
Vitamin D (1.50 micrograms/100 g,
or 0.75 micrograms/100 ml and
0.50 micrograms/100 kcal)
Vitamin E (2.4/100 g, or 1.2 mg/
100 ml and 0.8 mg/100 kcal)
Folic acid (60 micrograms/100 g, or
30 micrograms/100 ml and
20 micrograms/100 kcal)

Contains

Protein (7.5 g/100 g solid food, or
7.5 g/100 ml liquid food and 7.5 g/
100 kcal)
Dietary fibre (3 g/100 g, or 1.5 g/
100 ml and 1.5 g/100 kcal)
Zinc (1.05 mg/100 g, or 0.53 mg/
100 ml and 0.35 mg/100 kcal)
Calcium (105 mg/100 g, or 53 mg/
100 ml and 35 mg/100 kcal)
Iron (1.13 mg/100 g, or 0.56 mg/
100 ml and 0.38 mg/100 kcal)
Copper (0.09 mg/100 g, or 0.05 mg/
100 ml and 0.03 mg/100 kcal)
Magnesium (38 mg/100 mg, or
19 mg/100 ml and 13 mg/100 kcal)
Niacin (1.7 mg/100 g, or 0.8 mg/
100 ml and 0.6 mg/100 kcal)
Pantothenic acid (0.83 mg/100 g, or
0.41 mg/100 ml and 0.28 mg/100
kcal))
Biotin (6.8 micrograms/100 g, or
3.4 micrograms/100 ml and
2.3 micrograms/100 kcal)

	Vitamin A (68 micrograms/100 g, or 34 micrograms/100 ml and 23 micrograms/100 kcal) Vitamin B_1 (0.15 mg/100 g, or 0.08 mg/100 ml and 0.05 mg/100 kcal) Vitamin B_2 (0.17 mg/100 g, or 0.08 mg/100 ml and 0.06 mg/100 kcal) Vitamin B_6 (0.15 mg/100 g, or 0.08 mg/100 ml and 0.05 mg/100 kcal) Vitamin B_{12} (0.30 micrograms/100 g, or 0.15 micrograms/100 ml and 0.10 micrograms/100 kcal) Vitamin C (12 mg/100 g, or 6 mg/100 ml and 4 mg/100 kcal) Vitamin D (0.75 micrograms/100 g, or 0.38 micrograms/100 ml and 0.25 micrograms/100 ml) Vitamin E (1.2 mg/100 mg, or 0.6 mg/100 ml and 0.4 mg/100 kcal) Folic acid (30 micrograms/100 g, or 15 micrograms/100 ml and 20 micrograms/100 kcal)
Not contained	Calories (5 kcal/100 g of solid food, or 5 kcal/100 ml of liquid food) Fat (0.5 g/100 g, or 0.5 g/100 ml) Saturated fat (0.1 g/100 g, or 0.1 g/100 ml) Cholesterol (5 mg/100 ml, or 5 g/100 ml, with 1.5 g/100 g saturated fat, or 0.75 g/100 ml saturated fat and the energy from saturated fat must be 10% of total energy or less)[e] Sugars (0.5 g/100 g, or 0.5 g/100 ml) Sodium (5 mg/100 g, or 5 mg/100 ml)

Low	Calories (40 kcal/100 g of solid food, or 40 kcal/100 ml of liquid food) Fat (3 g/100 g, or 1.5 g/100 ml) Saturated fat (1.5 g/100 g, or 0.75 g/ 100 ml and energy from saturated fat must be at most 10% of total energy) Cholesterol (20 mg/100 g, or 10 mg/ 100 ml, with 1.5 g/100 g saturated fat, or 0.75 g/100 ml saturated fat and the energy from saturated fat must be 10% of total energy or less)[e] Sugars (5 g/100 g, or 2.5 g/100 ml) Sodium (120 mg/100 g, or 120 mg/ 100 ml)

Australia and New Zealand

Claim	*Applicable nutrient*
Increased	Mono- and polyunsaturated fatty acids
Low, Reduced or Light/lite, Diet	Low joule (energy)
Low, Free	Lactose
Low salt/sodium, Reduced or Light/ lite, No Added, Unsalted	Sodium/salt
Reduced or Light/lite, Increased	Carbohydrate
Low, Medium, High	Glycaemic Index
Low, Reduced or Light/lite, Low proportion	Saturated and trans fatty acids
Good source	Vitamin or mineral
Free, Low	Gluten
Low, Reduced or Light/lite	Cholesterol
Free, Low, Reduced or Light/lite, Low proportion	Saturated fatty acids
Good source, Increased	Omega-3
Increased	Omega-6 Omega-9

Good source, Excellent source, Increased	Dietary fibre
% Free, Low, Reduced or Light/lite, No added, Unsweetened	Sugar or sugars
% Free, Low, Reduced or Light/lite	Fat
Good source, Increased	Protein
Free, Reduced or Light/lite	Trans fatty acids

Brazil

Low (40 kcal/100 g for solid food or 20 kcal/100 ml for liquid food maximum) Free (4 kcal/100 g or 4 kcal/100 ml)	Energy
Low (20 mg/100 g and 1.5 g/100 g saturated fat and 10% energy derived from saturated fat maximum for solid food or 10 mg/100 ml and 0.75 g/100 ml and 10% energy derived from saturated fat maximum for liquid food) Free (5 mg/100 g and 0.75 g/100 g saturated fat and 10% energy from saturated fat maximum, 5 mg/100 ml 0.75 g/100 ml and 10% maximum)	Cholesterol
Source (15% RDI/100 g solid food or 7.5% RDI/100 ml liquid food) Rich (30% RDI/100 g or 7.5% RDI/100 ml)	Vitamins and minerals
Low (3 g/100 g or 1.5 g/100 ml maximum) Free (0.5 g/100 g or 0.5 g/100 ml)	Fat
Low (5 g/100 g maximum for solid food and meets criteria for low in energy or reduced in energy or 5 g/100 ml and same conditions for liquid food)	Sugars

Free (0.5 g/100 g and low energy or reduced energy or 0.5 g/100 ml and same conditions)	
Low (1.5 g/100 g or 0.75 g/100 ml and 10% total energy from saturated fat maximum) Free (0.1 g/100 g or 0.1 g/100 ml maximum)	Saturated fat
Low (120 mg/100 g solid food or 120 mg/100 ml liquid food maximum) Very low (40 mg/100 g or 40 mg/ 100 ml) Free (5 mg/100 g or 5 mg/100 ml)	Sodium
Free (0.2 g/portion trans fat and 2 g/portion saturated fat maximum)	Trans fat
Source (10% RDI/100 g for solid food or 5% RDI/100 ml liquid food) Rich (20% RDI/100 g or 10% RDI/ 100 ml)	Protein

Notes:

a. For use regarding protein, minerals, vitamins, fibre and potassium only.

b. For use regarding vitamins and minerals only.

c. Claims added after EC 1924/2006 Annex of Regulation (EC) No. 1924/2006 last amended by Regulation (EC) No. 116/2010.

d. Only valid for nutrients, not vitamins or minerals.

e. Must not have serving size of 15 g or less. Saturated fat content cannot exceed 15 per cent of the fat content.

Source:

United States of America: Derived from FDA (2008). A different kind of nutrient content claim is allowed to be made on dietary supplements (percentage of nutrient per capsule) (FDA, 2003).

Canada: Derived from CFIA and Health Canada (2009). Not permitted on NHPs, which have labelling that is distinctly different from food.

European Union: Derived from EC Regulation 1924/2006 and EC (2013a). Food supplements, as they are considered food, can use nutrition content claims. Since vitamins and minerals are the only acceptable food supplements, claims applicable to vitamins and minerals are the only acceptable claims.

Japan: Derived from MHLW (n.d.a). Unclear from sources whether nutrient content claims can be used on nutraceuticals. Given the fact that there is no regulatory or legal difference between nutraceuticals/supplements and food in the Japanese system (see text), it is probable that nutrient content claims can be used on nutraceuticals in addition to food.

Australia and New Zealand: Derived from Standard 1.2.7 (FSANZ, 2013a). Nutraceuticals are regulated separately in Australia and New Zealand from joint regulation on food. As such, nutrient content claims as currently developed are only applicable to food.

Brazil: Derived from CFS (2008) and FAS (2012a).

Note: Unclear from sources whether or not nutrient content claims can be used on nutraceuticals/supplements in Brazil. However, given Brazil's stricter regulatory regime for nutraceuticals/supplements than for food, it is unlikely that Brazil permits nutrient content claims on nutraceuticals.

Appendix 2: Medical foods and food for special dietary use in the USA

In addition to dietary supplements, the USA recognizes two additional categories of foods: medical foods and food for special dietary use. Medical foods are defined as a food product that is manufactured to be consumed or administered under the supervision of a physician and is intended for the specific dietary management of a disease or condition for which distinctive nutritional requirements, based on recognized scientific principles, are established by medical evaluation (Orphan Drug Act 1988) (FDA, 2010).

Medical foods do not have to undergo pre-market review or approval by the FDA and individual medical food products are not permitted to make health claims and, as such, do not have to be registered with the FDA. According to the FDA, ingredients used in medical foods must be approved food additives or a food additive that is the subject of an exemption for investigational use. Medical foods are exempted from the labelling requirements for health claims and nutrient content claims under the Nutrition Labeling and Education Act of 1990. They can be sold in food stores and pharmacies. However, they must follow the same labelling regulations as conventional food with exemptions such as:

- 'If it is a specially formulated and processed product (as opposed to a naturally occurring foodstuff used in its natural state) for the partial or exclusive feeding of a patient by means of oral intake or enteral feeding by tube;
- If it is intended for the dietary management of a patient who, because of therapeutic or chronic medical needs, has limited or impaired capacity to ingest, digest, absorb, or metabolize ordinary foodstuffs or certain nutrients, or who has other special medically determined nutrient requirements, the dietary management of which cannot be achieved by the modification of the normal diet alone;
- If it provides nutritional support specifically modified for the management of the unique nutrient needs that result from the specific disease or condition, as determined by medical evaluation;
- If it is intended to be used under medical supervision;

- If it is intended only for a patient receiving active and ongoing medical supervision wherein the patient requires medical care on a recurring basis for, among other things, instructions on the use of the medical food' (FDA, 2010, 21 CFR 101.9(j) (8)).

Foods for special dietary use are defined as 'a particular use for which a food purports or is represented to be used, including but not limited to the following:

- Supplying a special dietary need that exists by reason of a physical, physiological, pathological, or other condition ...;
- Supplying a vitamin, mineral, or other ingredient for use by humans to supplement the diet by increasing the total dietary intake;
- Supplying a special dietary need by reason of being a food for use as the sole item of the diet ...' (Federal Food, Drug and Cosmetic Act, Section 411(c)(3)).

Examples include infant foods, hypoallergenic foods such as gluten-free foods and lactose-free foods and foods offered for reducing weight.

Food for special dietary use must also comply with the nutrient and health claims that are approved for conventional foods with health benefits (functional foods) or with those that are approved for specific products like diet and hypoallergenic foods (Kurpiewski, 2008). As with medical foods, food for special dietary use do not undergo FDA approval before they are marketed, with the exception of infant formula which falls under the category of food for special dietary use but must be pre-approved by the FDA. However, infant formulas are not required to be used under physician supervision. The infant formula ingredients must also be approved food additives or be 'Generally Recognized as Safe' by the FDA.

Appendix 3: Canadian and US nutrition facts labelling exemptions

List of exemptions for US nutrition facts labels (FDA, 2008):

- food is manufactured by a small business
- food served in restaurants or delivered for immediate consumption
- delicatessen or bakery-type foods prepared and sold at the same location
- Foods with no significant nutrition (for example, instant coffee, spices)
- infant formula and food intended for consumption by children up to the ages of four (other labelling requirements for these foods)
- dietary supplements
- medical foods
- bulk foods shipped for further processing or packaging before retail sale
- fresh produce and seafood
- custom processed fish or game meat (voluntary labelling on shelves in store)
- certain egg cartons
- individual packages labelled 'This unit not intended for retail sale' that make up a larger package that has a nutrition label
- self-service bulk foods (voluntary labelling on shelves in store)
- donated food given free to consumer.

List of exemptions for Canadian nutrition facts table labelling (CFIA and Health Canada, 2009):

- for spices and some bottled waters, when much nutritional information is by values of '0'
- beverages with an alcohol content of more than 0.5 per cent
- fresh fruits and vegetables with no added ingredients (also fresh herbs)
- raw, single ingredient meat and meat by-products (not ground meat)
- raw, single ingredient marine or freshwater animal products

- food is sold only by a retail establishment that prepares the food on-site
- food sold at a fair, farmers' market and so on by an individual who made the food or product
- individual servings of foods that are sold for immediate consumption (and have not been specially processed/packaged to prolong their shelf life)
- if the product has an available display surface of less than 200 cm^2 and is sold at the same retail establishment as it is packaged
- one-bite confections (never loses exemption)
- pre-packaged individual portions of food served by a restaurant with other food (for example, creamers, crackers) (never loses exemption)
- different kinds of goat and cow milk products vended in refillable containers (never loses exemption).

Appendix 4:   Codex Alimentarius guidelines

The Codex Alimentarius Commission was established by the Food and Agriculture Organization (FAO) of the United Nations and the World Health Organization (WHO) in 1963. It develops harmonized international food standards, guidelines and codes of practice. The two main objectives of the Codex are to ensure the protection of consumer health and to facilitate international food trade (CAC, 1993). The Codex standards are not binding but they are referenced in World Trade Organization (WTO) disputes.[1] Many countries are moving to align their food regulations with the Codex guidelines. This appendix provides a brief outline of Codex standards pertaining to health claims, nutrition claims, nutrient content claims and nutrition labelling.

Health Claims

Codex defines health claim as 'any representation which states, suggests or implies that a relationship exists between a food or a constituent of that food and health' (Subirade, 2007, p. 13). There are three different types of health claims: a nutrient function claim describes the physiological role of the nutrient in growth, development and normal function of the human body; an enhanced function claim refers to specific beneficial effects of the consumption of food and their constituents in the context of the total diet; a disease risk reduction claim relates the consumption of a food or its constituents to the reduced risk of developing a disease or a health-related condition. The risk reduction claim should be presented in a way that will not make consumers presume them to be preventative claims (Subirade, 2007).

Codex has established some criteria for the substantiation of the health claims that apply to all types of health claims[2]:

1.   Health claims should be based on evidence provided by human studies. These studies should not be only observational but also based on animal model studies that substantiate the relationship between the food and the health effect;

2. The totality of the evidence should be identified and reviewed. This must include unpublished data if applicable, evidence supporting the claim, evidence contradicting the claim and any unclear evidence;

3. Human-based evidence should demonstrate a consistent relation between the food and the claimed effect with little or no evidence to the contrary;

4. Nutrient function claims may be substantiated based on generally accepted authoritative statements by expert scientific bodies that have been verified over time;

5. Observational evidence such as epidemiological studies can also be used to substantiate some health claims such as those that involve a food category and a health effect.

Nutrition Claims (Codex Alimentarius)

The guidelines for the use of nutrition and health claims proposed by Codex defines nutrition claim as 'any representation which states, suggests or implies that a food has particular nutritional properties including but not limited to the energy value and to the content of protein, fat and carbohydrates, as well as the content of vitamins and minerals'.[3] Nutrition claims are divided into two categories: a nutrient content claim describes the level of a nutrient contained in a food, while a nutrient comparative claim is a claim that compares the nutrient levels and/or energy value of two or more foods.

Nutrient content claims (Codex Alimentarius)[4]

- If a food by its nature is low in or free of the nutrient that is the subject of the claim, the term describing the level of the nutrient should not immediately precede the name of the food but should be in the form of 'a low (nutrient name) food' or 'a (nutrient name)-free food'.

Nutrient comparative claim (Codex Alimentarius)[5]

- The foods being compared should be different versions of the same or similar foods. The foods should also be clearly identified;
- The amount of difference in the nutrient content should be stated and must appear in proximity to the comparative claim;
- Full details of the comparison should be given. They must be stated in the same quantity or unit of measurement;

- The comparison should be based on a relative difference of at least 25 per cent in the nutrient content except for micronutrients where a 10 per cent difference would be accepted;
- The use of the word 'light' should follow the same criteria as for 'reduced' and include an indication of what make the food 'light'.

Nutrition Labelling

Codex Alimentarius provides guidelines on food labelling that is purported to provide consumers with information about a food to facilitate informed consumption decisions. Food labelling according to Codex is a means of conveying information on the nutrient content of a food. To ensure that nutrition labelling does not describe a product or present information that is misleading, deceptive or insignificant in any manner, the Codex prescribes principles about nutrient declaration, supplementary nutrition information and nutrition labelling (Subirade, 2007). Nutrient declaration information is intended to provide consumers with a profile of the nutrients contained in the food that are considered of nutritional importance. Nutrient declarations should not lead consumers to believe that there is exact quantitative knowledge of what individuals should eat in order to maintain their health. Codex guidelines also recommend that nutrition labelling should not deliberately imply that a food that carries such labelling necessarily has any nutritional advantage over a food without the labels. Finally, the Codex guidelines recognize that the content of supplementary nutrition information will vary between countries and from one target population group to another.

NOTES

1. http://www.codexalimentarius.org/.
2. Nutrition and Health Claims CAC/GL 23-1997, p. 3 (CAC, 1997).
3. Nutrition and Health Claims CAC/GL 23-1997, p. 1 (CAC, 1997).
4. Nutrition and Health Claims CAC/GL 23-1997, p. 2 (CAC, 1997).
5. Nutrition and Health Claims CAC/GL 23-1997, pp. 2, 3 (CAC, 1997).

Appendix 5:   Literature summaries

This appendix contains literature summary tables. Table A5.1 presents a summary of studies examining the regulation of the health foods sector in various countries. A more detailed discussion of this literature is provided in Chapters 3, 4 and 5. Table A5.2 presents a summary of selected industry and market analyses of the health foods sector, as discussed in Chapter 6. Table A5.3 summarizes literature examining consumer attitudes towards health foods, WTP for health attributes and credibility of health claims, which is examined in more detail in Chapter 7.

Table A5.1   Summary of selected regulatory analysis

Author, year, location	Title, area	Objective, Method	Citation, prepared for
Bech-Larsen and Scholderer 2007 Europe	Functional foods in Europe: consumer research, market experiences and regulatory aspects Functional foods	To review consumer research, market experiences and the regulatory aspects regarding the use of health and nutrition claims for functional foods in Europe Descriptive Analysis	*Trends in Food Science & Technology*, **18**, 231–4

The EU functional food and supplements industry suffered from inconsistencies in the regulations across European countries prior to harmonization. A proposed harmonized regulation on nutrition and health claims is discussed (later came into effect in December 2012). The 'proposed' regulation involves the distinction of health claims that are scientifically proven and those that lack scientific evidence. Novel food will require individual scientific evaluation and pre-market approval. Health claims that are not clear and accurate will not be permitted. The legislation was expected to reduce the uncertainty facing firms but will constrain the potential positioning strategies for functional foods. Companies that are attempting to enter the functional food industry in Europe lack the necessary successful marketing skills. Consumer acceptance has received little attention. Inconsistencies between the new health claim legislation, consumer preferences and marketing forces makes the new legislation unlikely to enlarge the European functional food market.

Bureau of Nutritional Sciences Food Directorate (BNSFD) 2000 Canada	*Standard of Evidence for Evaluating Food with Health Claims: A Proposed Framework* Food	To propose a framework for the evaluation of foods with health claims Descriptive Analysis	http:// diabetestype2.ca/ diary/research/ finalproposal.pdf Health Canada

Argued that there should be appropriate evidence to support health claims that will ensure product safety, claim validity and quality assurance, as well as production methods and procedures for product testing. All foods should undergo at least a basic evaluation to determine the safety of the product. Further evaluations may be required when the product is novel and/or there are uncertainties surrounding the safety of the product. There will be a three-step process to demonstrate the efficacy and effectiveness of the product, validating its claims. For quality assurance purposes, there should be a demonstration of the reliability of the tests performed.

Bureau of Nutritional Sciences Food Directorate (BNSFD) 2001 Canada	*Product-specific Authorization of Health Claims for Foods* Food	To propose approaches to regulating health claims for food (proposed in a regulatory framework) Descriptive Analysis	Health Canada

The proposed regulatory framework was based on the recognition that consumption of a reasonable quantity of a food containing a biologically active substance could affect the physiological function or structure of the body. The approach taken was 'product-specific authorization' for health claims whereby the product (functional food) with the intended claim is assessed on its own merit. The health claims approved were generic. Key elements of the proposed regulatory framework: all food (modified and non-modified) that affect the structure of the body or claim to reduce the risk of disease would be required to carry a claim identification number (CIN); the manufacturer should provide product information and the proposed claim and information required for assessing product safety, claim validity and quality assurance; CIN may be cancelled or suspended when there is a violation of the specified conditions; applicants should notify the directorate of any changes in specified conditions. There should be transparency in the product review process.

Farrell, Ries, Kachan and Boon 2009 Canada	Foods and natural health products: gaps and ambiguities in the Canadian regulatory regime Functional food and NHP	To analyse the current regulatory framework governing (functional) foods and NHPs in Canada, as well as highlight the confusion and ambiguities surrounding the regulatory framework Descriptive Analysis	*Food Policy*, **34**, 388–92

The regulation of food, drugs and NHPs is under the Canadian Food and Drugs Act. NHPs are defined by the NHPR based on function (for example, diagnose, treat, mitigate or prevent a disease) and substance (for example, vitamins, minerals, amino acids, probiotics). The regulatory distinctions between food, NHPs, functional foods and nutraceuticals are unclear. The influx of NHPs in conventional food format in the Canadian market has become a source of confusion. The NHPR require clinical trials involving NHP to obtain approval from Health Canada, food does not. NHPs require a pre-market approval, while foods in general do not, with the exception of novel foods (foods with no history of use), food additives and infant formulas. NHP health claims are therapeutic claims, disease risk reduction claims and structure/function claims. The case of probiotic yoghurt and green tea illustrates the confusion surrounding regulations in Canada. There is the need for closer collaboration between the food and NHP Directorate as well as regulatory reform as the research and commercial interest in functional food and NHP continues to grow.

| Hawkes 2004 Global | Nutrition labels and health claims: the global regulatory environment Labelling and health claims | To provide an overview of international, regional and national regulations regarding nutrition labelling and health claims Descriptive Analysis | http:// whqlibdoc.who. int/ publications/ 2004/ 9241591714.pdf World Health Organization (WHO) |

The global regulatory environment around nutrition labelling and health claims is characterized by a certain amount of harmony but there is also a lot of variation. Nutritional labelling helps consumers make informed choices. Nutrition claims are more accepted than function and disease risk reduction claims because referencing a disease in a claim might imply the ability of food to treat or prevent diseases. There are constant changes in health claims due to ongoing developments in national, regional and international regulations and the possibility of misleading and confusing claims have made regulatory authorities recommend international harmonization of health claims. Nutrition labels and health claims will improve public health if regulations are developed to ultimately improve the long-term dietary intake of consumers.

Health Canada 1998 Canada	*Nutraceuticals/ Functional Foods and Health Claims on Foods* Nutraceuticals/ functional foods	To analyse the Canadian environment for nutraceuticals/ functional foods and health claims, review alternative policy options and recommend a framework for regulations Descriptive Analysis	http://www.hc-sc. gc.ca/fn-an/label-etiquet/claims-reclam/nutra-funct_foods-nutra-fonct_ aliment-eng.php

No definition existed for 'health claims' prior to 1998, hence all products with health claims were regulated as drugs (structure/function claims exempted). Health claims were categorized into three distinctions: thera-peutic; risk reduction; and structure/function claims. The final policy decision asserted that structure/function and risk reduction claims for 'food' and 'food components' (functional food and nutraceuticals) should be permitted; all other products with therapeutic health claims should be regulated as drugs. The proposed recommendations included communi-cating the policy to stakeholders, development of an implementation strategy and standards of evidence and composition in consultation with stakeholders in the industry.

Health Canada 2000 Canada	*Consultation Document on Generic Health Claims* Food	To examine proposals on five selected health claims and stakeholders' opinions on the format of the claims, credibility of claims, consumer education and scientific review of the claims Descriptive Analysis	http://www.hc-sc. gc.ca/fn-an/alt_ formats/hpfb-dgpsa/pdf/label-etiquet/health_ claims-allegations_ sante-eng.pdf

Proposals were based on the policy framework developed by Health Canada (1998) to permit risk reduction claims and structure/function claims on foods. Proposals were made on conditions for the use of five generic health claims: sodium and hypertension; calcium and osteoporosis; saturated and trans fat and cholesterol and CHD; fruits and vegetables and cancer; and sugar alcohols and dental caries. Proposals included: food should fall into one of the four food groups of *Canada's Food Guide* to healthy eating; be consistent with Nutrition Recommendations for Canadians and its update on Dietary Fat and Children; claims should not be permitted on foods that fall into the 'Other Foods' category of *Canada's Food Guide* to healthy eating; saturated and trans fat to CHD claim should also be permitted on fats and oils that meet the conditions of the claim; specific requirements for a claim should be included in the claim; and health claims should not be permitted on food for infants and children under two years. The core list of nutrients and any nutrient mentioned in the claim except alcohol should be declared. To clarify risk reduction benefits, information on an accepted diet–health relationship and information on the composition of the product relevant to the relationship should be included. Stakeholders expressed their opinions on the health claims in the areas of claim format, claim credibility and consumer education and scientific review.

| Health Canada 2004 Canada | *A Regulatory Framework for Natural Health Products* NHPs | To provide a snapshot of the new NHP regulatory framework in Canada Descriptive Analysis | Health Canada |

NHP regulations included provisions on a product licensing system that requires all NHPs to display a product identification number; site licensing that involves the licensing of all manufacturers, packagers, labellers and importers; GMPs to ensure product safety and quality; standard labelling requirements that include basic information such as product name, quantity in container, recommended use and storage conditions; and an adverse reaction reporting system to help monitor adverse reactions associated with products. In two years, all manufacturers, importers, packagers and labellers will employ GMPs and have site licences; it was envisioned that in six years NHPs would have an NPN or a DIN-HM (homeopathic medicine).

| Kim, Kim and Lee 2006 South Korea | Regulations on health/ functional foods in Korea Health functional foods (HFFs) | To report on the scope of functional foods, the strength of the evidence required for their effectiveness, safety considerations and future perspectives in South Korea Descriptive Analysis | *Toxicology,* **221**, 112–18 |

The Health Functional Food Act (HFFA) in South Korea was enacted in 2002 and came into effect in 2004. The main goal of the Act was to improve public health. The Act defines HFF as food supplements containing nutrients or other substances that have a nutritional or physiological effect with the purpose of supplementing normal diet in measured doses (for example, pills). The Act made HFFs a new food category separate from conventional foods. HFFs are divided into generic and product-specific HFFs. Product-specific HFFs refer to all products that are not in the 37 generic products. Claims on nutrients, other functions and disease risk that are compatible with the Codex Alimentarius Commission may be used for labelling. Labelling standards should be in conformity with those of other countries. Health claims and regulations should be focused on the protection of public health.

Laeeque, Boon, Kachan, Cohen and D'Cruz 2006 Canada	The Canadian natural health products (NHP) regulations: industry compliance motivations NHPs	To explore the motivation of corporations to comply with new natural health products (NHPs) regulations in Canada Survey/ Descriptive Analysis	*Evidence-Based Complementary and Alternative Medicine*, **4** (2), 257–62

Four main motivations for firms to comply with the new NHP regulations in Canada are identified. First is the general deterrent of fear: large firms fear negative media coverage and small/medium firms fear government actions. Second, the duty to comply as a legal responsibility and a civic duty. Third, social motivations that will enhance public perception of NHPs. Fourth is the ability of firms to comply: large firms with the resources and access to information pertaining to the regulations are better able to comply. Policymakers should factor in consumer perceptions and media coverage when planning compliance strategies. Enforcement policies such as premise inspections are expensive. Strategies that can stimulate motivation such as making public or publishing approved products and companies with site licences could enhance the likelihood of compliance.

| Malla, Hobbs and Sogah 2013 Multiple countries | *Functional Foods and Natural Health Products Regulations in Canada and Around the World: Nutrition Labels and Health Claims* Functional food, NHPs, supplements, nutraceuticals | Analyses regulatory developments in various countries and assesses implications for Canada Descriptive Analysis | Canadian Agricultural Innovation and Regulation Network, Report No. 36 |

Charts the development of regulations in a number of countries, including Canada, the USA, EU, Japan, Australia and New Zealand, UK, Sweden, Russia, Brazil, China, India, Singapore, Taiwan, South Korea, Thailand, the Philippines, Malaysia and Hong Kong. Describes health claims regulations, nutrient content and nutrition labelling regulations.

| Mariotti, Kalonji, Huneau and Margaritis 2010 EU | Potential pitfalls of health claims from a public health nutrition perspective Functional food | To analyse and review discrepancies between consumer perceptions of health claims and the reality of public health nutrition Descriptive Analysis | *Nutrition Reviews,* **68**, 624–38 |

The paper indicates there were over 10 000 health claim applications based on 4185 main relationships for inclusion in the EU register. Six potential incongruities related to health claims in the EU are identified: 'lexical terms' that consumers find difficult to understand; 'beyond scientific truth', discrepancies between scientific meaning of a claim and consumer perception; 'consumer understanding and reality', which includes confusion between the concepts of food and diet; consumers' misguided belief that 'more is better', multifactorial effects and target population. Solutions should reduce the risk of consumer misperceptions that can lead to inappropriate food choices. Recommendations include banning or limiting certain claims, restriction on wording of claims and the inclusion of general disclaimer statements in health claims.

Mine and Young 2009 Canada	Regulation of natural health products in Canada NHPs	To provide an overview of the Canadian natural health product regulatory situation Descriptive Analysis	*Food Science Technology Research*, **15** (5), 459–68

Increased interest in NHPs by Canadians and the need for regulations and accessibility led to the formation of the NHPD. The NHPD introduced the NHPR in 2004. The NHPR outlines the requirements regarding product licensing, site licensing, GMPs, adverse reaction reporting, clinical trials, labelling and packaging, health claims and safety issues. In 2009, Health Canada developed an approach where NHPs are assessed and issued a product licence based on their risk level (risk-based approach: Class I (low risk), II (high risk: requires thorough assessment for safety, efficacy and quality)). NHPs whose effects on humans have not been investigated may be required to undergo a 'clinical trial' to ascertain the safety and efficacy of the product (other range of evidence could also support an application). A major challenge facing Health Canada is to clarify which regulations should govern products that have both food and NHP characteristics (NHPR, FDR). NHPR provide safe and effective NHPs. The study recommends that Health Canada continue maintaining a transparent and open dialogue with all stakeholders in the sector.

| Palthur, Palthur and Chitta 2009 India | Emerging product categories in India: a regulatory view Functional food and nutraceuticals | To examine the development of new functional food and nutraceutical regulatory regime, make speculations on the regime's implementation and make recommendations on the approach to regulating functional food and nutraceuticals in India Descriptive Analysis | *Food and Drug Law Journal*, **64**, 677 |

Before 2006, there was no regulatory body or food law in India. The FSSA 2006 gives definition to foods for special dietary uses or functional foods or nutraceuticals or health supplements. Implementing the FSSA raises challenges that include: the inability of small and medium-scale firms to identify the procedural and compliance changes in the Act; the regulatory vacuum that will be created when the old regime is repealed; education and competency requirements for firms and regulators. The capacity gaps include: lack of qualified technical personnel; inadequacy of skills of existing personnel; lack of well-equipped laboratories for analysis. The study recommended the development of over-arching objectives for regulation; greater collaboration between departments and agencies; non-prescriptive types of regulations; sufficient resources; harmonization with major trading partners; comprehensive and *ex post* evaluation of regulation.

Smith, Marcotte and Harrison 1996 Canada, Japan, EU and USA	*A Comparative Analysis of the Regulatory Framework Affecting Functional Food Development and Commercialization in Canada, Japan, the European Union and the USA* Functional food	To analyse the opportunities and challenges of current regulatory frameworks affecting functional foods in Canada, Japan, EU, USA Descriptive Analysis/ Interview (personal and telephone)	Inter/Sect Alliance Inc. Agriculture and Agri-Food Canada

Canada has a relatively restrictive regulatory framework environment for the development and marketing of functional food compared to the USA, EU and Japan. The regulatory system in Japan is the most supportive, well defined, predictable and has established collaboration between government, industry, academia and research organizations; the US regulatory framework, though restrictive, is supportive with specific well-defined regulations; the EU has restrictive regulations but in the past has been ineffective because enforcement in member states was voluntary. The study recommended the establishment of health food associations in Canada to involve the private sector in the regulation of functional food as it exists in Japan; collaboration of government and the industry for regulatory reform (with consumers in mind); differentiation of disease risk reduction health claims from wellness claims (structure/ function claims) to reduce the processing time for functional food claims approval; and harmonization of health claims with that of the USA.

| Subirade 2007 Europe, USA, Canada, Japan and other Asian countries | *Report on Functional Foods* Functional foods | To present an overview of the functional foods regulatory systems for healthy nutrients and functional claims in Europe, USA, Canada, Japan and other Asian countries Descriptive Analysis | Food Quality and Standards Service (AGNS), Food and Agriculture Organization (FAO) of the United Nations |

There is confusion and distrust among health professionals and consumers about functional food and nutraceuticals/supplements generated by the proliferation of health claims. Most regulations have been on health claims (disease risk reduction claims). Canada and the USA permit disease risk reduction health claims, nutrient content claims and structure/function claims. Disease risk reduction claims relate the consumption of a food or ingredient to health; structure/function claims describe the importance of nutrients in promoting normal and healthy growth and functioning; and nutrient content claims describe the level of nutrients in a food. In Canada, health claims on food are generic; however, health claims on NHPs are product-specific. In the EU, disease risk reduction claims on food are prohibited (this has since changed). Nutrient content claims and structure/function claims are permitted. Japan is the most developed market for functional food, allowing FOSHU claims, which refer to food with ingredients that affect health; Qualified FOSHU claims for foods that have a function with no conclusive scientific evidence; Standard FOSHU for food processing ingredients that are well established in FOSHU claims; and food nutrient function claims. In South Korea, health/functional food have been standardized into generic and product-specific categories. Products that contain ingredients named in the Food Act are generic and those that contain new ingredients are product-specific. Uniform descriptions of types of nutrition, health claims and terminologies internationally were recommended, as were: a clear distinction between functional and disease risk reduction claims; health claims should be scientifically validated; protection of consumers; promotion of fair trade; and innovation in the sector.

Veeman 2002 Global	Policy development for novel foods: issues and challenges for functional food Functional foods	To compare the international regulatory situation to Canada and make recommendations Descriptive Analysis	*Canadian* *Journal of* *Agricultural* *Economics*, **50**, 527–39

Recognizes that the market for functional food and the nutraceutical sector is growing globally because of consumers' motivations for healthier diets. There are market failures due to the uncertainty and information asymmetry associated with health claims on these products. Health claim policies were well advanced in countries like Japan and the USA compared to Canada. However, there are some differences in approaches to national policies and regulations internationally. For example, S-adenosylmethionene (SAMe) was regarded as a dietary supplement in the USA but classified in Canada as a drug that needed a DIN and licence from Health Canada and available in Europe as prescription medication. However, policies on health claims in some nations are converging; for example, the Australia and New Zealand Food Standards. The study concluded that there should be government intervention to deal with inefficiencies and failures and there should be a balance in the interest of both consumers and producers through designed mechanisms to verify claims and information provided by producers.

Table A5.2   Summary of selected industry and market analyses

Author, year, location	Area, title	Objective, method	Citation, prepared for
AAFC 2009 Canada	Functional foods *Consumer Trends: Functional Foods*	To provide insights for stakeholders in the functional food industry Descriptive Analysis	http://www.gov.mb.ca/ agriculture/market-prices-and-statistics/ food-and-value-added-agriculture-statistics/ pubs/consumer_trends_ functional_foods_en.pdf International Markets Bureau

- Annual growth rate for the functional food market in Canada is estimated at 8–14%.
- R&D in the industry is resource-intensive.
- New firms struggle to gain market share and customer loyalty in the industry; industry is highly concentrated with the dominance of a few large companies.
- Industry is growing; firms should seek partnerships with other stakeholders that consumers trust to be a credible source of information.
- Recommends the development of products for niche markets and also educating consumers about the health benefits of products in a way consumers find credible, such as the use of public and health institutions.

| Arias-Aranda and Romerosa-Martinez 2010 Spain | Functional foods Innovation in the functional foods industry in a peripheral region of the European Union: Andalusia (Spain) | To examine the effect of the relationship between public sector research and industrial development in the functional food sector on innovation Descriptive Analysis | *Food Policy*, **35**, 240–46 |

- There are over 200 functional food products in the Spanish market.
- In 2007, there were 29 functional food firms and 19 research institutions devoted to functional food in the Andalusia region. Annual growth rate of the functional food sector is 14% compared to only 3% for conventional food; growth has been attributed to increased consumer interest in functional food.
- There have been significant public policies on functional food research but these have not translated into innovative activities and application.
- Very limited relationship between academic research groups and functional food companies investing in R&D; most firms outsource research functions to public and private institutions outside Andalusia.
- Recommendations include the creation of relations between stakeholders that will lead to innovation in the sector; increasing entrepreneurial activities on the part of researchers; promotion of international research groups; and stimulating the sector with government support to increase economic growth.

Bleiel 2010 N/A	Functional foods Functional foods from the perspective of the consumer: how to make it a success?	To discuss potential market failures of functional food Descriptive Analysis	*International Dairy Journal*, **20**, 303–6

- Failure of functional food products common because of consumer rejection.
- Firms ignore consumer insights at the innovation stage.
- Consumers seek the wellness benefits of functional food ingredients, so firms should emphasize the benefits from consuming the product rather than the ingredients used in making the product.
- Product development should be based on consumers' behaviour, needs and desires about functional food.

Cinnamon 2009 Canada	Functional foods and NHPs *Results from the Functional Foods and Natural Health Products Survey – 2007*	To provide indicators that will help with innovations in the sector Survey/ Descriptive Analysis $N = 689$	Statistics Canada Catalogue 88F0006X, No. 1

- In 2007 in Canada, there were 689 functional food and NHP firms, 290 NHP-only firms, 174 functional food-only firms, 177 firms producing both functional food and NHP and 48 firms providing services.
- Total revenue in 2007 amounted to CDN$3.7 billion with NHP generating more revenue (CDN$1.8 billion).

- There were approximately 22 062 product lines in the market; the majority of the product lines were NHPs.
- The USA is the major export destination for Canadian functional food firms, while China, Europe and Japan are the major export destinations for NHP firms.
- NHP firms preferred wholesalers compared to retailers by functional food firm as distribution channel.
- Total spending on R&D was approximately CDN$209 million in 2007 with approximately CDN$148 million spent on functional food and NHP R&D.
- Both functional food and NHP firms indicated health purposes in the areas of vascular health, weight control, energy, immune system and overall health and wellbeing were of major importance in terms of R&D.
- Most firms (87%) did not have patents and trade secrets was the common form of IPR protection used by firms; NHP firms had the most patents.
- Compared to the Tebbens' 2005 study there has been significant growth in the sector: the number of firms increased by 77%; revenue increased by 28%; revenue from trade increased by 34% and expenditure on R&D increased by 98%.
- Recommends government support in the area of regulations.

Evani 2009 USA	Functional foods Trends in the US functional foods, beverages and ingredients market	To provide an overview of the US functional food and beverage market and its potential Descriptive Analysis	http://www.ats-sea.agr.gc.ca/ Institute of Food Technologists and AAFC

- North American functional food market grew from approximately 200 products in 2006 to over 800 in 2008.
- US functional food and beverages market is estimated to have a retail value of US$59 billion in 2008 with estimated annual growth rate of 6.1% from 2007–2012.
- An ageing population, increasing health care costs, belief in the

correlation between diet and health and the convenience to meet nutritional needs by consumers are the major determinants of demand for functional products.

- Consumer demographics are very important for product development.
- Ingredients mostly used in the US market are low-calorie sweeteners, fibre, probiotics, omega fatty acids, antioxidants and sodium substitutes.
- Younger consumers represent an important market segment that affects sales; seeking out healthy convenience-oriented products that provide quick health solutions.
- New products need to be easy to understand and use less scientific vocabulary to avoid confusion.

| Herath, Cranfield, Henson and Sparling 2008 Canada | Functional foods and nutraceuticals Firm, market and regulatory factors influencing innovation and commercialization in Canada's functional food and nutraceutical sector | To develop a better understanding of the drivers of functional food and nutraceuticals innovation. Survey/ Econometrics $N = 576$ | *Agribusiness*, **24** (2), 207–30 |

- Increasing number of product lines and products positively affect the market but negatively affect product development/innovation; firms focus more on product commercialization than new product development.
- Existing regulations regarding composition and label requirements have a negative impact on innovation in Canada. Firms face the risk of unsuccessful new product development and commercialization because products may not be accepted in the market or not meet consumers' desires and clinical trial failures because of difficulties proving the efficacy of products and/or regulatory evaluations approval. Harmonizing health claims and composition and labelling

regulations with the USA will encourage firms to innovate at the product level.

- IPRs do not have a significant positive impact on innovation but patents have a significant negative impact on product lines. IPRs positively affect biotechnologically-produced products' R&D. Firms focused on patents have less product lines, which might be due to significant substitution effects where, instead of developing their own products, firms acquire products from other developers. The number of products on the market is not affected by the choice of target market.
- Recommends fewer product lines as important for successful innovation; and the development of policies and regulatory reform to enable the efficient use of generic health claims on functional food and nutraceuticals.

| Hobbs 2002 Canada | Functional foods and nutraceuticals Evolving supply chains in the nutraceutical and functional foods industry | To discuss factors that influence the evolution of supply chains in the functional food and nutraceutical sector; how firms in the industry get started and the challenges they face Descriptive Analysis | *Canadian Journal of Agricultural Economics*, **50** (4), 559–68 |

- The functional food and nutraceutical sector is resource-intensive.
- The absence of well-established property rights system discourages R&D by firms.
- Firms form partnerships to raise resources, while there are some contractual rights issues.
- Disputes over property rights hamper firms' abilities to capture rents.
- Developing more healthy products based on consumer interests and through scientific discoveries.

- Closely coordinated supply chains will reduce transaction costs and facilitate credible quality assurance.
- Supply chain development hampered by upstream raw materials supply and downstream food processing.
- Further research is needed in the role of labelling and quality assurance within supply chains.
- Health claims regulations are important for the growth of the sector.

IFT 2005 USA	Functional foods *Functional Food: Opportunities and Challenges*	To further the understanding of the opportunities and challenges posed by functional food development Descriptive Analysis	http://members.ift.org/ NR/rdonlyres/ 20B9EBDD-93B9-4B1B-B37B-3CF15066E439/0/ FinalReport.pdf Institute of Food Technologists (IFT) Expert Report

- Belief of the correlation between diet and disease prevention/health, availability of food technology and increased consumer desires for healthier food products provide an opportunity for growth in functional food.
- Lack of exclusivity in health claims discourages companies from investing, absence of a well-established property rights system for effective patent protection and cost of product development are major challenges facing the sector.
- Government should invest in basic and applied research to promote product development.
- Policies recommended include period of exclusivity for health claims and patents or tax incentives to encourage food companies to pursue functional food development.
- Contributions required from academia, government and industry.
- Health claims increase consumer confidence and enable consumers to select products that satisfy their desire to promote self-care and improve health.
- Recommends the establishment of scientific, regulatory and business frameworks to review new functional ingredients and their health claims for efficacy and safety; communicating the findings of the regulators to educate consumers will ensure informed decision-making, which is important for the success of functional

food; research is needed in the areas of bioactive compounds identification and their effects on health.

Kham- phoune 2013 Canada	Functional foods and NHPs Results from the 2011 Functional Foods and Natural Health Products Survey	To provide new statistical information on the functional food and NHP sector; and a profile of firms engaged in functional and/or NHP-related activities in Canada Survey/ Descriptive Analysis $N = 276$	Statistics Canada Working Paper, Catalogue 18-001-X, September, http:// www.statcan.gc. ca/pub/18-001-x/18-001- x2013001-eng.pdf

- 750 establishments were involved in activities related to functional foods and NHPs, with revenues from these activities totalling CDN$11.3 billion in 2011.
- NHP firms and product lines dominate, accounting for 85% of product lines in the sector and the majority of exports originated from NHPs (CDN$1.3 billion), mostly to the USA.
- CDN$238 million in functional food and NHP-related R&D activity in 2011.
- Trade secrets still dominate as the primary means of protecting intellectual property, more so than patents.

Krakar and Gao 2006 Canada	Functional foods and nutraceuticals *Summary of the Functional Foods and Nutra-ceuticals Survey*	To provide new statistical information on the functional food and nutraceutical sector; and a profile of firms engaged in functional and/or nutraceutical-related activities in Canada Survey/ Descriptive Analysis $N = 276$	http://publications.gc.ca/ collections/Collection/ A38-4-5-2005E.pdf Publication No. 10080B Catalogue A38-4/5-2005E-PDF Project 05-019-r Strategic Research Policy and Planning Team AAFC

- Firms mostly made up of small Canadian controlled firms, with more firms engaged in nutraceuticals than functional foods.
- Almost 90% of responding firms were engaged in partnerships or seeking partnerships.
- Trade secrets seem to be the most commonly used method to protect intellectual property.
- Existing patents are registered with the European patent office, followed by the USPTO and CIPO with the remainder registered in other countries.
- Pending patents are distributed across the globe.
- Most firms believe the allowance of health claims on their products will have a positive impact on sales.

Malla, Hobbs, Sogah and Yeung 2013 USA, EU, Japan, Canada	Functional foods, NHPs *Assessing the Functional Foods and Natural Health Products Industry: A Comparative Overview and Literature Review*	Assessment of key industry trends in major markets and literature review Descriptive Analysis	CAIRN Report No. 35, Canadian Agricultural Innovation and Regulation Network, April, http.www. ag-innovation.usask.ca

- Overview of industry trends in the USA, Canada, EU and Japan.
- Differences in definitions and terminology across countries high-lighted.
- Summarizes literature on consumer acceptance, industry developments and product-specific studies.

Mark-Herbert 2003 Sweden	Functional foods Development and marketing strategies for functional foods	To develop strategies for developing and marketing functional foods Descriptive Analysis	*AgBioForum*, **6** (1–2), 75–8

- Three strategic plans are proposed for product development: acquisition of property rights to ingredients that have undergone independent clinical studies, giving exclusive rights to sales; development of brand products to achieve customer recognition and/or alter consumption; involvement of health experts in product evaluations to increase product credibility among consumers.

- Firms should promote functional food efficiency and create awareness through market segmentation and specific marketing channels:
'sufferers' segment marketing via health professionals; 'at risk'
utilize health-related news and talk shows; 'prevention and mass
market' utilize print media and radio.

Palinic 2007 Canada	Functional foods and nutraceuticals *Results from the Functional Foods and Nutra- ceuticals Survey – 2005*	To provide a benchmark measurement of the industry and a better understanding of the scope and nature of the sector Survey/ Descriptive Analysis $N = 389$	Statistics Canada Catalogue 88F0006XIE, No. 003

- An estimated 389 firms in the functional food and NHP sector in
Canada; NHP: 174 firms; functional food: 118 firms; and 94 firms
involved in both product categories.
- Total revenue from the functional food and NHP industry was
CDN$2.9 billion in 2005: functional food-only firms CDN$823
million; NHP-only firms CDN$1.6 billion; and both functional food
and NHP firms CDN$442 million.
- Majority of functional food firms (85%) undertake R&D as compared to 66% of NHP. Total spending on R&D was CDN$162.8
million (CDN$74.5 million on product development; CDN$88.3
million on other areas including marketing, distribution and consumer research activities).
- Most firms export to the USA, South Korea and Japan.
- Common form of distribution in the sector is wholesalers (70%
NHP; 50% functional food) (retail: 31% NHP; 45% functional
food; direct sale to customer: 25% of functional food and NHP
firms). Most firms in the sector seek partnership in the areas of
R&D, production, marketing and access to distribution channels.
- Majority of firms in the sector did not have patents. For firms that
did, 30% were registered with the USPTO, 16% with the CIPO,

11% with the EU patent office and the rest were with other jurisdictions.

- The ability to make health claims on products boosted sales.
- Compared to an earlier study (Tebbens, 2005), firms in the sector had increased by 32%, revenue rose by about 15% and R&D on products increased by 29%.
- Recommends the allowance of product-specific health claims.

Spence 2006 USA	Functional foods Challenges related to the composition of functional foods	To discuss the challenges firms face in the development of functional foods Descriptive Analysis	*Journal of Food Composition and Analysis*, **19**, S4–S6

- The increase in the number of products makes it difficult for consumers to keep track of the particular composition of products, which can shape attitudes towards functional food.
- Maintaining accurate information about functional food composition is a difficult task as firms face a challenge of balancing variety and nutrients and may not know all the functions of dietary ingredients.
- Functional food designers should be cautious when developing products because of the possibility of consumers misunderstanding the role of bioactive food components.
- There is a need for accurate information about functional food composition to maintain industry credibility.

Stein and Rodríguez-Cerezo 2008 EU	Functional foods *Functional Food in the European Union*	To provide a comprehensive overview of functional foods in the EU Descriptive Analysis	http://europa.eu/ JRC 43851, EUR 23380 EN, doi: 10.2791/21607 European Commission, Joint Research Centre, Institute for Prospective Technological Studies

- The market for functional food within the EU is estimated to be €6–20 billion.
- Markets differ because of country-specific health and dietary needs.
- The most consistent reason for increasing demand for functional food in the EU was to stay healthy.
- Dairy products have the greatest market share followed by beverages, cereals, confectionary, fats and fat supplements, infant foods, bakery, convenience and miscellaneous products.
- Functional food ingredients: probiotic bacteria are the dominant bioactive ingredient followed by dietary fibres and plant extracts; consumption of functional food in Japan and the EU was considered to be more sustainable because of a genuine consumer interest in these products.
- Dominance of established conventional food product companies in the functional food sector, which is taken as a sign of barriers to entry.
- The withdrawal rate of products from the market is roughly 75% within the first two years.
- Demand is high for products that help in weight loss, digestion improvement, immunity enhancement and women's health.
- Recommends collaboration among firms in the areas of research, distribution channels and supply agreements.

Tebbens 2005 Canada	Functional foods and nutraceuticals *Functional Foods and Nutra- ceuticals: The Development of Value-added Food by Canadian Firms 2002*	To provide a benchmark measurement of the industry and a better understanding of the scope and nature of the sector Survey/ Descriptive Analysis $N = 576$	Statistics Canada Catalogue 88F0006XIE, No. 016

- 294 firms engaged in functional food and NHP activities in Canada: 75 in Ontario; 72 in Québec and British Columbia; 33 in Saskatchewan.

- 37% were small sized; 31% medium sized; 33% large sized.
- Common methods of distribution: wholesalers; third party distributors; retailers; direct sales; internet sales mail orders.
- Most firms privately owned, Canadian.
- 57% of firms exported to the USA, Japan, EU, Asia and Australia and New Zealand.
- 46% of firms were nutraceuticals only; 28% functional food; just over 25% engaged in both.
- 51% of NHP firms deal with plant-based nutraceuticals; 37% with marine-based nutraceuticals; 28% with animal or microorganism based nutraceuticals.
- 44% of functional food firms use active ingredients; the remainder use plant breeding, genetic modification and special livestock feeding.
- Further research is needed to document trends and growth in the sector.

Table A5.3   Summary of selected consumer behaviour literature

Author, year, location	Area, title	Objective, method	Citation, prepared for
Ares, Gimenes and Deliza 2010 Uruguay	Functional food Influence of three non-sensory factors on consumer choice of functional yoghurts over regular ones	To study the influence of type, brand, price and health claim on consumer choice of functional yoghurt Survey/Conjoint Analysis $N = 103$	*Food Quality and Preference*, **21** (4), 361–7

The type of yoghurt, brand, price and health claim has a significant effect on consumer choices and also depends on attitudes towards health issues. The influence of brand and type of yoghurt was significantly higher than the effect of price and health claims. The likelihood of consumers choosing functional yoghurt is increased when functional ingredients like fibre and antioxidants are present. Consumers also prefer familiar brands to unfamiliar brands. Consumers had mixed reactions to price, but most consumers are concerned about an increase in price. Health claims had very little effect on consumers; this was the least important attribute. The factors are important considerations in the development of new functional foods.

Arnoult, Lobb, Chambers, Traill and Tiffin 2007 UK	Functional foods *Consumers' Willingness to Pay for Functional Agricultural Foods*	To examine and measure consumers' WTP for enhanced foods Survey/ Interviews $N = 200$	University of Reading, Project Document No. 09, Work package No. 2, Report No. 05, June Research Council UK and Rural Economy and Land Use

There is a viable market for health food products. However, there is a strong polarization against any product perceived by consumers as artificial or GM. Urban professionals, women, younger consumers and those with smaller households are more willing to pay for enhanced products. Pill supplements were mostly rejected by women, white collar workers and households with children. Large households with higher incomes or education levels have a positive WTP for pills (supplements). WTP is stronger for animal than for plant-enhanced food products.

Bech-Larson and Grunert 2003 Denmark, Finland and USA	Functional foods The perceived healthiness of functional foods: a conjoint study of Danish, Finnish and American consumers' perception of functional food	To assess the extent to which consumers' perception of food healthiness depends on different types of health claims, functional enrichments, base products and processing methods Survey/Conjoint Analysis $N = 500$ in each country	*Appetite*, **40**, 9–14

The conjoint results clearly indicate that perceptions of the healthiness of functional foods are more dependent on perceptions of the nutritional qualities of the base product than on any type of health claim or functional properties. Finnish respondents were generally more positive towards functional foods than American or Danish respondents. The three samples showed only small differences regarding the determinants of the perception of the healthiness of functional foods. In addition, the Danish and Finnish consumers had a negative attitude towards GM products compared to American consumers.

Cox, Koster and Russell 2004 Australia	Functional foods and supplements Predicting intentions to consume functional foods and supplements to offset memory loss using adaptation of Protection Motivation theory	To determine what characteristics of a product message would impact on the motivations to purchase functional foods to prevent memory loss Survey/Protection Motivation Theory $N = 290$	*Appetite*, **43**, 55–64

Consumers make no clear distinction between functional food and supplements. The health benefits of these products were the most important predictor of purchase intentions. However, enhancing these products through genetic modification was not acceptable, particularly amongst women. Sweetening functional foods to offset bitterness was not acceptable.

Dean, Shepherd, Arvola, Vassallo, Winkelmann, Claupein, Lahteenmaki, Raats and Saba 2007 UK, Italy, Finland, Germany	Functional foods Consumer perception of healthy cereal products and production methods	To evaluate consumer perceptions concerning bread, pasta and biscuit enriched with health attributes; and their production methods Survey/ ANOVA $N = 2000+$	*Journal of Cereal Science*, **46**, 188–96

The study defines functional cereal products as grains such as wheat, maize, rice, oats and so on that have been modified to provide health benefits over and above basic nutrition. Consumer responses to cereal products with either 'cholesterol lowering' or 'fibre added' as health claims were tested. Bread, pasta and biscuits were the products used in the study. The results showed that people preferred staple foods such as bread and pasta as base products for modification rather than occasional food like cookies. Consumers illustrated gender and country-specific preferences in terms of which health benefit is desired, types of delivery product, as well as means of enhancing the product. British, Finnish and Italian consumers perceived bread that lowers cholesterol as more beneficial than did German consumers. Cholesterol-lowering pasta was perceived to be more beneficial by the British and Italians than the Finns and Germans. Finnish consumers perceived fibre-added bread as more beneficial than did consumers in the other countries. Moreover, production methods such as fortification and traditional cross-breeding were preferred over genetic modification. Men tended to value products with specific health claims while women perceived more benefits in products with general health claims.

Hailu, Boecker, Henson and Cranfield 2009 Canada	Functional food and nutraceuticals Consumer valuation of functional foods and nutraceuticals in Canada: a conjoint study using probiotics	To measure consumers' preferences over attributes (mode, health claim, health claim source and cost) of functional food and nutraceuticals with probiotics as the functional compound Survey $N = 200$ Statistics/Conjoint Analysis	*Appetite*, **52**, 257–65

Health claim/benefit is an attribute that mainly influences consumer acceptance and preference. Government-verified health claims are preferred by consumers. 'Pill lovers' place much value on the health claim source compared to 'pill loathers'. Carrier (base product) of the functional ingredients has a large effect on consumers' valuation of functional food. Cost of usage has a negative effect on consumer preferences. The study recommends further research into potential substitution effects between functional foods and nutraceuticals with attention on specific products or health benefits.

| Henson, Cranfield and Herath 2010 Canada | Functional food and nutraceuticals Understanding consumer receptivity towards foods and non-prescription pills containing phytosterols as a means to offset the risk of cardiovascular disease: an application of Protection Motivation theory | To better understand consumers' willingness to purchase food and/or non-prescriptive pills containing phytosterols as a means to reduce the risk of CVD in Canada Survey/Protection Motivation Theory $N = 446$ | *International Journal of Consumer Studies,* **34** (1), 28–37 |

Factors that affect intentions to consume food and/or nutraceuticals containing phytosterols are twofold: 'response efficacy' and 'self-efficacy'. Response efficacy refers to how effective the product is or if consumers believe the efficacy of the product. Self-efficacy refers to the ability of consumers to consume the products in the prescribed manner. Fear of CVD and/or the use of biomarkers like blood cholesterol as an indicator of CVD does not significantly affect consumers' purchasing intentions. Functional food and nutraceuticals should be promoted as one of the effective ways to reduce the incidence of CVD. Communication efforts should focus on efficacy and the ease with which products can be used; and target the entire population rather than focusing on high-risk individuals. Format matters: functional food and nutraceuticals should be presented in a format that is acceptable to consumers.

Herath, Cranfield and Henson 2008 Canada	Functional foods/ nutraceuticals Who consumes functional foods and nutraceuticals in Canada? Results of cluster analysis of the 2006 survey of Canadians demand for food supporting health and wellness	To identify consumer segmentation in relation to consumption of functional food and nutraceuticals Survey/ Cluster Analysis/ANOVA $N = 1753$	*Appetite*, **51**, 256–65

Among Canadian consumers there is a difference in the likelihood to consume functional foods and nutraceuticals: age, location, education, income are the most prominent distinguishing factors. The more receptive groups are the elderly, low-income households and the less educated. The less receptive group is younger consumers with higher education and income levels who mostly live in urban areas. More receptive consumers are interested in knowing the health benefits of these products before they commit themselves. Segmentation of consumer markets will facilitate the use of different strategies to change attitudes towards these products.

Ipsos Reid 2005 Canada	NHPs *Baseline Natural Health Products Survey Among Consumers*	To determine NHP awareness, attitudes, knowledge and behaviour among Canadian consumers Survey/Descriptive Analysis $N = 2000+$	Ipsos Reid Reports Health Canada

More Canadians are unfamiliar (45%) than familiar (36%) with NHPs; and more women (41%) compared to men (30%). Among reasons to use NHPs, the desire to control or influence personal health accounted for 52% of responses, followed by an assumption that it is safer than conventional medication (29%) or due to recommendation from a friend or a medical doctor (20%). Reasons for non-use were mainly due to lack of enough information about NHPs. Key recommendations for government include focusing on the dissemination of NHP information to educate Canadians about their use (manage health); collaboration between government and informed sources about safety and appropriate use of NHPs; informing the public about the importance of NHP regulations

Krystallis, Maglaras and Mamalis 2008 Greece	Functional foods Motivations and cognitive structures of consumers in their purchasing of functional foods	To identify the most frequently purchased functional food products; to define the most important attributes of functional foods; to gain insights into consumers' functional food-related buying motives; and to model consumers' functional food selection-relevant cognitive structures, in other words, the way that functional food consumption-relevant knowledge is stored and organized in consumers' memories Survey/Means End Chain Analysis $N = 100$	*Food Quality and Preference*, **19**, 525–38

The young adult group prefers functional food juices, while the older group prefers functional spreads, indicating the possibility of a fragmented functional food market. Both young adults and the older group share some similar preferences; the most important attributes were quality related (for example, pure, safe, healthy and high quality), label information related (for example, best before and packaging dates, nutritional value and health/functional claim), price and brand name. Motives for buying functional foods vary; young adults were concerned about enhancing their health status, while the older group was concerned about reduction of disease risks. The success of functional foods depends on how well they satisfy consumer needs. The study recommends that health claims about functional foods should be honest and presented in an attractive format.

| Labrecque, Doyon, Bellavance and Kolodinsky 2006 USA, France, Canada (French) | Functional foods Acceptance of functional foods: a comparison of French, American and French Canadian consumers | To identify whether acceptance of functional foods varies across cultures; and the extent to which attitudes influence acceptance of functional foods Survey/Regression Analysis $N = 611$ | *Canadian Journal of Agricultural Economics*, **54**, 647–61 |

Minor differences in attitudinal beliefs associated with functional foods exist between Canadian and American consumers. Health and product-related benefits, credible information and knowledge about products are the major determinants of acceptance. The promotion of other product benefits in addition to health attributes can increase market development. French students reported less favourable attitudes towards functional food than French Canadian and American students. The attitude difference is small across countries so product development should be approached from a global market perspective.

Marette, Roosen, Blanchemanche and Feinblatt-Meleze 2010 France	Functional food Functional food, uncertainty and consumers' choices: a lab experiment with enriched yoghurts for lowering cholesterol	To evaluate the effect of health information on consumers' functional food choices Survey/Discrete choice experiment/ Lab experiment $N = 107$	*Food Policy*, **35**, 419–28

Food consumption is significantly impacted by health concerns. Health claims and labels serve as a signal for healthy products and functional food. Information about cholesterol-reducing properties of plant sterols increases consumers' WTP. Uncertainty regarding functional ingredients and possible side-effects of plant sterols does not significantly reduce consumers' WTP. Due to consumers not focusing much on scientific uncertainties when choosing these products, there is the possibility of the proliferation of unsubstantiated claims in the market. Thus, there is the need for a stringent approval process for health claims and the consideration of these effects in any cost–benefit analysis of changes to health claims.

Markosyan, McCluskey and Wahl 2009 USA	Functional food Consumer response to information about a functional food product: apples enriched with antioxidants	To measure consumers' responses to apples with enriched coatings and analyse the factors that affect consumers' choices Survey/Interviews/ Contingent valuation $N = 730$	*Canadian Journal of Agricultural Economics*, **57**, 325–41

Consumers value the health attributes of functional foods and are willing to pay more for them. Consumers are responsive to functional food health claims so dissemination of information to educate consumers about the benefits and safety of these products is vital for the growth of this industry. Reason for rejection was mainly due to the use of new technology (additives), which respondents perceive is unnatural and risky.

| Maynard and Franklin 2003 USA | Functional foods Functional foods as a value-added strategy: the commercial potential of 'cancer-fighting' dairy products | To evaluate the commercial viability of functional dairy foods containing high levels of CLA Survey/Contingent valuation $N = 111$ | *Review of Agricultural Economics*, **25** (2), 316–31 |

Dairy products containing high levels of CLA (cancer-fighting properties) have good market prospects but there is the need for more scientific evidence of the health benefits. On average, consumers are willing to pay US$0.41 per gallon more for high-CLA milk; $0.38 per pound more for high-CLA butter and $0.15 per 8 ounce cup more for high-CLA yoghurt; 80% of respondents were willing to pay at least $0.20 more per gallon of milk for the cancer-fighting benefits of CLA. Currently, there is a paucity of information on CLA-enriched products, which hinders the ability to communicate with and develop attitudes and behaviours of consumers.

Nepote, Olmedo, Mestrallet and Grosso 2009 Argentina	Functional foods A study of the relationship among consumer acceptance, oxidation chemical indicators and sensory attributes in high-oleic and normal peanuts	To determine the relationship between overall acceptance and chemical indicators in roasted peanuts harvested from high-oleic peanut genotypes Survey/Sensory Analysis $N = 100$	*Journal of Food Science,* **74** (1), S1–S8

High-oleic acid peanuts have an overall higher acceptance amongst consumers over conventional peanuts. High-oleic acid peanuts possess high stability against the lipid oxidation process leading to health benefits such as the reduction in the risk of cardiovascular diseases. High-oleic peanut oil has the benefit of offering protection against cardiovascular disease by lowering low density lipoprotein-cholesterol. The study recommended the replacement of normal peanut cultivars with high-oleic acid peanut lines as there do not appear to be negative effects on consumer acceptance but health benefits are gained.

Peng, West and Wang 2006 Canada	Functional foods (CLA-enriched dairy products) Consumer attitudes and acceptance of CLA-enriched dairy products	To identify factors important in explaining consumer attitudes towards and acceptance of CLA-enriched dairy products Survey/Ordered Probit Model – probability of purchase $N = 803$	*Canadian Journal of Agricultural Economics,* **54**, 663–84

Healthiness of conventional milk was found to be the main determinant of the acceptance of CLA-enriched dairy products in Canada. There is not a significant correlation between gender, education and consumer acceptance of CLA-enriched dairy products. The target consumer segment for this product should be health-conscious, middle-aged consumers who believe in healthiness of conventional milk products. Interest in a product that is perceived by consumers to be less healthy can be increased through the introduction of a functional health claim.

Siegrist, Stampfli and Kastenholz 2008 Switzerland (German-speaking)	Functional foods Consumers' willingness to buy functional foods: the influence of carrier, benefit and trust	To examine the factors that influence willingness to buy functional foods Survey/WTP estimates $N = 249$	*Appetite*, **51**, 526–9

Physiological/health benefits of functional food are the main determinant of the willingness to buy or accept functional foods. The use of an already accepted product, with a positive health image as a carrier and trust in the food industry, positively influences consumers' willingness to buy functional food. Older consumers are more interested in functional foods than younger consumers.

Stein and Rodríguez-Cerezo 2008 EU	Functional foods *Functional Food in the European Union*	To examine consumer awareness, attitudes and WTP for functional food in the EU Survey/Descriptive statistics $N = 626$	IPTS Technical Report Series EUR 23380 EN–2008 Institute for Prospective Technological Studies (IPTS) and Joint Research Centre (JRC) of the European Commission

The consistent reason for buying functional food is to stay healthy. There is not one unique determinant of consumer acceptance, but the consumption of functional food should improve the health of consumers. Functional food must fulfil the general expectations regarding food products: good taste; convenience; reasonable price; attractive design; and practical packaging. Consumer understanding of functional food depends on mediated information that hinges on the credibility of that information. The food industry's communication policy is weak and food retailers have limited knowledge about the functional food products they sell. Reasons for not buying functional food differ across countries: in Poland and Spain, price was the main reason; in the UK and Germany, consumers were more concerned about taste; Polish consumers fear side-effects. Recommendations include further research into functional food as a way of achieving cost-effective ways of addressing health problems in Europe.

| Surai and Sparks 2001 Europe | Functional foods Designer eggs: from improvement of egg composition to functional food | To discuss how eggs can be turned into a functional food Descriptive Analysis | *Trends in Food Science & Technology*, **12**, 7–16 |

Eggs are the only food of animal origin consumed by many people worldwide and can be considered a functional food as nutrients such as docosahexaenoic acid (DHA), vitamin E, lutein and selenium can be enhanced. Consumption of 1–2 omega-3 eggs daily can increase n-3 fatty acids in blood lipids. Consumers are willing to pay a premium for the health benefits of designer eggs. Research into improving designer egg quality, benefits of designer eggs and consumer education are recommended. Egg consumption also benefits from the change in experts' opinions countering the belief that egg consumption increases dietary cholesterol and heart disease.

| Teratanavat and Hooker 2006 USA | Functional foods Consumer valuations and preference heterogeneity for a novel functional food | Examine consumer valuation and preference heterogeneity for novel functional food attributes and how they are affected by health benefits, organic ingredients, source of nutrients and price Survey/Discrete choice experiment $N = 3000+$ | *Journal of Food Science,* **71** (7), S533–S41 |

Consumers value health attributes of functional foods and are willing to pay more for them. Consumers who regularly purchase food groups such as functional foods, organic foods and food with natural ingredients react more positively and are more interested in novel functional foods compared to those who never purchase these types of food. Consumers, in attempts to maintain health and prevent disease, are more open to functional foods and novel foods with health claims. Further research should segment population groups that are more interested in novel functional foods.

| Tuorila and Cardello 2002 USA | Functional foods Consumer responses to an off-flavor in juice in the presence of specific health claims | To determine consumer willingness to compromise on taste for health benefits Survey/Descriptive Analysis $N = 78$ | *Food Quality and Preference,* **13**, 561–9 |

Consumers are unwilling to compromise on taste for health benefits. Consumer acceptance of functional food depends on the specific health benefit. Cognitive and physical performance improvements are more likely to motivate acceptance of functional food than emotional well-being.

Urala and Lahteenmaki 2004 Finland	Functional foods Attitudes behind consumers' willingness to use functional foods	To measure/predict the determinants of consumer WTP Lab experiment $N = 1158$	*Food Quality and Preference*, **15**, 793–803

The reward (health benefits) associated with consumption of functional food is a major determinant of WTP. The reward from consumption overshadows the perceived risks associated with consumption. Consumers will compromise on taste if there is a clear promise of disease risk reduction.

Verbeke 2005 Belgium	Functional foods Consumer acceptance of functional foods: socio-demographic, cognitive and attitudinal determinants	To assess the determinants of consumer acceptance of functional foods Survey/Probit Model – probability of purchase $N = 215$	*Food Quality and Preference*, **16**, 45–57

Health benefits was found to be the main determinant for accepting functional foods, far outweighing the impact of socio-demographic determinants such as age, literacy, location, income and so on and attitudinal and cognitive factors such as knowledge and beliefs. In Belgium, the level of household education (households with higher education) negatively affects functional food acceptance whereas high-income households have a positive attitude towards functional food. The paper argues that a rational/cognitive-oriented decision-making process exists for functional foods, including active reasoning.

Verbeke	Functional	To investigate the	*Food Quality and*
2006	foods	determinants of	*Preference*, **17**,
Belgium	Functional	consumer willingness	126–31
	foods:	to compromise on	
	consumer	taste for health	
	willingness to	Survey/Descriptive	
	compromise	statistics	
	on taste for	$N = 255$ in 2001;	
	health	$N = 205$ in 2004	

Belgian consumers exhibited a sceptical attitude towards functional food in general. This attitude was evident in their unwillingness to compromise on taste for health. The acceptance of functional food is being conditioned on taste; consumers are likely to reject functional foods with a taste inferior to that of conventional food. This will be one of the challenges for future acceptance of functional foods.

West,	Functional	To assess consumers'	*Canadian Journal*
Gendron,	foods/GM	valuation of functional	*of Agricultural*
Larue and	foods/organic	properties of food in	*Economics*, **50**,
Lambert	foods	Canada	541–58
2002	Consumers'	Survey/Discrete	
Canada	valuation of	choice experiment	
	functional	$N = 1008$	
	properties of		
	foods: results		
	from a		
	Canada-wide		
	survey		

Consumers have a positive attitude towards functional foods and are willing to pay a premium for them, especially for plant-derived functional foods. However, there is the need for credible information about the safety and benefits of these products. This information should come from reliable sources outside the food industry; government experts and health care experts are the preferred choices. The success of functional foods should not only be based on consumer belief in their safety and composition but also on their efficacy. It is suggested that the majority of Canadians are taking vitamins and herbal supplements. In addition, the probability of Canadians purchasing GM and organic products with added functional property increases at the expense of conventional food.

West and Larue 2004 Canada	Functional foods Profiling consumer trend-setters in the Canadian healthy-foods market	To identify and measure the impact of variables affecting consumers' likelihood of being among the first to purchase new health food products Survey/Discrete choice experiment $N = 1008$	*Current Agriculture, Food and Resource Issues*, **5**, 65–82

Consumers most interested in foods with enhanced functional health properties and, hence, the first to purchase are those who believe strongly in the link between food and health and who already believe in current nutritional content claims. Older consumers and consumers with negative attitudes towards GM foods are less likely to be among the first to try functional foods. Demographically, men, metropolitan consumers and consumers with children are more receptive to novel foods in Canada as opposed to women. Consumers should be convinced that claims about these products are not gimmicks but scientifically proven.

Zou 2011 Canada	Functional food Canadian consumers' functional food choices: labelling and reference dependent effects	To assess the credibility of full health claims, implied health claims and sources of verification Survey/Discrete choice experiment $N = 740$	PhD dissertation, University of Saskatchewan

Examines consumer responses to the use of implied health claims on dairy products in the form of a red heart symbol (partial labelling) versus full labelling of structure-function, risk reduction and disease prevention health claims. Uses several discrete choice models to estimate WTP. Full labelling is preferred over implied health claims (for example, the use of a heart symbol to imply a health claim), but primarily for risk reduction claims. There is no significant difference in consumer responses to a function claim, such as 'good for your heart' and partial labelling in the form of a red heart symbol. Latent Class models reveal considerable heterogeneity in consumer attitudes towards the source of verification for health claims. Socio-demographic (for example, income, education and health status) and attitudinal factors (for example, attitude, trust and knowledge) are significant in shaping attitudes. Since Canadian consumers are receptive to implied health claims, policymakers should be cognizant of the risk of consumers being misled in regulating allowable health claims and forms of messaging.

| Zou and Hobbs 2010 Canada | Functional food The role of labelling in consumers' functional food choices | To assess the credibility of full health claims, implied health claims and sources of verification Survey/Discrete choice experiment $N = 740$ | *Proceedings of the 1st Joint EAAE– AAEA Seminar on the Economics of Food, Food Choice and Health* |

Examines consumer responses to the use of implied health claims on dairy products in the form of a red heart symbol (partial labelling) versus full labelling of structure-function and disease risk reduction health claims. Full labelling is preferred over partial labelling, but primarily for risk reduction claims. There is no significant difference between WTP for a function claim and an implied health claim in the form of a red heart symbol. Verification of health claims by a government agency (Health Canada) or by a third party (Heart and Stroke Foundation) is viewed positively but considerable heterogeneity in consumer attitudes towards the source of verification exists.

References

AAFC (2009), *Consumer Trends: Functional Foods*, Ottawa: International Markets Bureau, Agriculture and Agri-Food Canada, December, http://www.gov.mb.ca/agriculture/market-prices-and-statistics/food-and-value-added-agriculture-statistics/pubs/consumer_trends_functional_foods_en.pdf (accessed 17 March 2010).

AAFC (2011), *Health and Wellness Trends in Russia*, Market Analysis Report, Ottawa: International Markets Bureau, Agriculture and Agri-Food Canada, January, http://www.ats-sea.agr.gc.ca/eur/5696-eng.htm (accessed 20 June 2014).

ADA (2004), 'Position of the American Dietetic Association: functional foods', *Journal of the American Dietetic Association,* **104** (5), 814–26.

Altaffer, P. and G. Washington-Smith (2011), 'From the corners of the world: Russia – is the bear riding a bull?', *Nutraceuticals World*, 1 October, http://www.nutraceuticalsworld.com/issues/2011-10/view_columns/from-the-corners-of-the-world-russia-is-the-bear-riding-a-bull/ (accessed 23 September 2013).

AP (2007), 'China introduces new novel foods regulation', Associated Press, Food Technology, http://www.ap-foodtechnology.com/Formulation/China-introduces-new-novel-foods-regulation (accessed 8 December 2010).

Ares, G., A. Gimenes and R. Deliza (2010), 'Influence of three non-sensory factors on consumer choice of functional yoghurts over regular ones', *Food and Quality Preference*, **21** (4), 361–7.

Arias-Aranda, D. and M.M. Romerosa-Martinez (2010), 'Innovation in the functional foods industry in a peripheral region of the European Union: Andalusia (Spain)', *Food Policy*, **35**, 240–46.

Arnoult, M.H., A.E. Lobb, S.A. Chambers, W.B. Traill and R. Tiffin (2007), *Consumers' Willingness to Pay for Functional Agricultural Foods*, University of Reading, Project Document No. 9, Work Package No. 2, Report No. 5.

Bailey, R. (2007a), *Identifying Functional Food and Natural Health Products (FF and NHP) Trade and Investment Opportunities in Japan*, Oregon: California Functional Foods (CFF) Inc.

Bailey, R. (2007b), *Identifying Japanese Trade and Investment Business Requirements for Functional Food and Natural Health Products (FF and NHP): A Survey of 30 Japanese Companies*, Oregon: California Functional Foods (CFF) Inc.

Bailey, R. (2008), 'Japan: an established market for nutraceuticals', *Nutraceuticals World*, November, S50, http://www.nutraceuticalsworld. com/articles/2008/11/japan (accessed 9 August 2010).

BCC Research (2011), *Nutraceuticals: Global Markets and Processing Technologies*, FOD013D, http://www.bccresearch.com/market-research/ food-and-beverage/nutraceuticals-markets-processing-technologies-fod01 3d. html (accessed 12 March 2014).

Bech-Larsen, T. and K.G. Grunert (2003), 'The perceived healthiness of functional foods: a conjoint study of Danish, Finnish and American consumers' perception of functional food', *Appetite*, **40**, 9–14.

Bech-Larsen, T. and J. Scholderer (2007), 'Functional foods in Europe: consumer research, market experiences and regulatory aspects', *Trends in Food Science & Technology*, **18**, 231–4.

Blakeney, M. (2009), *Intellectual Property Rights and Food Security*, Wallingford: CAB International.

Bleiel, J. (2010), 'Functional foods from the perspective of the consumer: how to make it a success', *International Dairy Journal*, **20**, 303–6.

BNSFD (2000), *Standard of Evidence for Evaluation of Foods with Health Claims: A Proposed Framework*, Ottawa: Bureau of Nutritional Sciences Food Directorate, Health Canada, http://www.hc-sc.gc.ca /fnan/alt_formats /hpfb-dgpsa/pdf/label-etiquet/consultation_doc-eng. pdf (accessed 20 July 2011).

BNSFD (2001), *Product-specific Authorization of Health Claims for Foods*, Ottawa: Bureau of Nutritional Sciences Food Directorate, Health Canada, http://diabetestype2.ca/diary/research/finalproposal.pdf (accessed 20 June 2014).

CAC (1993), *International Food Standards*, Rome: Codex Alimentarius Commission, http://www.codexalimentarius.net/web/index_en.jsp, (accessed 14 June 2010).

CAC (1997), *Guidelines for Use of Nutrition and Health Claims*, Rome: Codex Alimentarius Commission, CAC/GL 23-1997, pp. 1–3.

Canada Gazette (1998), *Novel Foods Interpretation*, 26 September, http://gazette.gc.ca (accessed 20 June 2014).

Canada Gazette (2003), *Natural Health Products Regulations*, 18 June, http://gazette.gc.ca (accessed 20 June 2014).

CFIA (2013), 'Discussion paper for food labelling modernization', Canadian Food Inspection Agency, http://www.inspection.gc.ca/food/ labelling/labelling-modernization-initiative/consultations/discussion-paper/eng/1369936679236/1370294142986 (accessed 6 March 2014).

CFIA and Health Canada (2009), *Guide to Food Labeling and Advertising*, Canadian Food Inspection Agency and Health Canada, http://

www.inspection.gc.ca/english/fssa/labeti/guide/toce.shtml (accessed 8 March 2010).

CFS (2008), *Comparison of Conditions for Nutrient Content Claims Between Hong Kong and Other Countries*, Centre for Food Safety, Government of Hong Kong, http://www.cfs.gov.hk/english/programme/ programme_nifl/files/Nutrient_Content_Claims.pdf (accessed 29 April 2010).

Cinnamon, B. (2009), *Results from the Functional Foods and Natural Health Products Survey – 2007*, Statistics Canada, Catalogue 88F0006X, No. 1.

CIPO (2010), Canadian Patent Database, Canada Intellectual Property Office, http://brevets-patents.ic.gc.ca/opic-cipo/cpd/eng/introduction. html (accessed 21 July 2010).

Coase, R. (1964), 'Discussion', *American Economic Review*, **54** (3), 194–7.

Coitinho, D., C.A. Monteiro and B.M. Popkin (2002), 'What Brazil is doing to promote healthy diets and active lifestyles', *Public Health Nutrition*, **5** (1A), 263–7.

Cox, D.N., A. Koster and C.G. Russell (2004), 'Predicting intentions to consume functional foods and supplements to offset memory loss using an adaptation of protection motivation theory', *Appetite*, **43**, 55–64.

Dean, M., R. Shepherd, A. Arvola et al. (2007), 'Consumer perceptions of healthy cereal products and production methods', *Journal of Cereal Science*, **46**, 188–96.

DH (2011), *Nutrition and Health Claims: Guidance to Compliance with Regulation (EC) 1924/2006 on Nutrition and Health Claims Made on Foods*, Department of Health, Government of the United Kingdom, November, https://www.gov.uk/government/uploads/system/uploads/ attachment_data/file/204320/Nutrition_and_health_claims_guidance_ November_2011.pdf (accessed 22 September 2013).

DOJ (n.d.), *Food and Drug Regulations, CRC, c.870*, Department of Justice, Government of Canada, http://laws.justice.gc.ca/eng/C.R.C.- c.870/page-1.html#anchorbo-ga:l_B-gb:s_B_01_001 (accessed 15 April 2010).

DSHEA (1994), Dietary Supplement Health and Education Act (1994), http://www.fda.gov/RegulatoryInformation/Legislation/FederalFoodDrug andCosmeticActFDCAct/SignificantAmendmentstotheFDCAct/ucm148 003. htm#sec4 (accessed 19 May 2010).

EAS (2009), *Marketing Health Supplements, Fortified & Functional Foods in Asia: Legislation & Practice*, Singapore: European Advisory Services.

EC (1990), Council Directive 90/496/EEC of 24 September 1990 on nutrition labelling for foodstuffs, European Commission, http://eurlex. europa.eu/smartapi/cgi/sga_doc?smartapi!celexapi!prod!CELEXnum doc&lg=EN&numdoc=31990L0496&model=guichett (accessed 15 April 2010).

EC (1997), EC Regulation No. 258/97 of the European Parliament and of the Council of 27 January 1997 concerning novel food and food ingredients, European Commission, http://eurlex.europa.eu/smartapi/ cgi/sga_doc?smartapi!celexapi!prod!CELEXnumdoc&lg=EN&numdoc =31997R0258&model=guichett (accessed 21 April 2010).

EC (1998), EC Regulation No. 258/97 of the European Parliament and the Council of 27 January 1997 concerning novel foods and novel food ingredients 043, European Commission, http://eur-lex.europa.eu/ smartapi/cgi/sga_doc?smartapi!celexapi!prod!CELEXnumdoc&lg=EN &numdoc=31997R0258&model=guichett (accessed 27 April 2010).

EC (2002), Council Directive 2002/46/EC of the European Parliament and Council of 10 June 2002 on the approximation of the laws of Member States relating to food supplements, European Commission, http://eur-ex.europa.eu/LexUriServ/LexUriServ.do?uri=CELEX:32002 L0046:EN:NOT (accessed 15 April 2010).

EC (2003), EC Regulation No 1829/2003 of the Parliament and of the Council of 22 September 2003 on genetically modified food and feed, European Commission, http://ec.europa.eu/food/food/animalnutrition/ labelling/Reg_1829_2003_en.pdf (accessed 21 April 2010).

EC (2006), EC Regulation No. 1924/2006 of the Parliament and of the Council of 20 December 2006 on nutrition and health claims made on foods, European Commission, http://eur-lex.europa.eu/LexUriServ/Lex UriServ.do?uri=OJ:L:2007:012:0003: 0018:EN:PDF (accessed 15 March 2010).

EC (2012), EC Regulation No. 432/2012 of 16 May 2012 establishing a list of permitted health claims on foods, other than those referring to the reduction of disease risk and to children's development and health, European Commission, http://eur-lex.europa.eu/LexUriServ/LexUri Serv. do?uri=OJ:L:2012:136:0001:0040:en:PDF (accessed 6 March 2013).

EC (2013a), *Community Register of Nutrition and Health Claims Made on Food – Authorized Health Claims*, European Commission, http:// ec.europa.eu/food/food/labellingnutrition/claims/community_register/ authorised_health_claims_en.htm (accessed 27 March 2014).

EC (2013b), *New EU Law on Food Information to Consumers*, DG Health and Consumers, European Commission, May, http://ec.europa. eu/food/food/labellingnutrition/foodlabelling/proposed_legislation_en. htm (accessed 20 September 2013).

EC (n.d.), *GMOs in a Nutshell*, European Commission, http://ec.europa.eu/food/food/biotechnology/qanda/e5_en.htm#e (accessed 27 April 2010).

EFSA (2010), *Food Supplements*, European Food Safety Authority, http://ec.europa.eu/food/food/labellingnutrition/supplements/index_en.htm (accessed 28 April 2010).

EUFIC (2012), *Nutrition Labelling Becomes Mandatory in Europe*, European Food Information Council, Food Today, May, http://www.eufic.org/article/en/artid/Nutrition-labelling-becomes-mandatory-in-Europe/ (accessed 22 September 2013).

EurActiv (2010), *EU Delays Decision of Food Health Claims*, http://www.euractiv.com/en/food/eu-delays-decision-food-health-claims-news-498261 (accessed 8 February 2011).

Evani, S. (2009), 'Trends in the US functional foods, beverages and ingredients market', Ottawa: Agriculture and Agri-Food Canada.

FAA (2007), Food Administration Act, 2007, Council of Agriculture, Executive Yuan, Government of Taiwan, R.O.C.

FAO (2004), *Report of the Regional Expert Consultation of the Asia-Pacific Network for Food and Nutrition on Functional Foods and their Implications in the Daily Diet*, RAP Publication 2004/33, Food and Agriculture Organization of the United Nations, Bangkok, 16–19 November.

Farrell, J., N.M. Ries, N. Kachan and H. Boon (2009), 'Foods and natural health products: gaps and ambiguities in the Canadian regulatory regime', *Food Policy*, **34**, 388–92.

FAS (2011), *Russian Federation Food and Agricultural Import Regulations and Standards – Narrative*, Gain Report No. RS1168, Washington, DC: US Department of Agriculture, Foreign Agricultural Service.

FAS (2012a), *Brazil Food and Agricultural Import Regulations and Standards – Narrative*, GAIN Report No. BR12017, Washington, DC: US Department of Agriculture, Foreign Agricultural Service.

FAS (2012b), *Taiwan: Food and Agricultural Import Regulations and Standards – Narrative*, GAIN Report No. TW12049, Washington, DC: US Department of Agriculture, Foreign Agricultural Service.

FAS (2013a), *New Japanese Food Labeling Law will Mandate a Nutritional Labelling*, GAIN Report No. JA3001, Washington, DC: US Department of Agriculture, Foreign Agricultural Service.

FAS (2013b), *Republic of China: General Rules for Nutrition Labeling of Prepackaged Foods*, GAIN Report Number No. CH13001, Washington, DC: US Department of Agriculture, Foreign Agricultural Service.

FDA (1992), 'Statement of policy – foods derived from new plant varieties', US Food and Drug Administration Federal Register, V.57 1992, http://www.fda.gov/food/guidanceregulation/guidance documents regulatoryinformation/biotechnology/ucm096095.htm (accessed 20 June 2014).

FDA (2001), 'Premarket notice concerning bioengineered foods', US Food and Drug Administration Federal Register, **66** (12), 18 January, http://www.fda.gov/ohrms/dockets/98fr/011801a.htm (accessed 20 June 2014).

FDA (2003), *Claims that Can be Made for Conventional Foods and Dietary Supplements, Food Labeling and Nutrition, Food Claims*, US Food and Drug Administration, http://www.fda.gov/food/ingredients packaginglabeling/labelingnutrition/ucm111447.htm (accessed 20 June 2014).

FDA (2005a), Federal Food, Drug and Cosmetic Act, Section 402, 2005, US Food and Drug Administration, http://www.fda.gov/Regulatory Information/Legislation/FederalFoodDrugandCosmeticActFDCAct/FDC ActChapterIVFood/ (accessed 3 May 2010).

FDA (2005b), *A Dietary Supplement Labeling Guide*, US Food and Drug Administration, http://www.fda.gov/food/guidanceregulation/guidance documentsregulatoryinformation/dietarysupplements/ucm2006823.htm (accessed 20 June 2014).

FDA (2008), *Food Labeling Guide*, US Food and Drug Administration, http://www.fda.gov/Food/GuidanceRegulation/GuidanceDocuments RegulatoryInformation/LabelingNutrition/ucm2006828.htm (accessed 20 June 2014).

FDA (2009a), Federal Food, Drug, and Cosmetic Act, Section 411(c)(3) 2009, US Food and Drug Administration, http://www.fda.gov/ RegulatoryInformation/Legislation/FederalFoodDrugandCosmeticAct FDCAct/FDCActChapterIVFood/ (accessed 3 May 2010).

FDA (2009b), *Guidance for Industry: Evidence-based Review System for the Scientific Evaluation of Health Claims – Final*, US Food and Drug Administration, http://www.fda.gov/food/guidanceregulation/guidance documentsregulatoryinformation/labelingnutrition/ucm073332.htm (accessed 20 June 2014).

FDA (2009c), *Structure/function Claims*, US Food and Drug Administration, http://www.fda.gov/Food/IngredientsPackagingLabeling/Labeling Nutrition/ucm2006881.htm (accessed 20 June 2014).

FDA (2009d), *Summary of Qualified Health Claims Subject to Enforcement Discretion*, US Food and Drug Administration, http://www. fda.gov/food/ingredientspackaginglabeling/labelingnutrition/ucm0739 92.htm (accessed 20 June 2014).

FDA (2009e), *Dietary Supplements*, US Food and Drug Administration, http://www.fda.gov/Food/Dietarysupplements/default.htm (accessed 16 May 2010).

FDA (2010), *Orphan Drug Act – Congressional Findings for the Orphan Drug Act*, US Food and Drug Administration, http://www.fda.gov/regulatoryinformation/legislation/federalfooddrugandcosmeticactfdcact/significantamendmentstothefdcact/orphandrugact/default.htm (accessed 28 May 2010).

FEHD (2005), *Updates on Overseas Practice on Nutrition Information on Food Labels*, Food and Environmental Hygiene Department, Government of Hong Kong Special Administrative Region, http://www.fhb.gov.hk/download/press_and_publications/otherinfo/050826_labelling/tech_meeting3_overseas_updates.pdf (accessed 30 April 2010).

FSA (1999), *Guidance Notes on Nutrition Labelling*, Food Standards Agency, Government of the United Kingdom, http://www.food.gov.uk/multimedia/pdfs/nutlabel2.pdf (accessed 27 April 2010).

FSANZ (2001), *Regulation of Novel Foods*, Food Standards Australia New Zealand, http://www.foodstandards.gov.au (accessed 20 June 2014).

FSANZ (2006), *Food Standards Development*, Food Standards Australia New Zealand, http://www.foodstandards.gov.au (accessed 20 June 2014).

FSANZ (2008a), *Final Assessment Report Proposal P293: Nutrition, Health, and Related Claims*, Food Standards Australia New Zealand, http://www.foodstandards.gov.au (accessed 20 June 2014).

FSANZ (2008b), *Nutrition, Health and Related Claims: A Short Guide to the New Standard*, Food Standards Australia New Zealand, http://www.foodstandards.gov.au (accessed 20 June 2014).

FSANZ (2009), 'Proposal P293: nutrition, health and related claims', Consultation Paper for first review, Food Standards Australia New Zealand, 20 March, http://www.foodstandards.gov.au (accessed 20 June 2014).

FSANZ (2010a), *Reviews for High Level Claims*, Food Standards Australia New Zealand, http://www.foodstandards.gov.au (accessed 20 June 2014).

FSANZ (2010b), *Standard 1.2.8: Nutrition Information Requirements*, Food Standards Australia New Zealand, http://www.foodstandards.gov.au (accessed 20 June 2014).

FSANZ (2010c), *What are Novel Foods?*, Food Standards Australia New Zealand, http://www.foodstandards.gov.au (accessed 20 June 2014).

FSANZ (2013a), *Standard 1.2.7 – Nutrition, Health and Related Claims*, Food Standards Australia New Zealand, Federal Register of Legislative Instruments F2013L00054, http://www.foodstandards.gov.au (accessed 20 June 2014).

FSANZ (2013b), *Nutrition Content Claims and Health Claims*, Food Standards Australia New Zealand, http://www.foodstandards.gov.au (accessed 20 June 2014).

FSANZ (2013c) *Notifying a Self-substantiated Food-Health Relationship*, Food Standards Australia New Zealand, http://www.foodstandards. gov.au (accessed 20 June 2014).

FSSA (2006), Food Standards and Safety Act – India (2006), General Provisions as to Articles of Food, Ministry of Law and Justice, Legislative Department, Government of India, http://www.fssai.gov.in/ portals/0/pdf/food-act.pdf (accessed 2 June 2010).

FSSAI (2013), *Strategy for Harmonisation of India's Domestic Food Standards with Codex Standards and Other International Best Practices*, Food Safety and Standards Authority of India.

FUFOSE (1999), 'Scientific concepts of functional foods in Europe: consensus document', European Commission Action on Functional Food Science in Europe, *British Journal of Nutrition*, **81**, S1–27, http://www.ilsi.org/Europe/Publications/1999Sci_Con.pdf (accessed 18 May 2010).

Galizzi, M.M. (2014), 'What is really behavioral in behavioral health policy? and does it work?', *Applied Economic Perspectives and Policy*, **36** (1), 25–60.

Gruenwald, J. (2013), 'Eurotrends: European health claim regulation takes effect: limits placed on claims for foods and supplements, as well as many sports nutrition products', *Nutraceuticals World*, January, http://www.nutraceuticalsworld.com/issues/2013-01/view_columns/ eurotrends-european-health-claim-regulation-takes-effect/ (accessed 10 April 2013).

Hailu, G., A. Boecker, S. Henson and J. Cranfield (2009), 'Consumer valuation of functional foods and nutraceuticals in Canada: a conjoint study using probiotics', *Appetite*, **52**, 257–65.

Hair, J.F., B. Black, B. Babin, R. Anderson and R. Tatham (2006), *Multivariate Data Analysis*, 6th edn, Upper Saddle River, NJ: Prentice-Hall.

Hawkes, C. (2004), 'Nutrition labels and health claims: the global regulatory environment', World Health Organization, http://whqlibdoc. who.int/publications/2004/9241591714.pdf (accessed 6 April 2010).

Hayashi, T. (2007), 'The current regulatory situation and future directions for nutraceuticals, functional foods and food supplements in Japan', *Nutraceutical Business and Technology*, **3** (1), January/February, 50–57.

HCDG (2009), *Administrative Guidance on Submissions for Safety Evaluation of Substances Added for Specific Nutritional Purposes in* the Manufacture of Foods, Brussels: Health and Consumers Directorate-General, European Commission.

Health Canada (1998), *Nutraceuticals/functional Foods and Health Claims on Foods*, http://www.hc-sc.gc.ca/fn-an/label-etiquet/claims-reclam/nutra-funct_foods-nutra-fonct_aliment-eng.php (accessed 20 June 2014).

Health Canada (2000), *Consultation Document on Generic Health Claims*, http://www.hc-sc.gc.ca/fn-an/alt_formats/hpfb-dgpsa/pdf/label-etiquet/health_claims-allegations_sante-eng.pdf (accessed 12 April 2010).

Health Canada (2004), *A Regulatory Framework for Natural Health Products*, Ottawa: Health Canada.

Health Canada (2006a), *Evidence for Safety and Efficacy of Finished Natural Health Products*, http://publications.gc.ca/pub?id=302894 &sl=0 (accessed 20 June 2014).

Health Canada (2006b), *Labeling Guidance Documents*, http://publications.gc.ca/pub?id=302894&sl=0(accessed 20 June 2014).

Health Canada (2009a), *Genetically Modified (GM) Foods and Other Novel Foods*, http://www.hc-sc.gc.ca/fn-an/gmf-agm/index-eng.php (accessed 19 April 2010).

Health Canada (2009b), *Guidance Document for Preparing a Submission for Food Health Claims,* http://www.hc-sc.gc.ca/fn-an/alt_formats/hpfb-dgpsa/pdf/legislation/health-claims_guidance-orientation_allegations-sante-eng.pdf (accessed 15 April 2010).

Health Canada (2010), *Food and Nutrition – Health Claims*, http://www.hc-sc.gc.ca/fn-an/label-etiquet/claims-reclam/index-eng.php (accessed 7 February 2010).

Health Canada (2012), *Regulatory Roadmap for Health Products and Food*, http://publications.gc.ca/pub?id=302894&sl=0 (accessed 20 June 2014).

Health Canada (2014), *Health Claim Assessments*, http://www.hc-sc. gc.ca/fn-an/label-etiquet/claims-reclam/assess-evalu/index-eng.php#fn b3 (accessed 5 March 2014).

Heasman, M. (2004), *Functional Foods in the European Union: Market Opportunities for Canada*, Ottawa, Unpublished report prepared for Agriculture and Agri-Food Canada (AAFC).

Henson, S., J. Cranfield and D. Herath (2010), 'Understanding consumer receptivity towards foods and non-prescription pills containing phyto-sterols as a means to offset the risk of cardiovascular disease: an application of protection motivation theory', *International Journal of Consumer Studies*, **34** (1), 28–37.

Herath, D., J. Cranfield and S. Henson (2008a), 'Who consumes functional foods and nutraceuticals in Canada? Results of cluster analysis of the 2006 survey of Canadians' demand for food supporting health and wellness', *Appetite*, **51**, 256–65.

Herath, D., J. Cranfield, S. Henson and D. Sparling (2008b), 'Firm, market and regulatory factors influencing innovation and commercialization in Canada's functional food and nutraceutical sector', *Agribusiness*, **24** (2), 207–30.

HFCA (2006), Health Food Control Act, Department of Health, Executive Yuan, promulgated on 3 February 1999, pursuant to the President's Order Hua Zong Yi Zi No. 09500069821 promulgated on 17 May 2006, translated to English by Baker and McKenzie Attorneys-at Law, Taipei, Taiwan.

Hoadley, J.E. and J.C. Rowlands (2008), 'FDA perspectives on food label claims in the USA', in D. Bagchi (ed.), *Nutraceutical and Functional Food Regulation in the United States and Around the World*, Burlington, MA: Elsevier, pp. 115–32.

Hobbs, J.E. (2002), 'Evolving supply chains in the nutraceutical and functional foods industry', *Canadian Journal of Agricultural Economics*, **50** (4), 559–68.

Hobbs, J.E., W.A. Kerr, J.D. Gaisford, G. Isaac and K.K. Klein (2004), 'Conflict and consensus-building: international commercial policy and agricultural biotechnology', in R.E. Evenson and V. Santaniello (eds), *The Regulation of Biotechnology*, Wallingford: CAB International, pp. 59–65.

IFIC (2009), *Background on Functional Foods*, International Food Information Council, http://www.foodinsight.org/Resources/Detail.aspx?topic=Background_on_Functional_Foods (accessed 9 March 2010).

IFT (2005), *Functional Foods: Opportunities and Challenges*, Expert Panel Report, Chicago, IL: Institute of Food Technologists.

Ipsos Reid (2005), *Baseline Natural Health Products Survey Among Consumers*, Ottawa: Health Canada.

Isaac, G.E. and J.E. Hobbs (2002), 'GM food regulations: Canadian debates', *ISUMA – Canadian Journal of Policy Research*, **3** (2), Fall, 105–13.

JHCI (2003), *Final Technical Report*, London: Joint Health Claims Initiative, http://www.food.gov.uk/multimedia/pdfs/jhci_healthreport.pdf (accessed 5 May 2010).

JHCI (2007), *Approved Claims*, London: Joint Health Claims Initiative, http://webarchive.nationalarchives.gov.uk/nobanner/20130404135254/http:/www.jhci.org.uk/ (accessed 20 June 2014).

JHCI (n.d.), *Code of Practice on Health Claims on Foods*, London: Joint Health Claims Initiative, http://webarchive.nationalarchives.gov.uk/nobanner/20130404 135254/http:/www.jhci.org.uk/ (accessed 20 June 2014).

JPO (2010), *Procedures for Obtaining a Patent Right,* Japan Patents Office, http://www.jpo.go.jp/cgi/linke.cgi?url=/tetuzuki_e/t_gaiyo_e/pa_right.htm (accessed 13 April 2010).

KFDA (2006), Health/Functional Food Act, Korea Food and Drug Administration, http://eng.kfda.go.kr/index.php (accessed 2 May 2010).

Khamphoune, B. (2013), 'Results from the 2011 Functional Foods and Natural Health Products Survey', Statistics Canada Working Paper, Catalogue 18-001-X, September, http://www.statcan.gc.ca/pub/18-001-x/18-001-x2013001-eng.pdf (accessed 20 February 2014).

Kim, J.Y., D.B. Kim and H.J. Lee (2006), 'Regulations on health/functional foods in Korea', *Toxicology,* **221**, 112–18.

Kim, J.Y., D.B. Kim and H.J. Lee (2008), 'Regulations on health/functional foods in Korea', in D. Bagchi (ed.), *Nutraceutical and Functional Food Regulation in the United States and Around the World,* Burlington, MA: Elsevier, pp. 281–90.

Klimas, M., C. Brethour and D. Bucknell (2008), *International Market Trends Analysis for the Functional Foods and Natural Health Products Industry in the United States, Australia, the United Kingdom and Japan,* Guelph, Final Report prepared for Nutri-Net Canada by the George Morris Centre.

Kotilainen, L., R. Rajalahti, C. Ragasa and E. Pehu (2006), 'Health enhancing foods opportunities for strengthening the sector in developing countries', Discussion Paper 30, The World Bank – Agricultural and Rural Development.

Krakar, E. and S. Gao (2006), *Summary of the Functional Foods and Nutraceuticals Survey,* Ottawa: Agriculture and Agri-Food Canada Publication No. 10080B, http://publications.gc.ca/collections/Collection/A38-4-5-2005E.pdf (accessed 20 June 2014).

Krystallis, A., G. Maglaras and S. Mamalis (2008), 'Motivations and cognitive structures of consumers in their purchasing of functional food', *Food and Quality Preference,* **19**, 525–38.

Kurpiewski, R. (2008), 'Overview of product categories and the pros and cons: food regulations in the United States', in N. Fortin (ed.), *Food and Drug Regulation: A Web Book of Student Papers,* Michigan: Institute for Food Law and Regulations, Michigan State University, http://www.iflr.msu.edu/uploads/files/Student%20Papers/Robin%20Kurpiewski.pdf (accessed 20 June 2014).

Labrecque, J., M. Doyon, F. Bellavance and J. Kolodinsky (2006), 'Acceptance of functional foods: a comparison of French, American, and French Canadian consumers', *Canadian Journal of Agricultural Economics,* **54**, 647–61.

Laeeque, H., H. Boon, N. Kachan, J.C. Cohen and J. D'Cruz (2006), 'The Canadian natural health products (NHP) regulations: industry compliance motivations', *Evidence-Based Complementary and Alternative Medicine*, **4** (2), June, 257–62.

Lajolo, M.F. (2002), 'Functional foods: Latin American perspectives', *British Journal of Nutrition*, **88** (Suppl. 2), S145–S50.

LFI (2006), *The International Market for Functional Foods: Moving into the Mainstream?*, Leatherhead, Surrey: Leatherhead Food International.

LFI (2011), *Future Directions for the Global Functional Foods Market*, Leatherhead, Surrey: Leatherhead Food Research, Leatherhead Food International, http://www.leatherheadfood.com/functional-foods (accessed 12 March 2014).

Liu, E. and V. Lee (2000), *Regulation of Health Food in Taiwan*, Research and Library Services Division, Legislative Council Secretariat, Government of Taiwan, R.O.C.

Liu, P.J., J. Wisdom, C.A. Roberto, L.J. Liu and P.A. Ubel (2014), 'Using behavioral economics to design more effective food policies to address obesity', *Applied Economic Perspectives and Policy*, **36** (1), 6–24.

Lloyd, S. and M.J. Leber (2008), 'Functional food patents – manufacturers starting to rely on patented technologies for protection', http://www.ezinearticles.com (accessed 12 April 2010).

Lusk, J.L. (2003), 'Effects of cheap talk on consumer willingness-to-pay for golden rice', *American Journal of Agricultural Economics*, **85** (4), 840–56.

Mailly, J. and I. Blaszkiewicz (2013), 'Six new general function health claims adopted: European Commission makes progress on a number of health claim dossiers', Hogan Lovells, 3 July, http://www.lexology.com/library/detail.aspx?g=b5d4ef34-450d-428a-93a8-9b28ab 5802f2 (accessed 22 September 2013).

Malla, S., J.E. Hobbs and O. Perger (2007), 'Valuing the health benefits of a novel functional food', *Canadian Journal of Agricultural Economics*, **55**, 115–36.

Malla, S., J.E. Hobbs and E.K. Sogah (2013a), *Functional Foods and Natural Health Products Regulations in Canada and Around the World: Nutrition Labels and Health Claims*, Canadian Agricultural Innovation and Regulation Network, CAIRN Report No. 36, http://www.ag-innovation.usask.ca/ (accessed 20 September 2013).

Malla, S., J.E. Hobbs, E.K. Sogah and M.T. Yeung (2013b), *Assessing the Functional Foods and Natural Health Products Industry: A Comparative Overview and Literature Review*, Canadian Agricultural Innovation and Regulation Network, CAIRN Report No. 35, http: www.ag-innovation.usask.ca (accessed 7 July 2013).

Marette, S., J. Roosen, S. Blancheman and E. Feinblatt-Meleze (2010), 'Functional food, uncertainty and consumers' choices: a lab experiment with enriched yoghurts for lowering cholesterol', *Food Policy*, **35**, 419–28.

Mariotti, F., E. Kalonji, J.F. Huneau and I. Margaritis (2010), 'Potential pitfalls of health claims from a public health nutrition perspective', *Nutrition Reviews*, **68** (10), 624–38.

Mark-Herbert, C. (2003), 'Development and marketing strategies for functional foods', *AgBioForum*, **6** (1–2), 75–8.

Markosyan, A., J.J. McCluskey and T.I. Wahl (2009), 'Consumer response to information about a functional food product: apples enriched with antioxidants', *Canadian Journal of Agricultural Economics*, **57**, 325–41.

Marshall, A.C., K.S. Kubena, K.R. Hinton, P.S. Hargis and M.E. Van Elswyk (1994), 'n-3 fatty acid enriched table eggs: a survey of consumer acceptability', *Poultry Science*, **73**, 1334–40.

Maynard, L.J. and S.T. Franklin (2003), 'Functional foods as a value-added strategy: the commercial potential of "cancer-fighting" dairy products', *Review of Agricultural Economics*, **25** (2), 316–31.

Medsafe (n.d.), *Dietary Supplements*, New Zealand Medicines and Medical Devices Safety Authority, Ministry of Health, Government of New Zealand, http://www.medsafe.govt.nz/regulatory/DietarySupplements/Regulation.asp (accessed 24 August 2013).

MHLW (2010), *FOSHU*, Ministry of Health, Labour and Welfare, Government of Japan, http://www.mhlw.go.jp/english/topics/foodsafety/fhc/02.html (accessed 22 February 2010).

MHLW (n.d.a), *Food with Health Claims, Food for Special Dietary Uses, and Nutrition Labeling*, Ministry of Health, Labour and Welfare, Government of Japan, http://www.mhlw.go.jp/english/topics/foodsafety/fhc/index.html (accessed 28 April 2010).

MHLW (n.d.b), *Food with Nutrient Function Claims (FNFC)*, http://www.mhlw.go.jp/english/topics/foodsafety/fhc/01.html, (accessed 16 September 2013).

MHW (2004), Health/Functional Food Act (HFFA 2004), Ministry of Health and Welfare, Government of Korea, http://www.kfda.go.kr/eng/eng/index.do?nMenuCode=43&searchKeyCode=122&page=1&mode=view&boardSeq=67026 (accessed 22 February 2010).

Mine, Y. and D. Young (2009), 'Regulation of natural health products in Canada', *Food Science Technology Research*, **15** (5), 459–68.

Mintel International (2006), *Functional Food and Beverages*, Chicago, IL: Mintel International Group Ltd.

MWCD (2010), Ministry of Women and Child Development, Government of India, http://wcd.nic.in (accessed 15 February 2010).

NBJ (2007a), 'The global nutrition industry VI', *Nutrition Business Journal*, May/June, http://newhope360.com/managing-your-business/global-nutrition-industry-vi (accessed 3 March 2010).

NBJ (2007b), 'NBJ functional foods IX: healthy foods issue', *Nutrition Business Journal*, February/March, http://newhope360.com/nutrition-business-journal/2007-02-01 (accessed 3 March 2010).

Nepote, V., R.H. Olmedo, M.G. Mestrallet and N.R. Grosso (2009), 'A study of the relationship among consumer acceptance, oxidation chemical indicators and sensory attributes in high-oleic and normal peanuts', *Journal of Food Science*, **74** (1), S1–S8.

NZTE (2007), *Market Profile for Functional Foods in the European Market*, London: New Zealand Trade and Enterprise.

NZTE (2009), *Market Profile for Functional Foods in Japan*, London: New Zealand Trade and Enterprise.

Ohama, H., H. Ikeda and H. Moriyama (2006), 'Health foods and foods with health claims in Japan', *Toxicology*, **221**, 95–111.

Ohama, H., H. Ikeda and H. Moriyama (2008), 'Health foods and foods with health claims in Japan', in D. Bagchi (ed.), *Nutraceutical and Functional Food Regulation in the United States and Around the World*, Burlington, MA: Elsevier, pp. 249–80.

OPSI (1996), *Food Labelling Regulations*, Office of Public Sector Information, Government of the United Kingdom, http://www.opsi.gov.uk/si/si1996/uksi_19961499_en_1.htm (accessed 20 April 2010).

Palinic, R. (2007), *Results from the Functional Foods and Nutraceuticals Survey – 2005*, Statistics Canada Catalogue 88F0006XIE.

Palthur, M.P., S.S. Palthur and S.K. Chitta (2009), 'Emerging product categories in India: a regulatory view', *Food and Drug Law Journal*, **64** (4), 677–92.

Patel, D., Y. Dufour and N. Domigan (2008), 'Functional food and nutraceutical registration process in Japan and China: similarities and differences', *Journal of Pharmacy and Pharmaceutical Sciences*, **11** (4), 1–11.

Peng, Y., G.E. West and C. Wang (2006), 'Consumer attitudes and acceptance of CLA- enriched dairy products', *Canadian Journal of Agricultural Economics*, **54**, 663–84.

PWC (2009), *Leveraging Growth in the Emerging Functional Foods Industry: Trends and Market Opportunities*, PricewaterhouseCoopers, http://www.pwc.com (accessed 8 May 2010).

Reuters (2008), 'China to improve nutrition labeling on food', 11 January, http://www.reuters.com/article/idUSPEK33779920080112 (accessed 7 May 2010).

Roberts, A. and R. Rogerson (2008), 'Chinese approach on regulating food additives, novel foods, functional foods and dietary supplements', in D. Bagchi (ed.), *Nutraceutical and Functional Food Regulation in the United States and Around the World*, Burlington, MA: Elsevier, pp. 291–303.

Ross, S. (2000), 'Functional foods: the Food and Drug Administration perspective', *American Journal of Clinical Nutrition*, **71** (Suppl.), 1735S–8S.

Siegrist, M., N. Stampfli and H. Kastenholz (2008), 'Consumers' willingness to buy functional foods: the influence of carrier, benefit and trust', *Appetite*, **51**, 526–9.

Smith, B., M. Marcotte and G. Harrison (1996), *A Comparative Analysis of the Regulatory Framework Affecting Functional Food Development and Commercialization in Canada, Japan, the European Union and the United States*, Ottawa, Inter/Sect Alliance Inc. for Agriculture and Agri-Food Canada.

Spence, J.T. (2006), 'Challenges related to the composition of functional foods', *Journal of Food Composition and Analysis*, **19**, S4–S6.

Stein, J.A. and E. Rodríguez-Cerezo (2008), *Functional Food in the European Union*, Seville: Institute for Prospective Technological Studies, Technical Report Series EUR 23380 EN–2008.

Stringueta, P.C., M.P.H. Amaral, L.P. Brumano, M.C.S. Pereira and M.A.O. Pinto (2012), 'Public health policies and functional property claims for food in Brazil', in A.A. Eissa (ed.), *Structure and Function of Food Engineering*, Rijeka, Croatia: InTech, pp. 307–36, http://www.intechopen.com/books/structure-and-function-of-food-engineering (accessed 19 June 2014).

Subirade, M. (2007), *Report on Functional Foods*, Rome: Food and Agriculture Organization of the United Nations.

Surai, P.F. and N.H.C. Sparks (2001), 'Designer eggs: from improvement of egg composition to functional food', *Trends in Food Science & Technology*, **12**, 7–16.

Tebbens, J. (2005), *Functional Foods and Nutraceuticals: The Development of Value-added Food by Canadian Firms 2002*, Statistics Canada Catalogue 88F0006XIE, No. 016.

Teratanavat, R. and N.H. Hooker (2006), 'Consumer valuations and preference heterogeneity for a novel functional food', *Journal of Food Science*, **71** (7), S533–S41.

TGA (2001), Therapeutic Goods Order No. 69, Therapeutic Goods Administration, Government of Australia, http://www.tga.gov.au/industry/legislation-tgo.htm#.U6NWz5RdXmc (accessed 20 June 2014).

TGA (2006), *Australian Regulatory Guidelines for Complementary Medicines (ARGCM) Part II: Listed Complementary Medicines*, Therapeutic Goods Administration, Government of Australia, http://www.tga.gov.au/industry/cm-argcm.htm#.U6NXkpRdXmc (accessed 20 June 2014).

Thaler, R.H. and C.R. Sunstein (2008), *Nudge: Improving Decisions about Health, Wealth, and Happiness*, New Haven, CT: Yale University Press.

The Gazette of India (2006), The Food Safety and Standards Act, 2006: Chapter IV, Article 22, Registered No. DL-(N) 04/0007/2003-06.

Toledo, M.C.F. and F.M. Lajolo (2008), 'Supplements and functional foods legislation in Brazil', in D. Bagchi (ed.), *Nutraceutical and Functional Food Regulation in the United States and Around the World*, Burlington, MA: Elsevier, pp. 349–64.

Train, K. (2003), *Discrete Choice Methods with Simulation*, Cambridge: Cambridge University Press.

Trueman, S. (2009), *Functional Foods, Patents and Health Claims*, IP Strategist Publication, Tolland: Nerac Inc.

Tuorila, H. and A.V. Cardello (2002), 'Consumer response to an off-flavor in juice in the presence of specific health claims', *Food Quality and Preference*, **13**, 561–9.

Tutelyan, V.A. and B.P. Sukhanov (2008), 'The legislative regulation of biologically active food supplements circulation in the Russian Federation', in D. Bagchi (ed.), *Nutraceutical and Functional Food Regulation in the United States and Around the World*, Burlington, MA: Elsevier, pp. 305–21.

Urala, N. and L. Lahteenmaki (2004), 'Attitudes behind consumers' willingness to use functional foods', *Food Quality and Preference*, **15**, 793–803.

Veeman, M. (2002), 'Policy development for novel foods: issues and challenges for functional food', *Canadian Journal of Agricultural Economics*, **50**, 527–39.

Verbeke, W. (2005), 'Consumer acceptance of functional foods: socio-demographic, cognitive and attitudinal determinants', *Food Quality and Preference*, **16**, 45–57.

Verbeke, W. (2006), 'Functional foods: consumer willingness to compromise on taste for health', *Food Quality and Preference,* **17**, 126–31.

Viju, C., M.T. Yeung and W.A. Kerr (2012), 'The trade implications of the post-moratorium European Union approval system for genetically modified organisms', *Journal of World Trade*, **46** (5), 1207–38.

Walji, R. and H. Boon (2008), 'Natural health products regulations: perceptions and impacts', *Food Science and Technology*, **19**, 494–7.

West, G.E. and B. Larue (2004), 'Profiling consumer trend-setters in the Canadian healthy-foods market', *Current Agriculture, Food and Resource Issues*, **5**, 65–82.

West, G.E., C. Gendron, B. Larue and R. Lambert (2002), 'Consumers' valuation of functional properties of foods: results from a Canada-wide survey', *Canadian Journal of Agricultural Economics*, **50**, 541–58.

WHO (2002), *Globalization, Diets and Noncommunicable Diseases*, Geneva: World Health Organization, whqlibdoc.who.int/publications/9241590416.pdf (accessed 20 June 2014).

WHO (2012a), *World Health Statistics 2012*, World Health Organization, http://www.who.int/gho/publications/world_health_statistics/2012/en/ (accessed 23 March 2014).

WHO (2012b), *10 Facts on Ageing and the Life Course*, World Health Organization Fact files, April, http://www.who.int/features/factfiles/ageing/en/ (accessed 24 March 2014).

WHO (2012c), *World Global Health Expenditure Atlas,* World Health Organization, April, http://www.who.int/nha/atlas.pdf (accessed 23 March 2014).

WHO (2013), *Cardiovascular Diseases (CVD)*, World Health Organization Fact sheet No. 317, http://www.who.int/mediacentre/factsheets/fs317/en/ (accessed 24 March 2014).

Williams, P. and D. Ghosh (2008), 'Health claims and functional foods', *Nutrition & Dietetics*, **65** (Suppl. 3), S89–S93.

Wolf, C. (1979), 'A theory of non-market failure: framework for implementation analysis', *Journal of Law and Economics*, **21** (1), 107–39.

Wolf, C. (1987), 'Market and non-market failures: comparison and assessment', *Journal of Public Policy*, **7** (1), 43–70.

Yang, Y. (2008), 'Scientific substantiation of functional food health claims in China', *Journal of Nutrition*, **138** (6), June, 1199S–205S.

Zawistowski, J. (2008), 'Regulation of functional foods in selected Asian countries in the Pacific Rim', in D. Bagchi (ed.), *Nutraceutical and Functional Food Regulation in the United States and Around the World*, Burlington, MA: Elsevier, pp. 365–401.

Zou, N. (2011), 'Canadian consumers' functional food choices: labelling and reference dependent effects', PhD dissertation, University of Saskatchewan, http://ecommons.usask.ca/handle/10388/etd-06072011-194119 (accessed 14 June 2013).

Zou, N.N. and J.E. Hobbs (2010), 'The role of labelling in consumers' functional food choices', *Proceedings of the 1st Joint EAAE–AAEA*

Seminar on the Economics of Food, Food Choice and Health, Freising-Weihenstephan, Technische Universität München, http://purl.umn.edu/ 116421 (accessed 8 December 2012).

Index